Parody and Taste in Postwar American Television Culture

Routledge Advances in Television Studies

**1. Parody and Taste in Postwar
American Television Culture**
Ethan Thompson

Parody and Taste in Postwar American Television Culture

Ethan Thompson

First published 2011
by Routledge
270 Madison Avenue, New York, NY 10016

Simultaneously published in the UK
by Routledge
2 Park Square, Milton Park, Abingdon, Oxon OX14 4RN

Routledge is an imprint of the Taylor & Francis Group, an informa business

© 2011 Taylor & Francis

The right of Ethan Thompson to be identified as author of this work has been asserted by him in accordance with sections 77 and 78 of the Copyright, Designs and Patents Act 1988.

Typeset in Sabon by IBT Global.
Printed and bound in the United States of America on acid-free paper by IBT Global.

All rights reserved. No part of this book may be reprinted or reproduced or utilised in any form or by any electronic, mechanical, or other means, now known or hereafter invented, including photocopying and recording, or in any information storage or retrieval system, without permission in writing from the publishers.

Trademark Notice: Product or corporate names may be trademarks or registered trademarks, and are used only for identification and explanation without intent to infringe.

Library of Congress Cataloging-in-Publication Data
Thompson, Ethan.
　Parody and taste in postwar American television culture / by Ethan Thompson.
　　p. cm. — (Routledge advances in television studies ; no. 1)
　Includes bibliographical references and index.
　1. Television broadcasting—Social aspects—United States. 2. Television broadcasting—United States—History—20th century. 3. Parody. 4. Popular culture—United States—History—20th century. I. Title.
　PN1992.3.U5T48 2010
　302.23'45—dc22
　2010029422

ISBN13: 978-0-415-88638-3 (hbk)
ISBN13: 978-0-203-83293-6 (ebk)

To Maria
Together, anything is possible.

Contents

List of Figures ix
Acknowledgments xi

Introduction: The Parodic Impulse in the (Not-So) Fabulous Fifties 1

1 The New, Sick Sense: The Mediation of America's Health and Humor at Midcentury 15

2 What, Me Subversive? *MAD Magazine* and the Textual Strategies and Cultural Politics of Parody 45

3 The Parodic Sensibility and the Sophisticated Gaze: Masculinity and Taste in *Playboy's Penthouse* 76

4 Ernie Kovacs and the Logics of Television Parody and Electronic Trickery 98

5 Black Tie, Straightjacket: Oscar Levant's Sick Life on TV 125

Conclusion: Television for People Who Hate Television? 146

Notes 153
Index 163

Figures

1.1–1.4	Real-life comedian Shelley Berman walks onstage as fictional (and murderous) comedian Danny Holland for one final performance. Though he verbally and physically manifests his mental illness, his antisocial routine meets with unanimous laughter from the audience. (Frame Grab, *Peter Gunn*, "The Comic.")	16–17
1.5	Shelley Berman's performance as a homicidal comedian in *Peter Gunn* drew upon the content and style of Berman's actual routines. Here an outwardly "well" Holland performs atop a stool on a nightclub stage. (Frame Grab, *Peter Gunn*, "The Comic.")	29
2.1	"The Countynental" attempts to romance the television audience in *MAD*'s first Television Dept. parody, but fails due to technical glitches and an unreceptive male viewer.	57
2.2	*MAD*'s parody of *Disneyland*'s supposedly wholesome family entertainment portrayed the show as nothing but a marketing boondoggle.	63
3.1	Hugh Hefner welcomes the viewer into the television party in *Playboy's Penthouse*.	77
3.2	Lenny Bruce and Hefner enjoy champagne with a couple of the magazine's "Playmates" before sitting down for a proper chat.	78
3.3	Hefner looks on approvingly as Bruce talks about TV standards, sick comedy, and the vagaries of good and bad taste.	84
3.4	Hefner, Nat King Cole, Bruce, and author Rona Jaffe smoke, drink, and talk showbiz in *Playboy's Penthouse*.	85

3.5	Surprise! Hefner is notified jazz icon Ella Fitzgerald just arrived.	90
4.1	Ernie Kovacs the TV comic and auteur introduces a segment parodying the Western.	99
4.2	Frontier psychiatry in the "New Western."	102
4.3	A TV western in the "Serling Manner."	103
4.4	An incredible shrinking cowboy.	103
4.5	Despite his renowned electronic trickery and elaborate staging, Kovacs maintained an appreciation for simple sight gags and silly costumes. Here, a gunfighter meets his match in "Rancid the Devil Horse."	104
5.1	Frame grab from opening of *The Oscar Levant Show*.	135
5.2	Oscar Levant introduces himself as the "irreligious Billy Graham of Los Angeles" while wife and co-host June looks on.	136
5.3	Oscar squirms while June reads a *Time Magazine* article about his show. "Who do I repel?" he asks his audience.	137
5.4	Oscar's modestly sized in-studio audience offers reassurance.	138
5.5	"They LOVE you!" June tells Oscar.	139

Acknowledgments

This is a book many years in the making, and thanks are due to many who have helped, inspired, supported, and shaped it along the way.

I owe a debt of gratitude to colleagues I first encountered at the University of Southern California. In retrospect, I was very lucky to end up there when I did. Lynn Spigel first brought direction to my interests in parody and cultural history. Jeffrey Sconce's insights and guidance have been and continue to be invaluable. Dana Polan played a key role suggesting resources and shaping my early work. Thanks also to Marita Sturken for her critical comments and keen eye for editing. Many thanks to Jonathan Gray for his helpful notes on revising my manuscript, and to two anonymous reviewers for their productive criticisms as well. The number of media scholars working on comedy is currently booming, and I am indebted to my interactions with that community: at conferences, the comment sections on FlowTV.org and the Antenna blog—heck, on Facebook! I look forward to many collaborations and dialogues.

Thanks to the faculty of the Department of Communication & Theatre at Texas A&M University-Corpus Christi, particularly Kelly Quintanilla, Don Luna, and Bill Huie, for maintaining such a great environment for media studies research and teaching. The College of Liberal Arts and the Office of Research and Graduate Studies have dependably supported my work, and I have been fortunate to receive a number of grants for travel and course releases that have enabled me to continue and expand my research and writing. My thanks to the staffs of the Paley Centers for Media in Beverly Hills and New York, the UCLA Special Collections and Film and Television Archive, the USC Cinematic Arts Library, and the Peabody Archive at the University of Georgia.

Thanks to my parents for their unwavering support over the years. Thanks to my kids—Jenna, Dax, and Mia—for teaching me lessons in time management and priority-setting, as well as continuing to provide me glimpses of unbridled joy when it is needed the most. Finally, this book would have never been completed without the enduring support of my wife Maria.

Introduction
The Parodic Impulse in the (Not-So) Fabulous Fifties

On the last day of January 1960, the CBS television network broadcast a star-studded spectacular titled *The Fabulous Fifties*. The respected film actor Henry Fonda narrated the program's survey of "the ten years just left behind" as experienced through television. "This is you," he told the audience, as the TV screen zoomed in on a camera lens before fading into a montage of the decade's major events—from the realms of politics, news, and popular entertainment. Stars of music, theater, film, and, yes, television mixed with heads of state and other newsmakers. Looking forward to the decade ahead, the program, which was sponsored by General Electric, also introduced the audience to the "GE Golden Value Line of the Sixties."

The Fabulous Fifties celebrated the ability of television to bring the events of the decade into the home, even as it defined what those significant events were, juxtaposing Lucille Ball with an atomic blast and Grace Kelly's royal wedding with *Lassie*. Featured throughout the broadcast were comic sketches that parodied or satirized life in the fifties. Comic actor and stand-up comedian Shelley Berman talked with his "son" Howard about the morality of being deceitful and the possibility of using modeling clay as an outlet for his pent-up emotions. A film directed by Richard Avedon parodied the "new American woman" created in make-up ads. Other sketches on the program used parody to celebrate television as a cultural form by criticizing its main rival, cinema. At the beginning of the decade, the program recalled, Americans owned 10 million sets, so the Hollywood movie industry marshaled its forces and fought back. This brought innovations or gimmicks like Cinemascope, which was supposed to be a powerful visual spectacle, but could also result in characters spaced ridiculously far apart. The next step, the show suggested, might be "taste-o-vision" where a poor movie viewer would be locked in his chair and literally force-fed cinema through a tube in his mouth.

Eventually, in the interest of telling its own history, television got around to making fun of itself in *The Fabulous Fifties*. In a segment set up as an office water cooler conversation, the comic duo Mike Nichols and Elaine May talked about the quiz show scandal. The segment was an adaptation of an improvisational exercise the duo performed in nightclubs, for which audiences would shout out topics and they would form those into a comic conversation. For the special, however, Mike and Elaine chose their own topics: "quiz," "Van Doren," "moral issue," and "politics." Without explicitly saying what the subject of the conversation would be, Fonda had prefaced the water cooler sketch by referring to an event in the headlines that "seemed to affect the most." The name "Van Doren" alone would signify what that event was. Charles Van Doren had been transformed from Columbia University academic to the most famous quiz show contestant in 1957. He appeared on the cover of *Time* magazine, received hundreds of fan letters a week, and after his run on the quiz show *Twenty-One* met its premeditated end, he signed a lucrative contract with NBC television. Then, news broke that the quiz shows were rigged, rocking the industry and the television faithful. In early November 1959, just months before the broadcast of *The Fabulous Fifties*, Van Doren admitted before the House Committee on Interstate and Foreign Commerce, which was investigating the quiz show scandal, that he had been "deeply involved" in the quiz show's deceptions.[1] Because of the scandal, *The Fabulous Fifties*, in addition to marking the end of a decade, also occurred at a high point in public debates about the television medium. Just two months later, in March 1960, FCC chair John Doerfer would resign amid the rising complaints about sponsor censorship, program mediocrity, and, most importantly, the quiz show scandal.[2]

While the sketch isn't, strictly speaking, a parody, it shows how parodic performance could work both as criticism and as successful commercial content. In the sketch, Mike says Van Doren was his idol, and now he doesn't know what to think. His confidence in the truth of what he sees on television—what he can believe in—has been shaken.

> MIKE: Well, thank heaven for the investigation.
> ELAINE: Oh yes, yes, they're getting 'em. They're getting 'em.
> MIKE: When I feel worst I say to myself, "At least the government has taken a firm stand."
> ELAINE: Well, they can't fool around with this the way they did with integration.

Mike and Elaine agree that this, the quiz show scandal, is a "moral issue," which is "always more interesting than a real issue." Rather than being an indictment of television industry practices, the skit slyly mocks the government's investigation of the scandals. Mike and Elaine go on to have more fun with the notion that people assume what they see on television is "real." They discuss Edward R. Murrow's program *Person to Person*, which featured Murrow interviewing his guests remotely—the guests usually at home, and Murrow in his television studio. Mike says he was stunned "to find out that all of the people on *Person to Person* knew that they were on television." He claims he never knew a thing.

During the fifties, the television industry had promoted properties of the new medium that suggested it was more "real" than other media like film and radio. The "liveness" of television was promoted as an essential characteristic that enabled viewers to experience events as they happened. The qualities of "simultaneity," that viewers experienced things at the same time that they happened, and "presence," that the television actually brought an electronic manifestation of the people, places, and events into the home to a much greater extent than even radio, have been discussed as features promoted by the television industry.[3] Raymond Williams described this as the quality of "mobile privatization," television transporting the viewer to diverse spaces from within the comfortable, private confines of the home, dropping in on TV families, much as Murrow did on *Person to Person*.[4] All these qualities were promoted as unique characteristics of television, and they had now all been undermined for Mike, who could no longer believe that his hero Van Doren knew all the answers or that Murrow wasn't really just dropping in on his guests. Mike's faked naïve faith in the "truth" or "reality" of television had been undermined.

Of course, Nichols and May didn't *mean* any of it. Their somewhat scripted, somewhat improvised performance transforms criticism of the television industry into television content by way of parodying water cooler conversation. This prominent case of television making fun of itself would be seen as a self-critique by the contemporary popular press. *Life* magazine published a publicity photo of Mike and Elaine performing the skit, along with a partial transcript. The article, titled "TV Gets Laughs from Its Griefs," started by noting that although the TV industry liked to keep watch over the world's news, the industry had "for the most part kept its gaze modestly averted from the TV scandals." The Nichols and May water cooler skit had made up for those omissions, said the magazine, and was the best stretch of the show. As evidence, the magazine reported, "The day after the show they had 28 offers of high-priced work and even a bid to appear together on *Person to Person*."[5]

The water cooler skit was not Nichols and May's only performance on the show. Soon after the skit, the duo reappeared, now turning their sly, caustic humor on the GE refrigerators. In this case, the duo's comedy didn't focus on the commercialism of television (another subject of popular criticism of the medium); rather their humor *was* a commercial. "Refrigerators are my life," Mike tells Elaine as they inspect one of the GE Golden Value Line "stars." Both adopt haughty accents for the segment, and marvel at how well "those funny little half-cut hams" would fit in the new GE refrigerator as if they were inspecting the backseat of a new Cadillac. The comic tone of the commercial, which applies "highbrow" language to "lowbrow" commercialism, parodies both systems of speaking. Its similarity to the other Nichols and May performance blends the commercial segment seamlessly in with the other content of the spectacular.

From an industrial perspective, the duo's performance on the program can partially be explained simply as a case of getting funny new talent onscreen. However, the prominence of parody and ironic humor throughout

The Fabulous Fifties shows how important these comic styles were to celebrating an industry and commemorating a decade in a program self-consciously constructed as "quality" TV. The "hot talent" explanation doesn't account for the content of the performances or tell us much about how the duo's performances produced a discourse on TV that was not only comic, but critical and commercial at the same time. The water cooler routine directly addresses the quiz show scandal—something television did sparingly, and could be expected to avoid in a spectacular meant to celebrate itself. Their routine was a parody of the casual ways conversation could engage big, serious questions about the nature of television and the audience's relationship to television. And the routine had commercial appeal as well. The topic of conversation could promote the GE refrigerator in the same tone of ironic engagement without appearing to be blatant commercialism. In short, the style and content of their parodic performances were both a critique of television and consumer culture and a commercial discourse in service of television and consumer culture.

The "use" of parody as a critical and commercial strategy in *The Fabulous Fifties* suggests a number of questions for analyzing and evaluating how parody "fit" in American postwar popular culture. These questions can really tell us what produced the Nichols and May performances, both in terms of the content they drew upon and the chance they were given by the television industry to broadcast to an audience. In the most general sense, why celebrate the TV industry and commemorate the 1950s through parody? Parody was an enormously popular cultural mode during the decade, which especially flourished on TV and quite often took TV as its subject matter. But why was parody so popular and prevalent? One possible answer is that parody often worked within popular culture to reconcile criticisms about the commercial nature of that culture. This close relationship between parody and criticism of consumer culture is especially apparent in what is simultaneously a refrigerator advertisement and a Nichols and May *parody* of a refrigerator advertisement. In TV's earliest days, advertising was to a large extent merged with content as shows often had a single sponsor and shared a sponsor's name as part of their title. Or, an actor might step aside in the middle of a performance to tell us about a fantastic new appliance. But by the end of the 1950s, parody and irony were at work in advertising itself. Parody had developed as an acceptable mode of positioning oneself *vis-à-vis* consumer culture, whether that culture was TV shows, movies, magazine, stereos, or refrigerators. This is why the quiz show scandal (and broader discourse of TV criticism) is also the subject of parody. The TV industry scandal as comic source material is less an improvisation, and more a calculated choice to produce acceptable TV content *and* commentary. Such parodic criticisms had emerged during the 1950s as key elements of what was considered a sophisticated attitude toward television and commercial culture. A taste for parody allowed one to take pleasure in TV, meanwhile signaling one wasn't totally *taken in* by it.

The Fabulous Fifties celebrated television's growth as a technology and an industry during the 1950s, including its ability to deliver that decade into American homes and define what that decade "meant" for Americans. This book will explore the relationships between parody and television during that decade in which the medium, as *The Fabulous Fifties* noted, found its way into American homes in spectacular fashion. Along with that rapid growth, a simultaneous explosion of parodic discourse took place across a wide field of American culture—in magazines, comic books, film, comedy albums, and on television itself. This book will tell a story about how parody has responded to and influenced American culture—in particular, how parody has functioned in the circuits of production and consumption, of encoding and decoding, which produce meaning, as Stuart Hall describes the communication process. Although this is a history of American television and American humor, it is not an exhaustive catalog of 1950s comedians who performed parodies, or the television shows or publications in which parody could be found. Nor is it a schematization of all the possible "meanings" to be found through parodies in the 1950s. Instead, it is a history of comedy that examines the role of parody as a textual strategy in particular cases of television production and reception. It is a history of a certain kind of laughter produced through media culture that signifies an engagement with, rather than escape from, everyday life. Sometimes this laughter was produced by textual parodies, sometimes by broader social satire, sometimes by the emergent type of humor labeled "sick comedy." In all those cases, that laughter could be characterized as critical—not just finding the humor in postwar life, but suggesting there was something unacceptable about what was considered "normal."

A glance around the contemporary media landscape shows that parody remains a vital cultural form and this history of past TV culture should help us understand the present. Though its popularity ebbs and flows (like everything else), parody has maintained a presence in television culture since its beginnings, and at times has seemed keenly suited to address the cultural milieu *outside* of television. The civil rights movement, the Vietnam War, feminism, the sexual revolution—all these changed the consciousness of Americans and parody remained a useful tool to make sense of it all. First *That Was the Week That Was* and then *The Smothers Brothers* and *Rowan and Martin's Laugh-In* were key programs where viewers could find parodic and sometimes controversial takes on current events while the majority of television entertainment ignored the social upheavals of the 1960s. In the 1970s and 1980s, the sketch comedy programs *Saturday Night Live* and the Canadian *SCTV* made comic actors and their signature characters famous, but also commonly depended upon parody of current events, political figures, movies, and television. In the 1990s, the cable network Comedy Central recycled some of those shows, but ultimately emerged as *the* site for contemporary political comedy: first as the original home of *Politically Incorrect with Bill Maher*, then with *South*

Park—a program which immediately went to work brutally parodying the sanctimonious, as well as breaking all accepted notions of good taste. In the 2000s, television satire boomed like never before, with programs like *The Daily Show with Jon Stewart* and *The Colbert Report* taking on politicians in ways the "real" news seemed unable. Other cable programs like *Chappelle's Show* and *The Sarah Silverman Program* produced hilarious entertainment that sometimes doubled as scathing cultural critique—and also proved capable of generating additional revenue through DVD sales.[6] By the 2008 presidential campaign, parody and satire had become part and parcel of how Americans made sense of politics through media culture. An appearance on *The Daily Show* was regarded by the political establishment as nearly important in courting voters as one on *Meet the Press*. Even the old network stalwart *Saturday Night Live* recaptured the public's attention, both with its parodies and impersonations, as well as cameo appearances by the real-life candidates themselves.

While a television program appearing in the 1950s might have inspired a scathing *MAD Magazine* parody published some months later, the production and distribution of today's electronic parodies are almost immediate. Even the establishment political campaigns have gotten in on the act. When *The Sopranos* broadcast its final episode, Hillary Clinton's Democratic primary campaign quickly reimagined and refilmed its final scene. The stunt, starring this past and potentially future First Family, again became an Internet sensation. For some, the exhibition of this parodic impulse suggested a likeability that the overly scripted Hillary hadn't previously possessed, similar to the response to Al Gore following his appearances on *The Late Show with David Letterman* and *Saturday Night Live*.

How do we understand the cultural relevance of such high-powered parodic gestures? Do they, like everything else, just "poll well"? Should we be surprised that parody, with its inherent critical component, is so ripe for incorporation by the powers that be? After all, *The Daily Show* and *South Park* may create controversy or say things that aren't said elsewhere, but both air on Comedy Central, which is just one arm of media leviathan Viacom. Clinton, Obama, McCain, and Palin all eagerly jumped at the chance to appear on *Saturday Night Live*. How, then, can we evaluate the politics of parody? Does it maintain its essentially subversive nature, undermining the very structures that propagate it, or is it rendered harmless by incorporation into the culture industry? Examining how parody worked in television culture of the 1950s can help us address these questions without falling into such simplistically bifurcated, all-or-nothing, choices.

As for *The Fabulous Fifties*, the show was a big hit, winning an Emmy as well as the prestigious Peabody Award for television excellence. Apparently the airing of the spectacular stopped short of creating a public atmosphere healthy enough to save the job of Doerfer, who resigned less than two months later, but it does show that the industry could adopt self-parody to incorporate critique. William Boddy notes in *Fifties Television* that the industry had not undergone the same heated debates as radio over its status as a commercial medium. Advertising had been discussed as tactics, not part of a larger public debate over the general social role of television.[7] But in both academic and popular sites of cultural criticism, the commercial nature of television was still regarded as a primary signifier of its degraded cultural value, and the ubiquitous sponsor announcements and product placements did not go unnoticed by the public. The comic sketches in *The Fabulous Fifties* take on both the quiz show scandal and these critiques of industrialized, mass culture. The prevalence of parodic humor, rather than undermining the commercial structures of television, suggests that the producers of *The Fabulous Fifties* believed parody could be used both to take a swipe at the film industry as well as inoculate the TV industry against critiques about commercialism, at a tumultuous time for TV's public reputation.

PARODY AND POSTWAR TEXTUAL BOUNDARIES

The intellectual critique of television in the 1950s is perhaps best summarized by Dwight MacDonald's comments on the "spreading ooze" of mass and "middlebrow" culture. MacDonald dismissed works of popular culture as articles for mass consumption, just like chewing gum. As opposed to folk culture that was truly popular because it was produced by "the people," mass culture was imposed on them from above. "It is fabricated by technicians hired by businessmen; its audiences are passive consumers, their participation limited to the choice between buying and not buying."[8] MacDonald not only objected to the commercial nature of mass culture, but assumed that its "uses" were limited to "passive" consumption. Even worse was the "mid-cult" that watered down the avant-garde and then tried to pass itself off as a better kind of mass culture. This book suggests that had MacDonald been looking more closely at the parodic media culture examined here, popular culture that was produced contemporaneously with his "spreading ooze" critique, had he been reading the letters written to the editors of *MAD* or had access to what fans were writing early TV auteur Ernie Kovacs, he might have recognized some dissatisfied kindred spirits. Before anyone in 1960 could have pondered the ramifications of Nichols and May parodying the new GE line or getting laughs from TV's "griefs," Americans had become quite accustomed to media culture's capacity for self-critique through parody. Indeed, on both sides of the producer/audience divide, many had embraced parodic comedy as participatory culture existing within "Masscult."

This book is not intended to be a refutation of Dwight MacDonald's cultural hierarchies. Rather, it seeks to understand how and why parody was so prevalent in postwar television culture, and how it was useful for those many Americans who were fans of it. The point is not just to dig up some interesting examples of postwar media culture and say, "Ha!" Instead, it is to show how parody and sick comedy articulated cultural criticisms within popular culture, and then ask, so what? One of the most important ways to answer that question is to again "dig up" foundational cultural theorists such as Michel de Certeau (and work in media studies that has looked to him for inspiration) who challenge the tradition of looking at communication in terms that assume to write is to produce and to read is to receive. Instead, de Certeau says that a system of signs "is a reservoir of forms to which the reader must give a meaning."[9] One of the problems of reconstructing those meanings produced by the reader, he notes, is that there is a "lack of traces" left behind by reading practices. While the producer creates a message of record, the reading of that message doesn't often create its own by-products of evidence. Parody, because it always includes some earlier source material, provides evidence of reading practices. A parody is evidence of how at least one person made sense of some communication message or some cultural text. At the same time, the parody is an instruction for reading practices, a system for creating new reading strategies. This book seeks to understand how parodies become meaningful in the pleasures they produce and in the identities they construct for their readers.

The prevalence of parodic humor on *The Fabulous Fifties* (at the end of the 1950s) suggests the importance of investigating the history of how parody of television became a popular type of content *on television* (during the 1950s). How can we account for the popularity of parody from the perspective of a "nuts and bolts," industrial approach? How did television parody fit in the "logics" of early television production? The second component of this history of parody is analyzing the textual strategies of parody and theorizing how they functioned culturally. How did they influence the ways viewers produced meanings and pleasures from television? Writing about television parody, attempting to answer these questions, at times feels like a redundant gesture. Perhaps this stems from how comedy, and parody in particular, is too often considered a cultural form whose meaning is self-evident—hence the tendency of academics to begin a scholarly presentation by using a pithy video clip or comic strip to put the audience at ease before embarking on intellectual acrobatics. Textual analysis of parody usually doesn't seem necessary because the hermeneutics aren't that complicated. Indeed, parody depends upon the audience having the discursive knowledge necessary not just to read, but to laugh. However, it is the cultural hermeneutics of parody, how a parodic text is tied to the world outside its particular discursive structure, that is the puzzle. Parody demands that the reader "decode" by making connections not just within a text, but to that which resides outside it. For this reason, I believe the popularity of parody in the 1950s, and the relentless way in which it was employed to both propagate and interrogate fifties culture, begs historical and theoretical analysis.

The term "parody" is often used in conjunction with "satire," as I myself have already done here as well. However, critics have long drawn meaningful distinctions between the two. Margaret A. Rose's exhaustive history of parody and the differences between parody and related forms offers a useful, simple distinction. Parody is the comic refunctioning of preformed linguistic or artistic material.[10] A parody makes its target part of its own structure, in order to somehow refunction it. This contrasts with satire, which may have a target to criticize, but that target remains external to the structure of the satire. In the 1950s, the two types of comedy blurred, and the terms were often used interchangeably to describe humor that seemed to articulate a criticism that went beyond a text itself to the broader culture that produced it. In short, parody is often the most accessible route to satire available to producers and audiences alike.

The water cooler conversation of Nichols and May serves as a good example to explore the limits of these distinctions. If we say that the "targeted material" (the subject of the conversation) is the quiz shows, then a parody of the quiz shows would take the form of a restaging of the shows where the content would be changed to become the joke. Perhaps Van Doren would visibly cheat on air or the contestants would compete to see who would forget the answers they had been told. If, however, we say that the "targeted material" is not only the quiz shows themselves, but the scandals, the public uproar and debates, and the other discourses on television which played a part in producing the uproar, then the water cooler conversation can be seen as a cultural parody—a parody of public discourses rather than cultural texts. The skit "repurposes" a casual office conversation as well as the discourses on TV to critique television and, importantly, the naïveté of Nichols's particular TV viewer. While in Rose's terms the conversation might be described as a satiric critique of the quiz show scandals, the discourses on TV which Nichols's character articulates are systems of meaning—discourse as the preformed material to be refunctioned.

THE CHAPTERS

Google "fabulous fifties" today, and you will find a number of consumer items for sale, but not (at least as of this writing) the CBS network spectacular. These products include a Time-Life CD set of popular music from the 1950s, as well as video collections of sports and entertainment performances. Such products provide a nostalgic view of the 1950s that leaves out the uneasiness, skepticism, and *ennui* that, for many at the time, characterized the decade. The alternative proposition, that the 1950s were "not-so-fabulous," has been made in a number of important works. These included contemporary social criticism which ranged from William Whyte's indictment of the "organization man" whose life played out in service to bureaucracies at work and home, to Betty Friedan's critique of the "feminine mystique" which proposed that women find fulfillment through their role as queen of the household. Many of these works were bestsellers, a number of which I discuss in conjunction with the 1950s fascination with psychoanalysis and mental health. This combination suggested that fifties culture was a "sick" one, and such criticisms often found popular voices in American humor. During the 1950s, popular culture became a place where Americans learned they had anxieties, then were taught strategies for managing them. A new type of humor labeled "sick comedy" suggested that it was the shared American culture and value systems of the postwar period that were to blame for these anxieties.

The first chapter of this book traces out the tensions between appearances, expectations, and realities of living the supposed postwar good life, tensions which helped produce what was described as the "new" or "sick" comedy at the time. The chapter explores how humor was understood as a weapon to be deployed against repression in the Cold War context both at home and abroad, and how comedy that ostensibly broke boundaries of good taste was embraced as successfully engaging the rifts between expectations and realities. Despite going against many mainstream sensibilities, humor considered by many to be subversive, even dangerous, was successfully incorporated into media culture. The chapter thus explains the cultural contexts for examining parody and sick comedy in the following chapters: how the parodic impulse was tied to other aspects of postwar culture, and how it was suited to the particular tastes of audiences, and thus ripe for incorporation in television culture. While the name "Lenny Bruce" is for many synonymous with "sick comedy," this chapter considers Bruce but focuses more extensively on Shelley Berman, one of the most successful new comedians, whose everyman persona ran counter to Bruce's hipster, and, perhaps not surprisingly, brought him success in clubs, on LP records, and on TV. Rather than positing this as a typical example of the Culture Industry's co-optation and watering-down of subversive humor, this chapter seeks to understand why Berman's persona so successfully connected with postwar audiences through media culture.

When fifties TV viewers watched, read, or listened to parodies, they engaged in semiotic games loaded with cultural power. The second chapter of this book looks at the birth of the enormously popular—and culturally influential—*MAD Magazine* to closely examine those semiotic games and to consider the ways in which their potency might be manifested. *MAD*'s meteoric success coincided with that of television, and though it initially parodied comics before TV, it quickly became an indispensable weapon for youth audiences making sense of postwar popular culture, and in particular the commercialism and consumerism which so permeated and defined it. As defined earlier, parody typically critiques aesthetic conventions, while satire highlights social ones.[11] But in the 1950s, the separation between the aesthetic and the social was blurred more than ever before. Whether in *MAD*, the TV shows of Ernie Kovacs, or elsewhere, parody articulated this intersection between the aesthetic, textual world and the "real" social world outside the text. Nowhere is that more obvious than in the supposedly juvenile pages of *MAD*.

To understand the significance of *MAD* for its readers as TV viewers, it is necessary to take a dialogic approach, examining discourses on mass media, the production practices of early television, the changing regulations in the comic book industry, and the youth culture as an emerging market. The *MAD* chapter thus looks primarily to how these intersecting discourses impacted the creation and consumption of *MAD* parodies, rather than the particular artistic methods and attitudes of the artists and editors of the magazine. In addition to the broad critical attitude toward culture expressed in its anticonsumerist parodies, *MAD* specifically encouraged an active participation with media texts. *MAD* taught its readers how to find pleasure in cultural decoding and recycling through strategies of reappropriation, recycling, and recombination. In short, by examining *MAD*'s parodies and how readers (not to mention the FBI!) responded to them, we can recognize that parody influences how people use popular culture, not just what they use. *MAD*'s profound popularity in the 1950s suggests that we ought to fundamentally rethink what sorts of pleasures audiences were finding in postwar television culture. The magazine's fans sometimes made *MAD* part of their public identities, in formal and informal clubs. But beyond those explicit cases, *MAD* parodies encouraged individuals to produce pleasures from television in their own ways, and to construct identity in relation to media culture beyond an embrace of the magazine itself.

The third chapter turns to another 1950s upstart and megasuccess in the magazine industry, *Playboy*. Though *Playboy* quickly became notorious for its nude pictorials, its founder Hugh Hefner embraced parody as part of his prescription for sophisticated living from the beginning, even going so far as to hire away the first editor of *MAD*, Harvey Kurtzman, and much of his staff. This chapter examines how parodic reading strategies became one more method of attaining cultural capital for the readers of *Playboy*, alongside appreciating modern art and jazz and purchasing the proper wardrobe and furniture. Parodic texts like *MAD* and especially *Playboy*'s own parodic content were key to constructing the "sophisticated" *Playboy* consumer's engagement with mass culture, a taste that could include both a *Victory at Sea* dramatic television score and a Louis Armstrong jazz album. The embrace of parody by *Playboy* extended to a series of books parodying movies seen on TV, and even influenced *Playboy*'s own syndicated television show, *Playboy's Penthouse*. This chapter details how *Playboy* adopted parody in order to connect with readers and teach them how mass media consumption could be transformed into cultural capital. Parody, for *Playboy*, helped create a critical distance from popular culture, from which it could be safely enjoyed in a refined manner as part of a self-consciously "sophisticated" masculine identity.

Max Horkheimer and Theodor W. Adorno's foundational work on the "Culture Industry," which predated and influenced MacDonald's

"Masscult" critique, also remains an intriguing model for examining the function of parody in the cultural texts produced by and about television. The essay famously outlines an explanatory schema that describes the standardization of content across the culture industries, and suggests that deviations (such as Nichols and May's TV criticism on TV) are already accounted for in the structure of the industry. They are expected, even necessary. Horkheimer and Adorno cite Orson Welles as an example tolerated because his "departures from the norm are regarded as calculated mutations which serve all the more strongly to confirm the validity of the system."[12] In the case of early television, Ernie Kovacs has been canonized as the televisual analogue to Welles the cinema auteur. J. Hoberman's 1982 essay "Vulgar Modernism," for example, made a connection between the early *MAD*, Kovacs, and other popular media works he believed were "precursors, parallels, and analogues to local or European avant-gardism." Hoberman defined vulgar modernism as a "popular, ironic, somewhat dehumanized mode reflexively concerned with the specific properties of its medium or the conditions of its making" and described its presence in Kovacs' oeuvre, from his live, cheaply produced morning shows to his taped and elaborate video manipulations in his later specials.[13] Hoberman viewed this type of cultural work as oppositional, using comedy to interrogate mass media form, more so than interrogating mass media form in order to produce comedy.

Taking a different tack, the fourth chapter examines just how Kovacs's critically celebrated "electronic tricks" and parodies fit within the logics of early television production. This inevitably means rethinking the "oppositional" label applied to them by critics such as Hoberman. Kovacs has justly been celebrated as the first video artist by academics, and was indeed known for his singular approach to television as a visual and electronic medium. He also was particularly fond of parody, which was a fundamental component of his aesthetic. Kovacs' status as auteur, though it may distinguish him now as distinctive from the "standard" TV comics of the 1950s, served as valuable product differentiation for the TV industry. Though both his parodies as well as his "electronic tricks" worked to interrogate television as a technology and cultural form, these also are what made him a marketable commodity. Like Welles, his singular style worked to reinforce the larger, standard system of television production.

While parody may have had popular resonance, I argue, because of its tendency to critique the dominant, cheery accounts of cultural life, I don't propose viewing its ability to produce pleasures from textual manipulation to be strictly ideological. Textual manipulation, with or without explicit ideological overtones, can produce reading pleasure. Roland Barthes asks whether anyone has actually ever read Proust or Balzac word for word, and instead says that it is the rhythm of what is read and what is not read that produces pleasures. "Thus, what I enjoy in a narrative is not directly its content or even its structure, but rather the abrasions I impose upon the fine surface: I read on, I skip, I look up, I dip in again."[14] While Barthes, in this case, champions the abrasions made upon the "great narratives," similar pleasures may have been produced by parodying American popular culture. Repurposing, recycling, reappropriating were all "abrasions" upon texts that could produce individual pleasures and meanings. At the same time, these individual pleasures were tied to participation in alternative reading communities. By examining the dialogic contexts in which parody emerged from the cultural industry and was embraced by viewers/readers/consumers in the 1950s, we can see how parody as a textual strategy was integral *and*—sometimes—oppositional to postwar popular culture.

If parodies marked abrasions upon the surface of "normal TV" in the fifties, then Oscar Levant can be said to have taken a machete to the medium. Chapter 5 examines the peculiar career of this pianist, composer, actor, television host and performer, and all-around eccentric. Though Levant didn't usually deal ostensibly in parody or satire, his very "sick" wit and star persona created an altogether distinctive form of television considered an antidote to normal TV—"a show for people who hate TV" in the words of his producer. Certainly, Levant was considered an abrasive personality willing to say almost anything, but it was his sick, sophisticated wit that made him a national curiosity on network television and a subcultural TV hero among the fans of his local Los Angeles TV show. On network TV, Levant played "Name That Pill" with Steve Allen, made multiple appearances as a disheveled wreck on Jack Paar's show, and caricatured himself as a houseguest from hell on *The Joey Bishop Show*. But on his local Los Angeles show he was a hero not just for the acerbic wit he turned on Hollywood and himself (a prototype for today's celebrity snark), but for the spontaneous, unscripted nature of the show. In one famous spat, his anticommercial rhetoric and inclination culminated in flat-out telling his fans not to buy Philco—who happened to be his sponsor.

It is the distinction between Levant as national curiosity and Levant as subcultural hero that signals how local television in the 1950s did at times also generate its own, to borrow Hoberman's phrase, "precursors, parallels, and analogues" to the narrowcasting strategies of postnetwork television. Those narrowcasting strategies were also anticipated by MacDonald, who admitted that his dismissive attitude toward mass tastes was elitist, even un-democratic. But MacDonald saw potential in media culture: it was the "mass" that really disturbed him, and he suggested that there might be ways to exist above or outside the "ooze." Referring to such successes as quality paperbacks, art cinema houses, and off-Broadway theaters, he wrote:

> The mass audience is divisible, we have discovered—and the more it is divided, the better. Even television, the most senseless and routinized expression of Masscult (except for the movie newsreels), might be improved by this approach. One possibility is pay-TV, whose modest

concept s that only those who subscribe could get the program ... perhaps one would rather pay for bread than get stones for nothing.[15]

Whether MacDonald would have approved of HBO's promotional claim that "It's Not TV," he certainly endorsed its model, and Oscar Levant's success on local TV in LA showed both the potential for narrowcasted audiences and the market that existed because of shifting tastes in consuming media culture. It's relatively safe to say that MacDonald was not an official member of the Oscar Levant Fan Club nor did he march alongside the "*MAD* Readers of Plainville, Connecticut," in a local parade. But it was just those sorts of cultural formations that he endorsed and saw as the future of "quality" culture.

By virtue of their incorporation in a 1960 network television spectacular, the Nichols and May performances in *The Fabulous Fifties* existed at a nexus of discourses on what television meant for Americans at the end of the 1950s. Their presence on the program and their parodic, satiric form point to the insufficiency of labeling popular media culture subversive or oppositional. What matters is what that content meant to viewers and what they did with it. Certainly by 1960 there was nothing shocking about what they had to say around the water cooler. Their parodic banter about TV echoed the skeptical pleasure with which many Americans regarded the medium. For those viewers, and for the producers, writers, and comics commemorating the 1950s, parody went hand-in-hand with television's discovering, teaching, and critiquing of itself.

1 The New, Sick Sense
The Mediation of America's Health and Humor at Midcentury

In a 1959 episode of *Peter Gunn*, real-life comedian Shelley Berman stars as Danny Holland, a stand-up comic who hires the detective because he thinks his wife is trying to kill him. Gunn quickly finds out, however, that the wife believes *Danny* is the one with emotional problems—that she fears he is going to kill *her*. Gunn consults a psychiatrist, who can't tell him which person is lying, but we quickly discover that Danny is truly a "sick" comic. His paranoid delusions have led him to murder several men that he believed his wife sent to kill him. When Danny walks onstage to perform his routine for the last time, his head is overwhelmed with voices. He accuses the audience of being brainwashed, and tells them that they are laughing because they are told something is funny. Which is exactly what the audience does: Danny's onstage breakdown meets with uproarious laughter. It's unclear why the audience shows so much pleasure in Danny's mental collapse. Is it sadistic enjoyment at the sight of a man who has become sick, who has buckled under life's pressures? Maybe they truly find the few antisocial quips he aims at them funny. Perhaps they are indeed laughing because they are told he is funny, performing their proper roles as audience members. Whatever the reason, Danny the sick, murderous comic, leaves them in stitches.[1]

However unsettling this *Peter Gunn* episode is to see now, the audience in the club should not be understood as a *Twilight Zone*-styled alternate universe, where people laugh at what is hurtful or even sadistic. Rather, the episode links popularly discussed concerns about mental health on both individual and national scales with debates about the social relevance and propriety of a brand of humor commonly called "sick comedy." The episode portrays sick comedy literally, overtly connecting two postwar American preoccupations: humor and mental health. The audience, laughing maniacally, seems to signify that sickness is a widespread condition, not one existing only inside Danny's—or any specific individual's—head.

Television and film were key areas throughout the 1950s where concerns about what it meant to be normal versus neurotic were put into play. During the same time, a distinction between what constituted normal, healthy humor and what constituted sick comedy developed. The nation's sense

16 Parody and Taste in Postwar American Television Culture

1.1

1.2

The New, Sick Sense 17

1.3

1.4

Figure 1.1–1.4 Real-life comedian Shelley Berman walks onstage as fictional (and murderous) comedian Danny Holland for one final performance. Though he verbally and physically manifests his mental illness, his antisocial routine meets with unanimous laughter from the audience. (Frame Grab, *Peter Gunn,* "The Comic.")

of humor seemed to be changing. Television and the popular press took note that a new type of humor was developing: comedy was simultaneously becoming more socially relevant and breaking more social taboos. But this changing sense of humor was just a component of a much larger concern: what constituted a normal, well-adjusted individual in the postwar era? Was this new, sick humor a response to the social pressures of conforming to those accepted qualities, or at least pretending to?

This chapter examines a variety of television shows, comedy albums, and newspaper and magazine articles to attempt to understand how comedy in the late 1950s and early 1960s functioned in the articulation of identity. Comedy as a privileged area for popular social critique grappled increasingly during this period with the postwar standard of "normal." The "normal" of 1950s America was supposed to be unequivocally accepted as a great improvement over other recent "normals." After the struggles of the Great Depression and prolonged sacrifices of World War II, the economy boomed and Americans looked forward to sharing in the prosperity. The GI Bill made college education and homeownership possible for more people than ever before, swelling the ranks of the middle class. Those who had been living with extended families during tougher times moved out, bought a house, and filled it with the latest consumer goods—the television set foremost among them. The nuclear family was born, and with it, a particular version of the American Dream. For middle-class men, happiness and fulfillment were to be found through a reliable job, a wife and kids to come home to, and a hobby or other leisure activity for staying productive even during "down" time. Despite having entered the workforce in large numbers during the war, women were expected to go back home and find their happiness and fulfillment within it. The role of the middle-class woman as housewife was recast not as servant catering to husband and children, but as queen of her house in the suburbs and of the consumer wonders within it.

From the beginning, there were segments of the population for whom achieving this version of the American dream would prove more elusive. Desirable or not, for them the dream simply wasn't equally accessible. Though many African-Americans had experienced greater social freedom as veterans serving abroad, back home racial discrimination remained firmly entrenched. Biased loan and development practices effectively segregated the new suburban communities by excluding homeowners who weren't white. The Levitts, whose Levittown, New Jersey, is considered the prototypical postwar suburb, publicly refused to sell to blacks for two decades following the war.[2]

It wasn't long before even those with access to the dream began to identify its more nightmarish elements. Betty Friedan's *The Feminine Mystique* balked at the oppressive claim of popular culture (and advertising in particular) that women should be satisfied with staying at home and mastering their consumer goods. The book popularized social criticisms that would become early strains of feminism and helped trigger the women's movement. Almost from the moment the war ended and the postwar period began, men, too, expressed disaffection for this prescription for a normal, happy life. That disaffection is what bred sick comedy and Danny Holland's onstage breakdown.

Often, it was the new postwar "normal" which was understood to be sick in popular culture, as comics, artists, and writers took aim at subjects ranging from politics to child-rearing to bureaucracies—in short, the American way of life. Such potentially culturally subversive comedy can be documented as far back as one cares to go, but it was in the postwar period, particularly during the late 1950s and early 1960s, that it was built into the structure of the emerging medium of commercial television. Television was hungry for content; the networks needed to fill up their expanding programming schedules as well as find ways to make that content relevant to viewers. When a significant proportion of those viewers became critical of the cultural institutions of life in the suburbs and working for the organization, or at least began to feel uneasy and dissatisfied with them, television and American comedy became critical of them as well.

This does not mean that the presence of sick comedy on television was simply a reflection of what audiences already thought and felt. Nor does it mean sick or socially relevant comedy simply functioned as a safety valve, relieving pressures so that some larger social "explosion" wreaking radical change wouldn't take place. Whether or not political or socially topical humor was subversive is not inherent in the comedy itself, but depends upon individual interactions with the media texts. Criticism of one's culture, even at this early point in postwar America, wasn't necessarily a deviant act. One just needed to make appropriate criticisms in the appropriate places with the appropriate terms. Cultural criticism was at times an accepted sort of popular diversion, integrated into cocktail conversations, comics, and *The Reader's Digest*. The new, sick humor of postwar America is best understood in dialogue with other forms of social and cultural criticism at the time, which were eminently concerned with the changing psychological nature of American life. The articulation of normal health and humor took place through a variety of popular culture materials, and the documents I draw on cluster around the period of the late 1950s and early 1960s. In particular, I will examine how comedic texts mediated concerns about mental health and humor. Thus, this chapter is not just about classifying and writing the history of a different style of comedy or cultural mode, but thinking about how behavior, words, beliefs, attitudes, and individuals—not just comedians—can be labeled deviant, maladjusted, or sick. But this is not just a documentation of discipline by an abstract governmental or corporate "them." I also ask why such deviance—to be mad or sick—held such popular appeal, making financial successes of albums, magazines, television shows, novels, movies, and even sociocultural studies that interrogated the postwar "normal" and suggested it was something to be shunned, not emulated.

REPRESSED LAUGHTER: AT HOME AND ABROAD

To understand the term "sick comedy" and understand how that comedy became a popular form of social criticism, it is necessary to look at other ways in which American humor was described in the postwar period. One major theme in the discussion of comedy in the popular press from 1950 to 1962 made comedy a matter of national concern by speculating that a national sense of humor could be constructed to oppose the essentially humorless communists. "The stern, unsmiling faces of Malik, Mao and Malenkov are the outward signs of an inner attitude toward life," posed Richard Armour in *The Saturday Evening Post*. "The sourpuss is as much a trade-mark of communism as the hammer and sickle."[3] This characterization of the communist temperament was not a postwar invention. American pop culture had already suggested that this overly serious demeanor was symptomatic of an ideology that valorized sacrificing personal happiness and gain for the betterment of the larger community. In 1939, for example, Greta Garbo starred in *Ninotchka*, a film directed by Ernst Lubitsch and written by Billy Wilder that suggested its overly serious communist protagonist was so consumed by ideology that she was incapable of experiencing pleasure. This distinction between the demeanors of capitalists and communists became more acute in the 1950s as the pursuit of happiness and pleasure was increasingly tied to material consumption.

The employment of a sense of humor as an essentially American characteristic typifies much discussion surrounding controversial humor in the postwar press. When some comedians would subsequently be criticized for being too political, or potentially subversive, the response along these lines was that humor was a type of free speech, and that people should enjoy the right to laugh. In such a climate, it may be difficult to imagine that humor could subvert American culture, which was assumed (through the Bill of Rights) to have the capacity to contain dissident humor just as it tolerated disparate political viewpoints.

In humor, as in politics, one could go too far, of course. But when sick humor became dangerous, it wasn't because of any direct political content, or even because it upset a mainstream sense of good taste through bodily humor. Sick humor was deemed to be dangerous or subversive when it proposed that core American values and the American way of life were to blame for that very same "sick-ness." Sick comedy became culturally potent when it suggested the sick and the mad weren't aberrant characters, but what all Americans were inevitably heading toward. In the meantime, sick comedy implied, they were only pretending to keep themselves together, performing those social roles they were expected to in order to be considered normal.

Belying the reputation of the humorless commies, in a 1952 column in *The Saturday Review*, Richard Hanser wrote that the millions now living behind the Iron Curtain were finding out that humor was one of the few weapons they had in the struggle between freedom and oppression.[4]

Though the press and the airwaves could be censored for subversive content, regulating what people said amongst themselves was more difficult, and it was on this level that political jokes could circulate as "the only means by which the slave-citizen can express, however furtively, his defiance of his masters." Hanser gave examples from Rumania, Russia, and Poland, and especially pointed out the body of anti-Hitler *Flüsterwitze*—whisper jokes—that had proliferated under Nazi rule. The problem wasn't the nature of the Soviet people, but those people who enforced the communist ideology.

Hanser noted that the Third Reich had not collapsed because people made irreverent cracks about it, and nor would communism.

> But there is no way of estimating how many deluded Nazis and Fascists had their eyes opened, how many blind believers had their faith shaken, how many timid dissenters were strengthened by hearing a satirical, searing story that cut through the pretensions of propaganda to the truth of the matter.[5]

The political joke was an enemy of totalitarianism, said Hanser, because it was a symptom of opposition and a lack of the unthinking reverence that totalitarianism demanded. With other areas off-limits to oppositional speech, the political joke both evidenced the resiliency of the people under totalitarian rule, and provided a release for the frustrations of living under such restrictions.[6]

Though Hanser prescribed "Wit as a Weapon" to be used against totalitarians overseas, sick humor emerged as a stateside psychological response to repression. The changing American and Soviet senses of humor weren't so much at ideological odds as they were both responses to stifling social forces. Though communist totalitarianism was usually constructed as the antithesis of the American way of life, a number of popular critiques during the 1950s pointed to the stifling nature of postwar suburban and corporate citizenship. John Keats's *The Crack in the Picture Window* lambasted suburban developments for destroying the American landscape to make way for row upon row of anonymous boxes. Additionally, while the academic critics of the Frankfurt School, fresh from fleeing Nazi Germany, theorized that the mass media standardized consciousness, more widely read books such as Vance Packard's *The Hidden Persuaders* popularized the notion that advertising manipulated minds and desires through unseen mechanisms. For a time, both the high-flown language of academics and down-to-Earth language of popular culture seethed as an opposition beneath the sheen of postwar life. Not only were scholars writing about what postwar culture was doing to national and individual psyches, but lots of people were reading these critiques of the contemporary culture, and many more were aware of them. The same forces applying pressure to be normal, to conform, to be productive, evidently encouraged an interrogation of what "normal" meant.

These works tied the experiences of what were said to be prototypical individuals working for large corporations and living in the suburbs with a change in psychological nature on a national scale. In particular, William Whyte's *The Organization Man* gave a name to a cultural figure that would reappear in many venues, from novels to movies to television and popular magazines.[7] The organization man didn't just work for the organization, he belonged to it. Even when home in the suburbs, his leisure played out through other organizations such as the Lions Club or PTA. The term "organization man" came to describe the consummate bureaucrat, who experienced life not through his own individualism, but through these organizations. The organization man was the product of a society that rewarded conformity, not creativity. He was to be disdained, his lifestyle and identity avoided, not emulated.

Whyte, a writer and editor at *Fortune* magazine, theorized that this psychological tendency to look for purpose or life meaning through the organization had developed because the traditional roots of family life had been severed in modern life. It was no longer possible for anyone but lawyers and doctors to return to their hometowns, making extended families a thing of the past. In substitution for these, the organization was embraced to attempt to bring community life to the suburbs.

While Whyte provided the catchy name for this figure, David Riesman had already developed an extensive formulation of him in his book *The Lonely Crowd: A Study of the Changing American Character* in 1950.[8] Riesman theorized that there had been a recent shift from inner-directed individuals who pursued goals they had internalized early in life to other-directed individuals who were primarily sensitized to the expectations of others. His "contemporaries are the source of direction for the individual" and only the process of paying attention to the signals from them remains unaltered through his life. His outer-directed nature allowed him to function as the consummate bureaucrat, not only at work, but in the community as well.

In *The Organization Man*, Whyte argues that there had been an ideological shift in organization life toward "idolatry of the system." Personality tests, he says, were an attempt by the organization to use science to achieve this idolatry. Often given to prospective employees, the tests were distributed by companies with such generically ominous names as "The Psychological Corporation" and "The Attitude Research Laboratory." These tests effectively taught prospective employees how they could be expected to think or behave in order to be considered normal and productive. Whyte included an appendix to his book called "How to Cheat on Personality Tests," which warned that the goal on personality tests wasn't to get a good score, but to avoid a bad one. Safety would be found in answering questions as if you were like everybody else was *supposed* to be, landing yourself safely within the 40th and 60th percentiles. Whyte noted that many of the questions on such tests had evolved from tests originally designed to screen mentally disturbed people, and were a means of checking for employees' neurotic tendencies. However, the often-conflicting postwar drives to be both a productive worker and have a rewarding home life meant that neuroses weren't necessarily a completely negative force. It was better to land somewhere in the middle than appear completely neurosis-free. An employee's neuroses weren't necessarily a liability for the company if they made him more productive. So it would be better to selectively choose your afflictions. Whyte suggested that you would have the "the best margin for error if you err on the side of being 'hypermanic'—that is, too energetic and active."[9] Cheating on personality tests showed how performing neuroses could be just another element of performing normality.

Packard's *The Hidden Persuaders* was one of the most successful works to argue that science was being used by sinister corporate forces to regulate personalities, sparking a national furor over the psychological techniques used by advertising agencies. Though Packard took issue with the agencies' arrogant approach that the masses could be so easily influenced, he warned that there was a nefarious coalition between science and advertising that sought to produce easily manipulated consumers. Packard went on to publish a series of such cultural exposés, most of them with similar titles such as *The People Shapers*, *The Status Seekers*, and *The Pyramid Climbers*. Though some of his claims in *The Hidden Persuaders* were exaggerated, motivational research, as such psychological advertising techniques were known in the industry, had indeed become a key tool in postwar advertising as agencies sought more effective means to drive consumption.[10]

Although these works by social scientists and popular critics were well read, their criticisms were also incorporated into successful novels and films, such as *The Man in the Gray Flannel Suit*, which produced catchphrases themselves. The social criticism in these works did not function as subtle subtext. As the dust jacket on the 1955 book club edition of the novel noted:

> Although this novel is about the Rath family, the man in the gray flannel suit is a fairly universal figure in mid-twentieth-century America. The gray flannel suit is the uniform of the man with a briefcase who leaves his home each morning to make his living as an executive in the near-by city. Tom Rath's wife appreciates the security this job provides, though both she and her husband at times question whether this is the life they really wanted when they were first married.[11]

By the mid-1950s, the downside of life in the 'burbs and in the bureaucracy had not only been pointed out, it had become a popular stereotype, and the critique of the repressive nature of postwar life was well known. Almost immediately *MAD Magazine* took up *The Hidden Persuaders*' unveiling of the covert techniques of advertising companies through parody. But even these comic critiques were taken seriously because they complicated Cold War "us vs. them" dichotomies. Communist subversives weren't the only ones attempting to brainwash Americans, but advertisers and corporations as well. While wit was being prescribed as a weapon against the repression experienced by those living behind the Iron Curtain, American writers and social scientists were warning that Americans were experiencing repression and mind control at the hands of their own employers and culture. Tyranny at home could easily be found in the demand for normalcy at home and work.

It was in this distinctly *American* context of repression that the new, sick comedy arose. The label of "sick" was applied to a wide variety of comedians, from the overtly political material of Mort Sahl and satire of Lenny Bruce to the confessional stand-up routines of Berman and the loony antics of Jonathan Winters. Though Hanser had written that in the United States it "seems fantastic that a mere joke should be deemed a menace to the state and punished accordingly," the label of "sick" signified that this form of comedy upset notions of good taste, which could largely be relied upon to regulate what could or could not be said in public.[12] Though Bruce may have been the only well-known sick comic actually jailed, the label at least showed that there was something forbidden about the comedy, something that should not be said. And, like the German *Flüsterwitze*, sick comedy flourished as a popular response to less politically overt—but particularly American—social repressions.

Of course, there was also overt political repression in American culture of the 1950s. At the end of the decade, America was finally emerging from the deepest depths of McCarthyism and the fervent anticommunism that had fostered a notion that one's fellow Americans might be communist "fellow travelers." The postwar period was not only one in which Americans might be anxious over nuclear annihilation, but also nervous over whom they could trust, or what they might be forced to do to prove their own American-ness. Besides commercial controls over content and comedians who had trouble remaining funny under the pressing demands of the TV industry, the popular press acknowledged that this political climate influenced the tenor of American humor. Had our right to free speech and tendency to exercise that right through humor been harmed by McCarthyism? Was the postwar climate just too serious to laugh anymore, much less make fun of the government?

In December 1958, the *New York Times Magazine* collected short essays from a number of prominent comedians in order to assess the "State of the Nation's Humor."[13] James Thurber, Mort Sahl, Al Capp, Jerry Lewis, and Steve Allen all responded to the questions of whether Americans were taking themselves too seriously, and whether satire on private and public mores had become "unhealthfully scarce." The consensus was that McCarthyism had indeed created some lasting intimidation for writers and artists, and the networks, television sponsors, and interest groups did exert some censoring influence over American comedy. But the reality of the matter, most of these comic commentators pointed out, was that there was more American humor than ever before, thanks to mass media. Indeed, Al Capp went as far as to posit that this was a Golden Age of Comedy, at least for the "thousands of half-competents and incompetents" making so much money off humor. Allen noted that American brains were "humor-washed to an extent never before known in history. The Russians may be smarter, but we have the dubious distinction of being funnier."

Paradoxically, this and other hunts by the contemporary press for relevance in American humor confirmed that comedy was indeed considered a very serious matter by commentators and critics. Though the antics on *I Love Lucy* might get better ratings than a Mort Sahl talk show appearance (and anything else, for that matter), the widespread attention paid to prominent comedians, and the attempt to assess the politics of sick comedy or identify a "New American Comedy" clearly show that comedy was not seen as just another television genre by critics. While the vast majority of popular press articles on comedy during the 1950s focused on individual performers, by the end of the decade, attention had focused on the increasing social significance of a specific number of comedians.[14] A "new comedy" was declared, rising from the ashes of a period of comic burnout of television personalities such as Jackie Gleason, Milton Berle, and Sid Caesar. This burnout, blamed on early television's endless hunger for material and the demands of live production caused a "Crisis in Comedy" in the words of *Life* magazine.[15] Though there were still laughs to be found on television, they were mostly emanating from domestic situation comedies and too often in those cases, from prerecorded laugh tracks.

In addition to the view at the time that these comedians simply ran out of material and energy, Arthur Wertheim has shown how Milton Berle's downfall from "Mr. Television" coincided with, and was in many ways a result of, the changing demographics of television viewers during the 1950s. Wertheim notes that during the height of his popularity, from 1948 to 1951, Berle's audience was almost exclusively urban, and his comic aesthetic was distinctly that of a "New York Jewish stand-up comic from the urban vaudeville and nightclub circuits."[16] As television broadcasting spread from the cities into the hinterlands via coaxial cable and newly licensed TV stations, Berle was brought to more potential viewers, but his ratings declined as his "citified comic style was not really suited to the new small-town and rural audiences."[17] Given the choice between the vaudeville-styled fare of Berle and decidedly less urban programming such as *Death Valley Days*, the expanded audience chose the latter.

The attention paid to the "new" or "sick" comedy in the late 1950s by commentators in the popular press, signifies, if not a return to the dominance of urban comedy, at least a reaction against the perceived "dumbing down" of popular culture following the expansion of television broadcasting outside major urban areas. The new comedians were occasionally afforded the highbrow designation of satire, but usually and most famously labeled "sick." They were also distinctly urban, and television and LP records meant these urban comedians could be accessed by those who couldn't catch their act at a club in the big city. By the end of the decade, comedy was finding its way into more American homes, via television, LPs, and comic books, than ever before. It was this explosion in the market for comedy, in spite of McCarthyism and sponsor censorship, that brought about the search for social relevance. The concern of the television critics and commentators, rather than a popular one about sustaining good old-fashioned American satire, seems to have been an elitist one: that popular tastes (the same tastes for quiz shows, Westerns, and soap operas) would do a better job of wiping out socially relevant humor than McCarthyism had.

SICKNIKS AND OTHER MALCONTENTS

While the fictional character Danny Holland may have been the most literally sick comic to appear on television, sick comedy was certainly a familiar concept to the television audience. The "sickest of sick comedians," Lenny Bruce, had appeared on the *Steve Allen Show* several times. Though plagued by obscenity charges and narcotics abuse, Bruce remained popular and successful through a humor he himself said was based upon destruction and despair. By 1961, Bruce was generalizing that changes in comedy during the 1950s had altered audiences' expectations of what a comic performance was "about." Audiences were, therefore, more likely to get upset about what could be considered appropriate comic fodder. Said Bruce in a *Newsweek* interview: "A comedian of the older generation did an act, and he told the audience, 'This is my act.' Today's comic is not doing an act. The audience assumes he's telling the truth."[18]

And not just any truth, either. Rather, a nasty truth about the supposedly normal mainstream. This shift in the "new" or "sick" comedy was a big change, as Walter Blair and Hamlin Hill note in their history of American humor: "This seems to suggest a new perspective—humor can attack not only the misfits and peculiar variants from the norm, but also the norm itself, somehow universalizing its assault until it insults everyone—even the audience paying the standup comedian for the privilege of being insulted."[19] Social critiques, popular culture, and their own experiences had all suggested to fifties audiences that the norm and the middle were not "where it's at." The middle needed to be vacated. The place to be was in the margins, with the hipster Bruce, or at least there temporarily, laughing "with" rather than "at" him. The success of record albums by Bruce, Berman, and Bob Newhart suggests that these recordings didn't just provide access to jokes but to ways of thinking that could be accessed over and over for both laughter and identification.

Blair and Hill note that whatever the medium, popular humor has traditionally, and understandably, championed the values and norms of the middle class who constituted its audience.[20] In contrast, sick comedy was a visible sign of what they describe as an underground humor, one that shunned the middle class and its values. But this underground or counter-cultural humor also became a popular humor, gaining entrance to the venues and audiences it criticized. This entrance occurred while counterculture humor was forming during the 1950s and 1960s, so it would be misguided to speak of it having "sold out" to or being co-opted by popular (and corporate) media. Bruce serves as an emblematic underground comic figure that, despite success, maintained his countercultural status through his escalating drug abuse, legal struggles, and eventual death by overdose. But countercultural humor in the form of sick comedy was available to mainstream audiences, through corporate, consumer media from its beginnings. Bruce made his iconoclastic humor accessible to a broad audience outside the club or coffeehouse through touring, limited television appearances, and especially his long-playing albums. What made the humor "counter" was its content: criticizing the norms of mainstream, postwar life, including the media and interests responsible for propagating and profiting from those same "counter" attitudes and tastes.

An article in *Time* magazine in 1959 termed a group of comedians "The Sickniks" as a play on the equally derogatory term "Beatnik." "Although audiences unquestionably laugh at Bruce," the article begrudgingly acknowledged, "much of the time he merely shouts angrily and tastelessly at the way of the world."[21] While the magazine's explanation of Bruce's appeal is the same as Danny Holland's—that audiences are told what is funny—the more likely one, as cited by Bruce and established by *Time*'s discussion of the success and prevalence of the Sickniks, is that the comics were mediating very real, timely concerns, and that these often crossed the boundaries of good taste.

That is, the taste of middlebrow magazines like *Time*, anyway. In a famous 1949 *Harper's* magazine article, Russell Lynes speculated that in the postwar period, old class distinctions were no longer operative.[22] In their place, a stratified system of tastes would be the basis of social and cultural distinction. In this new social structure, the highbrows would be the elites, and their tastes would be formed in opposition to the mass media. Lynes split taste levels between highbrow, upper-middlebrow, lower-middlebrow, and lowbrow. *Life* magazine soon provided a graphic interpretation of his distinctions, making it possible for readers to quickly position themselves within his taste schema by charting whether they preferred red wine over a martini or musical extravaganza films to the theater.[23] Guessing one another's taste-culture thus became a popular cocktail game.

Michael Kammen writes that Lynes's essay, and the popularity of taste speculation that followed it, gave the sense that American tastes were becoming more stratified in the postwar period and that these distinctions reflected social and cultural realities.[24] However, Kammen notes more recent critical consensus that since midcentury, and especially because of television's prominence, cultural lines of stratification and distinct taste levels have actually blurred. Lynes did admit that in some of the areas distinctions blurred; for instance, the affinity of both the highbrow and the lowbrow for jazz. Another quality the taste groups shared was mutual contempt for the middlebrows: "The middlebrows are influential today, but neither the highbrows nor the lowbrows like them; and if we ever have intellectual totalitarianism, it may well be the lowbrows and the highbrows who will run things, and the middlebrows who will be exiled in boxcars to a collecting point probably in the vicinity of Independence, Missouri."[25]

It is important to consider "sick" within this model of stratified tastes, which establishes levels of cultural distinction, rather than good versus bad taste. Middlebrow magazines and critics deemed Bruce et al. "sick," but the contempt Lynes admits the high- and lowbrow feel for the middlebrow enabled sick (or what otherwise might be considered "low") humor to ironically become a marker of sophistication and distinction. In consideration of these levels of distinction, a 1962 article in *The Saturday Review* posed that after fans of Mort Sahl discovered that his tastes and point of view were as middlebrow as his targets, they turned to Bruce for satire.[26]

Though it was sometimes difficult to nail down a clear definition at the time, sick comedy was clearly comedy that had crossed *someone's* line of what was considered decent or polite. Comedy might be expected to transgress normal behavior, but sick comedy took those liberties a bit too far. The "Sickniks," as plotted by the *Time* article, included Mort Sahl, Jonathan Winters (who not only joked about but intermittently spent time in the "funny farm"), Elaine May and Mike Nichols, Don Adams, and Tom Lehrer. *Cosmopolitan* declared the existence of a new sense of humor in late 1958 citing many of the same individuals, but instead of "sick," more generously deemed them "cerebral comics."[27] These new comics wrote their own material, in contrast to the TV "joke tellers" such as Sid Caesar, George Gobel, and Jackie Gleason. This "cerebral" designation not only points to their ability to write their own material, but also signifies how the idea of "sickness" was tied to the mind and ways of thinking, rather than to the body and humor of bodily excess deemed to be lowbrow.

SHELLEY BERMAN'S CEREBRAL LAXATIVES

Lenny Bruce tapped a vital postwar nerve, a nerve which may have found its most caustic expression on the extremities but which ran all throughout the body politic. Ultimately, Bruce became more and more consumed by his legal problems and drug addiction, and he would remain on the margins of popular media, successfully maintaining his countercultural status. Network television might hold the occasional talk show appearance for him, but not much more. By contrast, Shelley Berman's career illustrates how the sick aspects of comedy could be incorporated into a tamer, more acceptable form than that offered by Bruce. This didn't happen because the topics of sick humor are inherently funny, and therefore make the dangerous acceptable, but because the potentially disruptive aspects of the humor were articulated into a more conventional cultural dialogue. Examining that articulation is a more constructive exercise to help understand the midcentury American humor than simply seeing Berman as the watered-down, safe, or mainstream version of Bruce's sick comedy. Instead, Berman articulated a sick comedy of middle—not countercultural—America in his comedy, as well as embodying the sick everyman in several only slightly disguised acting roles.

Indeed, much of Berman's appeal appears to have come from his embodiment of the everyman teetering on the brink, fighting to maintain mental and emotional balance in middle America. Whereas Sahl and Bruce were characterized as political or at least controversial, Berman was described as specializing in "monologues on life's minuscule embarrassments."[28] Much popular commentary of the time was concerned with whether sick comedy was actually funny or just shocking, whether new and creative things were being said or just things that shouldn't be.[29] But Berman offers an example of how comedy created a dialogue between concerns about individual mental health (whether a person was sick in the head) and national health (whether America was a sick society).

Figure 1.5 Shelley Berman's performance as a homicidal comedian in *Peter Gunn* drew upon the content and style of Berman's actual routines. Here an outwardly "well" Holland performs atop a stool on a nightclub stage. (Frame Grab, *Peter Gunn*, "The Comic".)

Berman often overtly dealt with the collision between modern psychological know-how and the mundane aspects of family life and child-rearing. A fine example comes from his highly successful, Grammy-winning 1959 album, *Inside Shelley Berman*. He begins the album by recalling having heard a child psychologist on a talk show answer questions from "worried, distraught, harried, insane parents." One parent complained that her daughter had developed a penchant for taking things that weren't hers. The psychologist's pithy diagnosis: The child was a thief. There was nothing to worry about; either the child would grow out of it or become more proficient. Perhaps this quip is typical of the age-old comic technique of exchanging an intellectual response for common sense. But Berman also reveals how the new awareness of psychology could threaten what had been presumed to be commonsense truths. The psychologist adds that the mother shouldn't discourage the daughter, "or you'll give her a trauma and she won't be able to adjust to society." It is the kleptomaniacal daughter who is in fact better adjusted to modern life. "I know many a liar who's doing very well these days," says Berman's psychologist, "like those who make airline schedules." Thus, Berman segues from his psychology bit into another about the terrors of flying (another anxiety he assumes the audience shares).

The "sick" aspects of Berman's routine on the album include the manner in which Berman confronts the audience's presumed fear of flying, from pointing out that the people waving hysterically in the airplane's brochure have already landed, to the innocent looking white bag that really says, "You feel good now, but wait until we get you up there, brother" to the captain who reveals over the intercom that he doesn't know where the plane is headed. His sick material includes his objection to the "pornographic" appeal that buttermilk apparently has for some people, and his discussion of the minor embarrassment of spitting on people while talking. Berman also discusses the appeal of nostalgia, which "recalls an existence that is sweet, warm and quietly thrilling . . . like returning to the womb." Berman says that everyone wants to return to the womb, but he wants to get off the subject, "because it is . . . disgusting." All of these illustrate Berman's teetering across boundaries of good taste, especially regarding bodily functions, working his way up from vomit and buttermilk to the womb.

Berman was perhaps best known for his telephone monologues; sitting alone onstage, he feigned a telephone conversation. In these, the humor derives not from Berman's contact with a specific, comic character, but with his connection with a more generally understood, shared condition or experience. *Inside Shelley Berman* includes three such phone bits. The first of these features a man calling a department store to report that someone is hanging from a ledge of the building. Of course, before he can report this he is immediately placed on hold, then encounters an employee who is going on break, then is transferred to the complaint department, then to the lingerie department, etc. The fantastic occasion of the person dangling from the ledge only serves as an illumination of the frustrating experience of dealing with the department store bureaucracy, a frustration with modern life that the audience is expected to share.

On his follow-up album, none too cleverly titled *Outside Shelley Berman*, he begins by firmly placing himself alongside other key "sick" or socially relevant comedians. He notes the talent that has come from the area's nightclubs, including his friend Mort Sahl, whom he points out is a Canadian, and jokingly adds that it bothers him that a foreigner should criticize the government so. He also mentions Lenny Bruce, to applause, then says that he recently had the pleasure of hearing Pope Pius on record, and was amazed to hear his frank indifference to Lenny Bruce. Thus having positioned himself among his fellow relevant comics, Berman can make a sick joke, in terms both physically and intellectually sick, calling his routine "a kind of cerebral laxative. People who see this act every night we call regulars." Having positioned himself amid these political or at least socially relevant comedians, he establishes his sick credentials, and can then delve into his, in comparison to Sahl's or Bruce's, more pedestrian material.

Berman again reprises the phone routines, notably in "Franz Kafka on the Telephone," which bears no literary allusions to the author's work, but simply consists of Kafka calling information and dealing with first an old operator who dies on him, then one named "Miss Freud" who attempts to analyze him over the phone. The album's only other phone bit includes Berman portraying his father after he has asked him for money to attend acting school in New York. The piece foregrounds the father's Jewishness as an old-world relic. This relic is something the modern men or bureaucrats Berman usually has on the line lack, and something Berman in comparison to his father lacks as well. The result is a poignant contrast between generations that amounts to one between cultures: the old, religious, and ethnic world of the father and the modern, white, secular world of the son.[30]

Such an affective, heartfelt treatment of parenting is quickly contrasted by the next (and final) bit on the album. Berman improvises a game with the audience in which he assumes the role of a child psychologist appearing at a Parent-Teacher Association meeting. For a daughter who won't take a nap, the psychologist advises filling up a bottle with brandy, etc., then the parent should drink it and will no longer care about the missed nap. Thumb-sucking, bed-wetting, IQ testing are also cursorily dealt with, and Berman ends by mentioning the psychologist's latest book: *Raising Children for Fun and Profit*. In this bit, Berman parodies the pop psychology of parenting that boomed following the publishing of Dr. Benjamin Spock's *The Common Sense Book of Baby and Child Care* in 1946. Spock wanted parents to be flexible and think of kids as individuals who might require individual styles of child-rearing. But the success of Spock also points to the fifties preoccupation with normality: a need to locate a common way to shape children into normal kids through normal parenting styles.

Psychology, parenthood, and modern life form the core of the comic source material in all of these bits and performances. Berman's material, which appears less "edgy" or controversial than Lenny Bruce's, is interesting because it is so seemingly mundane and popular—in other words, because it is so mainstream. The nightclub audience seems as middle of the road in its concerns as the television audience, and the audience buying the record. The bitterest expressions of midcentury sickness might have been successfully marginalized, but there remained the searing center of pop psychology and consumer culture Berman occupied. From nightclubs to talk shows to anthology television shows to LPs, this was still sick comedy for a sick culture.

In a 1961 episode of *The Twilight Zone* titled "The Mind and the Matter," Berman stars as Archibald Beechcroft, described in Rod Serling's introduction as "a child of the twentieth century, a product of the population explosion, and one of the inheritors of the legacy of progress."[31] We watch as the put-upon Beechcroft is pummeled by a crowd on the subway, then in the elevator on his way to the office. One of the recurring lessons taught by *The Twilight Zone* is to be careful what you wish for, and when Beechcroft complains that "If I had my way, I would eliminate the people . . . and there would be only one man left, me," we know where the episode is headed. As luck would have it, a lackey who spills coffee on Beechcroft attempts to make it up to him by giving him a book titled *The Mind and the Matter: How You Can Achieve the Ultimate Power of Concentration.* Beechcroft skips ahead to the third chapter on "intense concentration," and before long he is concentrating hard enough to get rid of everyone else on Earth. First the landlady demanding rent disappears, then the people on the subway and at the office. Before long, boredom sets in, and Beechcroft decides that rather than being alone, it would be better to have some people around, but only ones just like him. So, the city is repopulated with Archibald Beechcrofts who not only look like him but also share his embittered worldview. The original Beechcroft is shown how utterly unhappy the world would be if everyone was as bitter and angry as him, so he concentrates things back to normal. Serling's narration tells us Beechcroft has learned "that with all its faults, it may be that this is the best of all possible worlds. People not withstanding, it has much to offer."

Though the episode maintains a lighthearted tone throughout, there is little overt comedy. When the city is repopulated with Beechcrofts, Berman appears in drag as an old lady on the elevator, but besides that, his acting talents as the anxious and flustered everyman are primarily on display. The episode shows how Berman embodies a mainstream comic approach to the well-documented downsides of being a "child of the twentieth century." That it is Berman starring as Beechcroft matters because he is a recognizable comedian, known for expressing the everyday frustrations which reach their ultimate, logical manifestations in the fulfillment of Beechcroft's misanthropic wishes. To a certain extent, then, the episode teaches not only to be careful what you wish for, but what you complain about—or laugh at—as well.

The lesson to be learned, perhaps, is that it is okay to have misanthropic feelings and complaints about the nature of modern, urban life, so long as you don't act upon them. This was a lesson learned by one of the comedians clearly following in Berman's tracks, Bob Newhart. Berman's albums sold millions of copies and in many ways set off the boom in comedy LPs that would continue through the 1960s and 1970s. Newhart's first album, titled *The Buttoned-Down Mind of Bob Newhart*, was another enormous success in 1960. While Berman typified the everyman who regularly cracked under social pressures and couldn't quite stay "normal," Newhart famously kept his cool. Though he pointed out the absurdities and performative nature of midcentury life, Newhart seldom snapped. Instead, he acknowledged, then moved on. His prescriptive relationship with the ills of American culture is perhaps best evidenced by the success of his role as Chicago psychologist Dr. Bob Hartley in *The Bob Newhart Show* from 1972 to 1978.

A *Bell & Howell Close-Up* documentary, titled "What's So Funny?" that aired on ABC in 1962 explored the changing American humor by posing an apparently simple question: What was funny now, and why was it funny?[32] Following the spate of articles in popular magazines and newspapers in the late 1950s that had been attempting to catch hold of what was changing on the comic scene, the television documentary cast a wide net at a point in time at which television had already taken firm hold, and America was out of Ike's 1950s and into Kennedy's brief, but psychologically immense, Camelot. After having helped spread and develop the "new humor," television now stepped back to assess it.

A foremost characteristic of the "new humor" as determined by the documentary, was its overt political content and tendency toward satire. The first comic shown is Mort Sahl, known for reading from a newspaper onstage and who performed at the 1960 Democratic convention.[33] But the documentary recognizes that what is really "new" about this kind of humor is its popularity, its proliferation due to mass media, rather than any new content. "Never in history has any people valued its comedians more than we, the twentieth century Americans," the narrator says. "We give them fame, we give them fortune, we give them influence." This influence, he adds, is due to mass communication. Postwar humor has spread from the stand-up comics in nightclubs to those on record to the "new hip comic books" such as *MAD* magazine.

Al Feldstein, *MAD*'s editor after founder Harvey Kurtzman, offers an explanation for "What's So Funny?": "Satire arises at a time when there's a complacency and some people start chafing at the bit . . . A few malcontents start asking questions. Malcontents like us, for example."[34] In contrast to the repressive political climate of the 1950s, such as that in which his boss, William Gaines, testified before Senator Estes Kefauver about the threat of comics, Feldstein later explains the current interest in satire is "showing how far from McCarthyism we've come."

The documentary is an example of how television can serve as a site for opening up discussion about American culture and comedy rather than closing such discussions. As a historical document, it shows a variety of what was deemed not only political but controversial humor at the time. African-American comedian Dick Gregory does a bit in which he implores the audience not to clap for him: "Just take me to lunch when it's not Brotherhood Week." The Second City comedy troupe performs a skit of a *Life* magazine journalist on a tour guided by a colonel, who shows them the training of Southeast Asians and the accomplishments of the military in constructing an eight-lane highway to provide access to a pond. In contrast to these comedians, the documentary offers a comedy group who go by the not-at-all-funny moniker, "The Young Conservatives," founded by one Robert Caughlin, who objects to political satirists who are left of center. These self-described "voices crying in the wilderness" of American comedy are opposed to the political establishment. Rather than being a subversive force, Caughlin credits the popular satirists such as Mort Sahl as promoting the political status quo: "The establishment is firmly established in the United States and it is buttressed by our comedians." Unfortunately, Caughlin can't point to any conservative precursors during the Eisenhower era that shored up support in order to defeat Adlai Stevenson.

In addition to the insight of a couple of academics, the documentary concludes with several "man in the street" type interviews to gauge public opinion on the new humor. Most of these, like the newspaper articles on the freedom to laugh, link comedy to free speech, and in the relationship between the two, see a reflection of the national character. The interviewees note that "good American satire is refreshing," that it is "wonderful that as Americans we can enjoy . . . and get these perspectives." Another states that the president's sense of humor is one of his great qualities. Indeed, John F. Kennedy, who had been actively supported by Mort Sahl and whose first family was the subject of a wildly successful comedy album by Vaughn Meader, gave a parodic state of the union address in 1962 at the inaugural anniversary dinner. Meader's album reportedly sold 4 million copies in four weeks, and went on to sell a total of 7.5 million copies.[35] Parody and satire were not only socially acceptable, but incredibly popular ways to poke fun at the president. The president's predilection for parody both endeared him to Americans and inspired parodies about him as well. Indeed, historian Stephen Kercher, in his *Revel with a Cause: Liberal Satire in Postwar America*, marks 1962 as the high point of humor's transformation from subterranean counterculture to a profitable enterprise: "With the young, witty, urbane John Kennedy in the White house, satiric expression, long a resource for cultural dissent, became for many American liberals a source of affirmation and a sign of better days to come."[36] It may be that Kennedy's Camelot marks the ascendancy to cultural dominance of a hybrid humor which began coalescing in the mid-1950s: one sick enough to acknowledge the problems in postwar culture and express countercultural complaints (if not clearly articulated ideas), yet nurtured and promulgated through media that were both popular and corporate controlled. This humor was not fundamentally conservative or subversive; but inhabited many of the spaces where the private and public spheres were interacting in unprecedented ways. Americans were encountering comedy—critical or not—as never before, and making sense of their lives through it as never before, as well.

MAD IN THE U.S.A.

Kennedy's Camelot also marked an important point in the country's preoccupation with mental health. In 1963 he signed the Community Mental Health Centers Act, which gave state hospitals the power to discharge many patients into their communities, and the Maternal and Child Health and Mental Retardation Planning Bill, described as the first major national drive against mental illness and mental retardation. These both capped reforms begun in the 1950s as part of the growing interest in the nation's mental health.

Identifying the sick or mad aspects of postwar life in the 1950s thus was not a marginal act. It was both as mainstream as Vice President Richard Nixon and as countercultural as Beat poet Allen Ginsberg. Nixon named mental health the number one problem in America at the opening of "Mental Health Week" in 1955.[37] The eponymous "Man in the Gray Flannel Suit" from Sloan Wilson's novel did public relations for a mental health campaign. Holden Caulfield, who would become America's archetypical disaffected youth, was chased into a mental hospital by "Fuck you's" and phonies. Ginsberg's poem "Howl" opened with the line: "I saw the best minds of my generation destroyed by madness, starving hysterical naked."[38]

These cultural manifestations of a national state of madness were not without their real-life antecedents. Indeed, Nixon's pronouncement was related to Congress's formation of a Joint Commission on Mental Illness and Health with a mandate to recommend a national policy for the mentally ill.[39] The number of institutionalized Americans was cresting in the 1950s, following the large number of mentally ill veterans produced by World War II. The resident population of state and county mental hospitals peaked at 559,000 in 1955, then began a quick decline following a policy shift toward deinstitutionalization. In the years between 1960 and 1975, the institutionalized population fell from 536,000 to 193,000.[40] This is a remarkable shift when you consider how much the American population itself was increasing over this same period. The period of the 1950s, was, therefore, the last decade when Americans were institutionalized in such large proportions.

While the numbers of hospitalized patients peaked during the 1950s, the psychiatric establishment and American population paradoxically became accustomed to the notion that mental health problems were more present outside the hospitals than inside. During the interwar years, historian Roy Porter writes, American psychiatry became committed "to a vision of social integration and stability based on individual 'adjustment' and adaptation to healthy social forms."[41]

In time, the infiltration of broadly psychodynamic turns of thinking helped the idea to gain ground—it had become conventional by the 1950s—that mental disorder was not confined to the certifiable. Ordinary people might have "complexes'", and neuroses, it was now said, ran like a watermark through the population at large: housewife blues, family conflicts, alcoholism, adolescent adjustment problems, generational tensions, and so much more—the precursors of the depression, eating, and sexual disorders ubiquitous by the close of the century.[42]

Madness as a social concept was deinstitutionalized in the 1950s through popular culture, as a corollary to the literal deinstitutionalization of the hospitalized mentally ill. Porter also traces the tradition of the mad genius in literature and popular culture, a tradition that is interrupted by Michel Foucault's "great confinement." Porter summarizes Foucault's argument:

> Hitherto, the mad had exercised a particular force and fascination, be it as a holy fool, witch or as a man possessed. Halfwits and zanies had enjoyed the licence of free speech and the privilege of mocking their betters. Institutionalization, however, maintained Foucault, robbed madness of all such empowering features and reduced it to mere negation, an absence of humanity.

Porter resists Foucault's take, opting to see the rise of the asylum not as an act of state, but as a by-product of commercial and professional society.[43] But although the asylum might not have been "designed" as an agent of social control, this does not mean that it didn't act as one. Similarly, while television portrayed madness both negatively and positively, it put into play meaningful markers of identity: what it meant to be sick versus well-adjusted.

Could the 1950s, with its explosion of mass culture and the renewed cultural currency of madness, mark a regaining of productive, artistic connotations of madness? If so, this turning point that popularizes sick comedy presents a period of valorizing mental illness as an alternative to performative normality. Popular culture diagnosed madness as a widespread condition, either to be dealt with on the psychiatrist's couch and numbed with tranquilizers or embraced as the sensible response to modern, consumer-driven, postwar life. In the art world, the Dadaists and Surrealists had celebrated artistic genius as a form of insanity. But even as they sought to abolish the boundaries between art and culture, modernism mostly remained highbrow fare. Throughout the 1950s, however, madness was culturally deinstitutionalized, mobilized, and propagated by television, the burgeoning youth culture, and individuals, subcultures, and audiences who imagined themselves as countercultural—not normal and not willing to pretend to be normal. Hip, mad, sick—all these were embraced as alternatives to mainstream complacency in the performance of normativity. In the persona of the mad or sick, individuals—boys, girls, men, women—found an acceptable model for making sense of their lives in relation to the mass media and so many other aspects of postwar life.

Though pop culture might find space to valorize madness or at least call into question the legitimacy of social norms, the dominant structures of the state and conservative morality attempted to contain the potentially liberating, sometimes threatening aspects of madness. The hysteria over juvenile delinquency serves as a model for how madness could be used to characterize a segment of the nonconforming population. While Nixon may have proclaimed Mental Health Week to come up with a plan to manage the nation's anxieties, the Kefauver investigations into juvenile delinquency provided a clear example of how the state could brand and manage the behavior of populations threatening to the status quo.

While Nixon and Kefauver personified the state's power to police the American people, television and the mass media are more difficult to pin down as agents of social control. A survey of the representations of the mad and the madly funny on television during the late 1950s and early 1960s shows that the medium could simultaneously police madness as a social ill, exhibit the mad as a popular spectacle, and popularize sick comedy as socially acceptable humor. Profiting from all these approaches, television is bound to be ideologically inconsistent, presenting madness or the sick take on society both positively and negatively. Within this terrain, individuals could map their lives in respect to the ideological positions offered: mad or well adjusted, hip or square.

CHARTING THE MIRTH SPECTRUM

In the 1950s, comedy and mental health met perhaps most directly in psychological testing that examined what a sense of humor revealed about an individual. In *Scientific American* in 1956, Jacob Levine, an associate clinical professor of psychiatry at Yale, described a test that used comic illustrations to aid psychological analysis.[44] In collaboration with Frederick C. Redlich, chairman of the department of psychiatry of the Yale School of Medicine, Levine devised a "mirth response test." The test rated the response of subjects to 20 cartoons from magazines such as *The New Yorker* and *The Saturday Evening Post* on a "mirth spectrum" ranging from a negative grimace to a belly laugh. The subjects were then asked to sort the cartoons into those they liked or didn't like, and were interviewed about their understanding of each cartoon and its associations for them. These responses were then compared with what else had been compiled about the subject's background and personality.

In his introduction to the article (which would also be picked up and abbreviated by *Science Digest*), Levine cited Sigmund Freud as useful for explaining the meanings of laughter and subconscious thought. The article (and probably the researchers as well) condensed Freud's theories on the comic to the assertion that humor permits the momentary gratification of a forbidden pleasure, and simultaneously lessens the inhibiting anxiety. Thus, the basic element in humor is anxiety, which is disguised enough in the joke that it is not disturbing. In this theoretical model, a joke will seem funny to an individual only if it both arouses anxiety and relieves it. Denying that nations or classes of people differed greatly in their sense of humor, Levine's test emphasized that the significant differences were between individuals that reflected "deep-seated aspects of personality and emotional development." Simply put, laughter did or didn't reveal personal anxieties.

Freud indeed theorized that the main characteristic of the "joke-work" is liberating pleasure by getting rid of inhibitions, and that the release of distressing affects was the "greatest obstacle to the emergence of the comic."[45] More specifically, jokes lift critical inhibitions and allow a temporary return to the pleasures of free play enjoyed during childhood. When we participate in a joke-work, Freud theorized, our train of thought drops, then emerges from the unconscious as a joke. "The thought which, with the intention of constructing a joke, plunges into the unconscious is merely seeking there for the ancient dwelling place of its former play with words. Thought is put back for a moment to the stage of childhood so as once more to gain possession of the childish source of pleasure."[46] Levine's article noted that individual responses to jokes differ because different individuals have different inhibitions. These inhibitions could be as common and basic as the structure of language inhibiting pleasure from nonsense, or as individual and complicated as sexual inhibitions. Thus, personal inhibitions are also wound up in social restrictions, the evasion of both through laughter being pleasurable. Levine cited several examples of personal reactions and how these were related to the individual's background. One cartoon featured a sheik and a eunuch looking at a veiled woman: in a cloud representing his thoughts, the sheik pictures her naked, while the eunuch's cloud is empty. Levine's discussion of the responses of several subjects reveals how the test used humor to reinforce cultural characterizations. A "young woman who had been brought up in a rather strict home" responded with an embarrassed smile; a "spinster of 45 with a puritanical attitude toward sex" found the cartoon revolting; and a young schizophrenic woman reacted violently because of delusions caused by her unbearable sexual feelings toward her brother and other men. The fact that these individuals did not find the cartoon funny became further evidence that they were deviant or maladjusted.

Levine's subjects ranged from psychotic patients to those whom he deemed "normal" individuals. He admitted that the "mirth response test" was less of a test that produced data or diagnoses of individuals, but "a useful instrument for probing personality and bringing out personal problems." This did not stop Levine from making a sweeping statement that the lack of a good sense of humor could be a symptom of major problems for anyone: "The capacity to laugh is a measure of one's adjustment to his environment. It follows that inability to appreciate humor, or deviant responses to it, can be regarded as a sensitive indicator of maladjustment and inner disturbance." [47] Yale was not the only place attempting to study or employ humor scientifically during the period. In a 1960 article, *Today's Health* cited researchers across the country in order to show that a person's sense of humor was of vital importance and could especially tell whether or not they were well-adjusted.[48] Studies at Purdue and Vassar showed that intelligence and a well-developed sense of humor went hand in hand, and that those with a good sense of humor were harder to deceive. Other studies in London's University College reportedly showed a "definite relationship" between body build and type of humor enjoyed: "The short, heavy-set type enjoyed simple down-to-earth humor; while the tall and lanky individuals inclined toward subtleties, plays on words, and delayed action effects; and the athletic type preferred humor which was direct and lacking shade or nuance."[49]

Cultural judgments that one was "short" and "heavy-set" were thus easily tied to humor judged to be "down-to-earth." Levine's work at Yale was distilled by this same writer as solid evidence that the better adjusted a person was, the more readily he responded to humor, and maladjusted people simply showed a greater tendency to miss the point in a joke or to take them too seriously. This last point reveals not that scientific studies of humor were taken up and simplistically misrepresented in the popular press, but that those studies were both dependent on and helped to produce what it meant to be culturally or socially "maladjusted." Similarly, television and the movies could provide acceptable models of sickness to vent cultural anxieties, mediating and defining just how significant they might be.

Freud's ideas about humor, and especially his theories of the subconscious, would be familiar to readers encountering Levine's mirth response test. A number of authors have discussed the proliferation of psychological rhetoric in films of the forties and early 1950s. Ed Sikov, for example, uses Freud to analyze screen comedies of the 1950s, but he does so with an eye toward the familiarity of fifties film audiences with psychoanalysis.[50] Sikov explores the tensions in fifties film comedies between the calm surface of family and social life and their threatening, repressed underneath. What is significant about fifties comedies, he says, is not the existence of this underneath, but the popularity of its revelation.[51]

As public awareness and interest in psychiatry and psychoanalysis boomed, it's little surprise that the overt representation of psychiatry became a popular subject for Hollywood filmmakers. In their book, *Psychiatry and the Cinema*, Glen O. Gabbard and Krin Gabbard identify the period from 1957 to 1963 (roughly the same period as the emergence of sick comedy) as the "Golden Age" of psychiatry in cinema. They trace how historically in cinema psychiatrists had most often been portrayed as evil-minded or incompetent quacks, or simply as convenient tools for exposition. During this period, however, more films than ever represented psychiatrists as legitimate, capable of solving individuals' problems, or at least helping them.[52]

Besides the literal treatment of mental illness, psychological breakdown was a popular performance style. Even performers who weren't labeled sick comics have been read as manifestations of national neuroses. Method actors like James Dean and Marlon Brando incorporated anxieties and a sense of vulnerability into their performances, popularizing a different kind of hero who wasn't immune from the pressures of modern life. Instead, they articulated a personal rebellion against the stifling structures so popularly documented by social scientists. In *Rebel without a Cause*, for example, we see the compounding of many preoccupations, all tied one way or another to mental health. James Dean's "Jim" may display sensitivities and weaknesses, but these are only the surface symptoms of what havoc is being wrought on his identity by his emasculated, apron-wearing father and overbearing mother. Momism, juvenile delinquency, and the organization man are all bound up together, leading to outbursts within the family as well as knife fights and police shootings outside. Method acting was famous for presenting "real" human emotion rather than a representation of emotion. In contrast to the traditional actor who simulated emotion onstage or onscreen, the method taught actors to actually feel what their character was supposed to be feeling. Method acting thus blurred the lines between reality and performance. The analogy to Bruce's assessment about the changing notions of comedy is clear: just as audiences no longer expected an "act" but "reality" from a comedian, audiences now expected not "acted" but "real" emotion from actors.

Psychologically oriented films often included, Sikov points out, emasculated fathers and mixed up sons, such as in *Rebel without a Cause*.[53] White men were probably not those most in need of psychological reconstruction during the 1950s. Sexual and racial repression probably caused far more psychological harm than "momism" or the unbearable pressures of owning a home in the suburbs, or even the pains of genuflecting before the corporate boss. Nonetheless, given the culture of the producers of film and television and the writers of the contemporary social histories (white and male), it's not surprising that momism, juvenile delinquency, and run-of-the-mill ennui dominated much of the mental health problems portrayed in popular culture.

It was by and through these men that sick comedy was produced and consumed, and through them that the broader culture examined its sicker aspects, some of which would be common despite race, gender, or class, and some of which would not. Sick men like Shelley Berman could be used to explore what amounts to the domestic containment of the housewife in addition to that of the organization man. The popularity of psychological subject matter, method acting, and sick comedy suggests that the laughter of fifties film and television audiences was not so far removed from the night club audience's hysterical reaction to Holland's breakdown in *Peter Gunn*.

Of course, television was even hungrier for material than film in the 1950s, and we should not be surprised to find psychiatry and mental health as common topics in the medium. While mental health served as narrative material for television dramas such as *Peter Gunn* and the *Twilight Zone*, the topic also expectedly came up on variety and talk shows. Here, mental health as a public health issue again served as a distancing mechanism, allowing not just the discussion of mental health, but the display of individuals who were known to have mental problems. In other words, the mentally ill could be made into appropriate television spectacles. Comedy not only kept this from being too grim a spectacle, but its use suggests the potential reason for the spectacle's appeal.

The ability of comedy, and Berman in particular, to mediate uncomfortable fears about identity and health is evidenced in an episode of *The Jack Paar Show* from 1963, which featured the famous neurotic Oscar Levant, a pianist, television panelist, and actor in films such as *An American in Paris* (and who is discussed in-depth in a later chapter).[54] The appearance also exhibits the same sort of pleasure in pain provided by Danny Holland's breakdown, and sick comedy more generally. From the beginning of the show, it is clear that the focus will be on Levant's precarious mental health. Paar begins his monologue by discounting critics who say he abuses Levant by putting someone onstage who isn't emotionally well. Paar responds that he can't help it if Levant's an eccentric and a hypochondriac, and assures the audience that he would not bring out somebody who wasn't completely well. Before we can see for ourselves how "well" Levant is or isn't, Paar introduces Berman as the most financially successful of the "new comedians," and says he will perform a monologue on the "fad of psychiatry." Little is exceptionally interesting about the monologue itself; Berman mimes neuroses about his nose, for example, and mostly does a long bit about talking to his therapist about becoming forgetful, repeatedly forgetting whom he is on the phone with. What is interesting is Berman's function as a comedic buffer, helping to position Levant not as a freak show spectacle but as a neurotic humorist. Paar's and Berman's monologues set the stage for Levant as an eccentric and hypochondriac whose neuroses and mental illness are both funny and make-believe.

After another brief buffer, an odd short film on animals trained to balance apples on their heads and other such tricks, Levant is introduced by Paar as being well-known as a concert pianist, *Information, Please!* panelist, film actor, and "one of America's great geniuses." Levant appears physically uncomfortable and disheveled. He rocks in his chair and slurs his speech, sounding drunk or drugged. When asked how he has been doing, he replies "My behavior has been impeccable. I've been unconscious for the last six months." Paar asks whether it ever occurred to Levant that his illnesses could be in his mind, and talks about what patience his wife must have to put up with him. Levant responds that if he loses a fight with his wife, she has him committed to the psychiatric ward. Paar manages to get Levant to play a piece on the piano, and again counters accusations that he "uses" Levant by implying he's doing him a favor by forcing him back onstage: "This was one of our most gifted artists," says Paar. The operative word being "was," now Paar presents the spectacle of a sick former artist and genius.

Freud theorizes that comedy can be used by the powerless against the powerful: "A joke will allow us to exploit something ridiculous in our enemy which we could not, on account of obstacles in the way, bring forward openly or consciously; once again, then, the joke *will evade restrictions and open sources of pleasure that have become inaccessible.*"[55] Though we might connect inaccessible pleasures to the subversive German *Flüsterwitzen* or the antisocial sick humor of Bruce and Berman, the spectacle of the mentally unstable Levant might be thought of as comedy being used to evade the restrictions of laughing at the downtrodden or mentally ill. The key restrictions functioning aren't simply social decorum, because doing so is cruel. Rather, experiencing pleasure from the nonsense of the man who has cracked is taboo because, in the American 1950s, everyone is understood to be on the brink of mental illness. Everyone has neuroses. This pleasure is restricted not simply by decency, but by fear. If Berman performs the organization man who has snapped under life's pressures, Levant is offered as the celebrity who isn't equipped to stand up to the rigors of the spotlight. If it could happen to one of "America's great geniuses," then it could happen to anyone.

When considering the cultural role of comedy in the 1950s, in order to understand the stakes of sick comedy and the laughter of the *Peter Gunn* episode, we need to recognize the popularity of psychoanalysis, the period's preoccupation with mental health, and the fact that humor was widely recognized as an area where cultural anxieties could be safely expressed. Movies, television, and mass publications provided the ideal outlet for those anxieties to be mediated. Like Danny Holland's breakdown, Levant's appearance or the show seems less performance and more orchestrated spectacle of mental degradation, with humor used to keep it from becoming too straightforward and disturbing. Such spectacles gave access to social sickness in its advanced stages. Everyone may have had those sicknesses to some degree, but those who had completely succumbed were meant to be invisible. They needed to be kept safe inside the hospital out of which Paar dragged Levant. Paar's jokes and Berman's performance attempt to mediate such spectacles through laughter. Freud says successful comedy must both raise an anxiety, then relieve that anxiety. If a joke or comic spectacle doesn't, it is disturbing, not funny. Sick comedians fed upon popular cultural anxieties to walk this line: between making people laugh, and just making them sick.

CONCLUSION

Just how unique was this "sickness" and postwar age of anxiety? Were these gray-flannel-suited neurotics really a new figure on the American landscape? Atomic anxiety was, no doubt, a maddening factor, but it only added to others that had since the turn of the century been identified as uniquely American anxieties. Though mental health might have become the number one health concern for Americans in the 1950s (at least according to Nixon), it was not a new one. A popular "mental hygiene" movement had begun at the beginning of the century, and a bit further back, in the nineteenth century, "neurasthenia" was a popular diagnosis of American men who were unable to meet the challenges of the market that should be their making.[56] Neurasthenia, described as a general weakness of the nerves, was called the "American" disease because America was supposed to be the place where men were free to create their own livelihoods, to make themselves successful, without any of the old world hindrances of class, history, or controlled markets holding them back. The American ethos of rugged individualism thus laid the groundwork for a both a national sense of American character, and the psychological problems that would belie that myth and undermine that sense of character.

The mental health problems portrayed by the popular culture of the 1950s had thus long been built into the American character. Once identified as popular neuroses, mass media allowed the American disease to be displayed and explored like never before. Whether this undermined the dominant mythologies and ideologies of America is a question of whether that popular culture successfully inoculated America against those concerns. This would only be the case if mental health remained an individual concern—something to be dealt with in a private session with a psychiatrist. If popular culture caused a general reexamination of what it meant to be sick rather than successful, that would signal much more than a simple inoculation. Popular media would have then generated a threatening diagnosis of the nation's mental health. Nixon's ringing of the bell was the controlled attempt to keep mental health on individual terms. Lenny Bruce and Shelley Berman were, on the other hand, the spreading of sick consciousness.

Time noted in 1959 that the success of the sick comedians was giving amateur analysts and sociologists a field day. One popular theory was that faced with the possibility of nuclear annihilation, people were less likely to be shocked. "The future seems so precarious, people are willing to abandon themselves to chaos. The new comics reflect this," said comedian Irwin "Professor" Corey.[57] While it is tempting to frame both sick comedy and a renewed concern with mental health within the strict confines of the postwar *atomic* condition, this is ultimately more restricting than illuminating. Instead, we should explain postwar anxiety as not just about conflicting feelings about the bomb and impending nuclear annihilation, but as part of a longer trajectory about success in America. This trajectory becomes more visible due to the surge of popular media, especially television, but also magazines like *Playboy* and *MAD*. The search for content for television and the new lifestyle magazines coincided with the continued popularity of Freud within the psychiatric establishment as well as the society at large, coincided with the booming economy in which men were expected to succeed as never before, and coincided with a governmental acknowledgment of how mental health could undermine American prosperity. These breakdowns of sick individuals, while once confined to the asylum, could now be displayed and discussed in new ways, in new forums, before many more people. Reframing the issue of the "sick" American as a core part of the postwar culture, rather than a marginal or even countercultural part, is why an examination of the "sick" humor of Shelley Berman can ultimately explain more about American popular culture than focusing on Bruce. Bruce may have been the most countercultural of sick comedians, but Berman shows how sick comedy and its related issues were put into play before a broader, more mainstream audience.

In the disheveled genius Levant and the neurotic family man Berman, the television audience saw not someone to be pitied or ridiculed, but a possible reflection of their shadow selves—who or what they might become if their conscious minds were to give up the game. While comedy provided a tool for easing anxieties through temporarily releasing people from them, television provided a forum where midcentury Americans learned that they possessed anxieties, then were taught how to laugh at them. But rather than being a successful long-term evasion, sick comedy taught that managing anxiety was never easy, and probably futile. Though an individual might be sick inside, his sickness ultimately came from the outside, where it showed no sign of disappearing. That sick comedy offered no remedies should not be surprising. American humor was instead a coping mechanism for living in what was (as Archibald Beechcroft learned) the best, however sick, of all possible worlds.

2 What, Me Subversive?
MAD Magazine and the Textual Strategies and Cultural Politics of Parody

Dear Mr. Hoover,

> Lately all my friends at school, and even some of my teachers, say that Mad Magazine is communistic. I've even heard that its publisher is a proven Communist. They say so because it makes fun of the government. Of course, Mad makes fun of everything, even itself. I don't think there's anything bad about making fun of the government, myself, but other people seem to. I've always enjoyed Mad, but if its communistic, I certainly don't want to buy any more issues. I'm writing to you because my friends would believe what you say more than they would anyone else. If you would tell me whether these rumors are true, I'd be most appreciative.Yours sincerely,
>
> [name withheld] [1]

The above letter, written in early 1963, capped a flurry of similar inquiries to FBI Director J. Edgar Hoover that dated back to 1955. Whether written by twelve-year-olds, concerned mothers, youth-group leaders, or high school students, they all asked what they assumed was a simple question: Was *MAD Magazine* communistic? Was it dangerous, subversive propaganda, bent on undermining the American way of life, or just good fun?

The letter also marks the end of the first ten years of *MAD*'s existence. The magazine's meteoric rise to cultural prominence began in 1952, and *MAD* maintained a high—and somewhat notorious—profile throughout the decade. Being the target of a *MAD* parody quickly became a status symbol. Even as worried youngsters and concerned mothers wrote Hoover to condemn *MAD* or seek his advice, celebrities wrote *MAD* to publicly thank the magazine for honoring them with a parody. Jackie Gleason wrote to praise the "accurate portrayal" of his lifestyle in *MAD*'s parody of the celebrity magazine bio piece, and later wrote an article for the magazine.[2] Ed Sullivan wrote to ask if he could have the original artwork for one the early parodies of his show.[3] Host Garry Moore displayed *MAD*'s version of his show *I've Got a Secret* on the air.[4] Probably one American whom J. Edgar Hoover *did not* have a file on, Pat Boone, even said that one of his great accomplishments in 1958 was making *MAD*.[5] The contradiction between letters written in suspicion of the magazine's motives and its public embrace by celebrities highlights the existence of other conflicts between discourses of television, consumerism, and the American "good life" during the 1950s. *MAD* used parody as a strategy to negotiate these contradictions of postwar life, and in so doing, promoted parody and other forms of rewriting as strategies for its readers to use as well.

We've already seen how the new or "sick" comedy in the postwar period articulated cultural criticisms through popular, mass-produced culture. This reveals that critical comedy was indeed compatible with industrialized culture and could even support the very institutions it critiqued. This does not, however, explain what such comedy "meant" to its fans or consumers. This chapter seeks to answer that question by focusing on the parodic magazine *MAD* and theorizing not just why its readers related to its "sick" take on postwar culture, but what they did with that take, and how it might have influenced how they looked, listened, or made sense of other elements of postwar culture. In particular, this chapter looks at how *MAD* "looked at" television, and how that might have influenced the tastes and habits of television audiences.

A key cultural transition during this postwar period is the growth of the television industry and, as Lynn Spigel has shown, Americans' coming to terms with the new electronic medium in their homes.[6] During the 1950s, television grew from a technological curiosity owned by few to a nationwide tool of cultural dissemination, a fixture within the vast majority of American homes. As this new media form emerged, it was met with a variety of reactions, ranging from utopian promises of democracy through technology to fears of the undermining of American democracy and the end of culture with a capital "C"—whichever came first.

MAD firmly established its status as a monument to irreverence—as well as a cleverly disguised venue for cultural criticism—over the same period. By relying primarily on the parody of movies, television, and advertisements, *MAD*, which began as a comic book in 1952, was selling 500,000 copies by its sixth issue. By 1960, circulation had reached 1 million, with a pass-along rate estimated to be six times that. *MAD* quickly spawned a number of imitations, but remained the most popular mainstream satire magazine available to Americans in the 1950s. If the statistics cited by *MAD* historian Maria Reidelbach can be believed, by 1960, 58 percent of college students and 43 percent of high schoolers regularly read *MAD*.[7]

In retrospect, *MAD* serves as a critical counterpoint to fifties popular culture which is so often, with the notable exception of rock-n-roll, deemed complacent or conformist. (Even rock-n-roll had Pat Boone.) Such generalizations about the decade usually contrast it with the late 1960s and the blossoming of the counterculture. This points to another significant aspect of the letter's timing. In February 1963, the fifties and Eisenhower were technically several years gone by, but Kennedy's Camelot was still in full swing. With its sudden end that November, a new period in American culture would begin: the mythical 1960s, where cultural turbulence rather than tranquility and cynicism rather than optimism are more often described as the norms. A publication like *MAD* might seem to fit in *that* decade better, but it was the popular culture of the 1950s that provided the content for *MAD*'s success, and paved the way for the politicization of the youth culture and popularization of "underground" or "countercultural" humor such as Paul Krassner's *The Realist* or the stand-up comedy of Lenny Bruce and, later, George Carlin.

It was in 1958, not 1968, that Fred Astaire danced in an Alfred E. Neuman mask on a network TV special.[8] This last anecdotal connection between the magazine and television may help to confirm the breadth of *MAD*'s grip on the popular imagination in the 1950s. It does not, however, indicate the critical and often complicated stance *MAD* took toward television and consumer culture. While many voices urged Americans to join in the consumption of television and the products it advertised, and others sought to reaffirm the value of so-called "high" culture, *MAD* negotiated a critical stance toward television and consumer culture from within popular culture. In particular, *MAD* pitted itself against the commodified culture of television. Through parodies and published letters to the editor, *MAD* readers encountered criticisms and engaged in conversations over the ethics of advertising and the commercial nature of television. As the decade continued, *MAD*'s criticisms of television became more textually oriented, engaging television as its own unique story world. Rather than meaning that debates about commercial culture were abandoned, this emphasized that television was not just another consumer good, but a key way in which Americans told stories about and understood themselves.

MAD readers shared a popular culture: They all had ads, products, entertainment, and American life in general to ridicule. They had television and film narratives to rewrite to their liking, and they had the language of parody to produce meaning and make sense of that shared culture. Many *MAD* articles overtly encouraged such a "Do-It-Yourself" (DIY) approach to producing culture. This was usually done through parody and the assumption that some category of text had a simple structure and anyone could create it. The overt DIY type of article was present very early in *MAD*, probably suggested by the processes of the artists and writers, who found they themselves had created their own formulas for producing the magazine's parodies. The first of these articles, in 1954, was about writing a movie parody for a magazine, explaining how a lampoon works by rewriting the recent film *Julius Caesar*, starring Marlon Brando.[9] First, the name of the actor had to be changed (Marlon Branflakes), background details added to destroy the main idea, modern things mixed in, huge bullet holes added, detectives, Bop-style talk (a Bop dictionary had been a very popular early *MAD* article), women who were either real good or real bad looking, and so forth. The piece was one of the few times *MAD* needed to parody itself, because the DIY approach could be applied to just about anything in popular culture. This was, after all, the era of painting by numbers. But *MAD*'s numbering system was more than a little off, designed to subvert the expected rather than reproduce it.

In the October/November 1955 issue, "Sure Fire Dialogue" picked cutouts of overused phrases, which could be recombined in order to write screenplays for different films. A later article "Make Your Own Love-Story" similarly featured illustrated panels with cutouts of dialogue to recombine and rewrite scenes.[10] Spurred by the numerous *MAD* clones that quickly filled the magazine stands, *MAD* even published an article on "How to Put Out an Imitation of *MAD*."[11]

"Scenes We'd Like to See" is another excellent example of this DIY aesthetic. The first of these articles in May 1955 was featured in the Cliché Dept., and first showed the actual clichés (of kissing, fencing, burglary, escape), then the *MAD* version. "Scenes We'd Like to See" would never need to include the clichés again—readers knew them all too well—but the feature became one of the magazine's most successful and has been applied to television, advertising, movies, and everything in between. Later the articles featured specific television programs. In one example: the Lone Ranger, besieged by Indians, worries aloud what he and Tonto are going to do. In response, Tonto says—finally—"What do you mean . . . WE?"[12]

Another parody called "Go West, Old Format," replanted television shows as diverse as *Dragnet* and *The Phil Silvers Show* within the Western. Its natural counterpart, "Go East, Old Western," offered a programming possibility should the ratings of the Westerns, currently riding high and dominating programming, falter. In "Have Suit, Will Commute" Pallidin offers a new ad campaign for Kitzel Elevators. When the campaign doesn't work, Pallidin tries his alternate plan: He pulls a gun on the competition. But Pallidin assures him he won't kill him: "We're civilized here on Madison Ave.! I'd kill your DRUGGIST . . . cut off your tranquilizer supply!" Within these "recombined" types of parody, characters and tropes from individual shows were recombined to create a new text; in effect, *MAD* rewrote the originals, integrating "real world" issues (foreign policy, domestic "tranquility") in not so subtle ways.

For a publication in need of relevant content, television continued to make obvious comic fodder throughout the 1950s. But considering the magazine's enormous popularity, and its critical stance toward TV, *MAD*'s attitude toward television programming and the medium in general must have implications for considering the 1950s audience's reception of TV, as well as their attitudes toward consumer culture more generally. Of course, as *MAD* continues to be read today, continues to parody TV, and since those who read *MAD* continue to watch television, this investigation has implications for later audiences as well. Additionally, the types of parody in the magazine that were critical of television and other aspects of fifties American culture were not entirely unique to the magazine. Television parody boomed both on and off TV. In uncovering and evaluating the politics of *MAD*'s approach to TV in the 1950s, more than fifty years later, my concern is not whether or not *MAD* was "un-American" as the young letter-writer feared. Tracing out why the magazine's content could produce just such a dialogue can help theorize how parody influences the ways in which people watch TV. *MAD*'s parodies not only inspired cheers and jeers, but also influenced how audiences produced meanings and pleasures from television texts.

If the media are an important arena through which people understand and make sense of their lives, then it is necessary to consider how individuals form relationships with media, and how that influences the formation of identities in relation to other aspects of culture. J. Edgar Hoover had no easy answers for those *MAD* readers wondering whether they held dangerous, subversive propaganda in their hands. He could only point them toward previously published literature on the communist menace. Theorizing how parody of popular culture creates strategies of cultural decoding and works in the articulation of identity is another indirect answer to whether *MAD* was subversive. The answer is not in the text itself, nor the writers, artists, editors, or publisher responsible for producing it. Rather, the answer is in the actions of the consumers of that text—not just in what sense they made of that text, but how *MAD* may have influenced their decoding practices more generally.

This purposefully shifts the evaluation of what constitutes a "subversive" text from looking for its direct political effects to thinking about how such texts work in the formation of individual identities. In other words, we shouldn't essentialize the subversive nature of *MAD* by whether or not its creators were communist infiltrators (highly unlikely) or whether *MAD* directly encouraged some of the radical activism of the 1960s (possibly so). Instead, we should look at how the structure of parodic texts encourages a critical relationship to mediated culture, encompassing not just the television texts themselves, but the industries producing them, and the broader sense of American culture understood through them.

Cultural studies scholars customarily look to issues of identity (race, class, gender, sexuality) to theorize how subject positions lead to dominant, oppositional, or negotiated readings of popular texts. My hope is not to obscure the relevance of such differences to subject formation, but to consider what a particular publication (*MAD*) and a particular textual strategy (parody) might be able to tell us about the formation of reading strategies across a fairly large and diverse portion of the television audience. By focusing on the 1950s, when both *MAD* and the television industry were emerging, I hope to show *MAD* armed its readers with protocols for the reading of television texts based on strategies of recycling, reappropriation, and recombination. In stark contrast to the "new" literary criticism of the time, *MAD* demanded the reader go outside the immediate text to uncover its meaning. By making connections from text to text and from text to cultural context, *MAD* popularized such decoding strategies as humorous-but-necessary exercises.

"Counterculture" is perhaps a hopelessly overdetermined term, saddled with cultural baggage from the 1960s and meaning many different things to different people. It still is valuable, I believe, since many of the people reading *MAD* (and especially those writing Hoover for help) believed reading the magazine was a form of "going against" mainstream culture. *MAD*'s brand of subversion dealt not in directly instigating acts but in influencing ways of thinking. Its popularity, in some part at least, owed to a mounting disaffection with the status quo. The magazine became a site where such disaffections gelled, not with the effect of producing a coherent social movement, but of shaping ways of thinking about and against postwar culture.

Still, many individuals over the years have thought that *MAD* was outright subversive. Though they often spoke in a clean-cut, straightforward manner about the social threat of the magazine, this was still grounded in a concern with the notion of identity formation and the possibilities of individual agency. After all, the "children" that read this magazine, as one letter to Hoover noted, would be called upon to resist communist brainwashing. The FBI files on *MAD* (called "bufiles") began with a letter from a concerned mother and schoolteacher who discovered the magazine by the bed of her teenage son. Explaining that she was "shocked and horrified," she contacted Hoover to confirm her belief that *MAD* was "Communistic and should be taken off our stands."[13] The mother felt the need to "name names" of the various writers featured in the issue, including television comedian Ernie Kovacs and humor writer Roger Price. Hoover would continue to receive many similar letters, most from concerned parents, but from earnest youngsters as well, looking for a definitive answer to ease their internal conflicts between coveting the magazine's irreverent humor and fearing it was a tool of the evil empire. Repeatedly they asked whether *MAD* was part of an orchestrated communist plot or just innocent, American fun.

The inquiries and complaints peaked in 1961, with ten different files in that year alone. One father sent in an entire mutilated issue his son tore up after being told how terrible it was for ridiculing the president. Another son made a deal with his dad who had tried to convince him *MAD* was communist: "Write to Mr. J. Edgar Hoover. If he agrees with you, I'll go along with you, otherwise, let's forget it."[14] The director of the Greater Knoxville Youth for Christ spent some time examining issues of the magazine, and came to the conclusion that it had to be subsidized by communists because it had no advertisements and cost only twenty-five cents. Most damningly, however, was the magazine's tendency to attack every aspect of the American way of life. The concerned youth director testified, "I feel that this magazine is a diabolical form of Red Propaganda used to infiltrate the minds of our Teen-agers to destroy our American way of life. A word used at the bottom of the first page by their own admission is a good way to describe what they are trying to do. (Satiric)"[15]

Hoover stopped short of confirming their fears, instead pointing out that the FBI was a "fact-gathering agency" that did not "make evaluations or draw conclusions as to the character or integrity of any publication, organization, or individual."[16] He usually referred the letter writers to the "Guide to Subversive Organizations and Publications" put together by the House Un-American Activities Committee, or toward his own reports, such as "Communist Target—Youth" and "What You Can Do to Fight Communism and Preserve America." The FBI mostly kept its value judgments to itself, though it did make them. A bureau note attached to one letter said that the magazine was "satirical in its entirety and actually contains articles and pictures which are in very poor taste." Another note stated that "various comic books of this nature were brought to the Justice Department and its decision was that such books did not constitute a violation of the Sedition statutes."[17] According to its files, the FBI kept clear of *MAD*, except for complaining after the magazine published a board game parody in 1958 which said an official draft dodger ID card could be received by writing Hoover. This resulted in a visit from a couple of agents, who were assured that the magazine would not misuse the bureau or Hoover's name in the future—a promise quickly forgotten.

IT'S A MAD, MAD, MAD, MAD DECADE

Perhaps a large measure of the popular tendency to regard the 1950s as a time of blissful conformity has to do with the reruns of sitcoms on cable television. Several generations have now grown up on *Leave It to Beaver* and *Father Knows Best*, and while our readings of the shows may increasingly find pleasure via irony and camp, we probably think that such critical distance is something we can now enjoy, while the conformists of the 1950s simply soaked up the dominant ideology embedded in the texts. While we might lament the cynicism of our day, we are also dumbfounded that the saps back then swallowed such nonsense.

Which isn't to say that people today are the only ones who have thought of media consumption as a passive act. While conformity to mainstream values may have been considered a virtue by the majority during the 1950s, passivity was not. Passivity meant you were susceptible to the forces bent on undermining the American dream; passivity might turn you into a communist dupe. One place where public concerns over active/passive identities galvanized was in the debate over the influence of comic books on children, at a peak in the congressional hearings presided over by Senator Estes Kefauver as part of his crusade against the purported menace of juvenile delinquency. The catalyst of the hearings had been psychologist Frederic Wertham's book *The Seduction of the Innocent*. Wertham blamed crime and horror comics for prompting children to commit a number of crimes, in addition to eroding their desire to read proper literature. While comics may have been Wertham's primary target, his concern extended to other media, notably television. In both of these media, he reported, "the entertainment flows over the child."[18]

The emergence of children (and teenagers in particular) as a market coincided with the emergence of television, as well as a boom in the production and distribution of comics. James Gilbert has theorized that the wide appeal of Wertham's argument was based on its linking of "two observable changes: new and strange behavior of adolescents and rapid and sometimes threatening developments in mass culture."[19] As Hollywood and Madison Avenue both discovered the discretionary income of teenagers, more and more cultural products were produced with them in mind. Roger Sabin discusses how comics in particular got in trouble because their content had become much more mature than the superhero staples of the forties, which had established the comics as a juvenile form. In response to the G.I. market for comics that developed during World War II, the comics had become more socially relevant in order to reach a broader audience. In fact, at the time of the Kefauver hearings, most comics were read by adults.[20]

The star of the Kefauver hearings, in addition to Wertham, turned out to be William H. Gaines of EC Comics, a prominent publisher of crime and horror comics, and also of what at the time was the fledgling comic book *MAD*. Gaines's crime and horror titles had been so successful that they had subsidized the development of the innovative *MAD*, which at the time contained almost exclusively parodies of comic genres. While Wertham cited case after case of children committing crimes, murders, and suicides after reading comics, Gaines offered what has become the typical response of producers of media criticized for provoking antisocial behavior: Delinquency is the product of the real environment in which the child lives, not the fiction he reads.[21] It became obvious during the Kefauver hearings, however, that if the comics industry didn't censor itself, the government would. Though he had led the comics' counterattack, Gaines was offered as a scapegoat for the industry, which established a code that in effect made his highly profitable crime and horror comics impossible to distribute. Despite the growing popularity of comics with adults since World War II, the code outlawed sex, violence, and attacks on authority with no concessions to the age of the reader.

MAD's cultural prominence was in large part born out of this crusade against the dangerous effects of comics. Gaines agreed to let Harvey Kurtzman, the founding editor of *MAD*, his last remaining successful title, turn the comic into a magazine in order to get around the code, which carried the chilling stipulation that comics have no social relevance. Disgusted by the restrictions of the code, and the failure of their various attempts to produce successful comics both under and around it, Gaines and EC dropped comics entirely by 1956.[22]

EC was now in the business of producing horrors through parodic revelations about popular culture. Though *MAD* began by parodying other comic books, advertising parody quickly became a mainstay of the *MAD* arsenal, and this ironic and adversarial relationship to consumer culture would greatly influence the magazine's treatment of television. *MAD* began parodying ads from comics in 1955, and soon thereafter began phasing out advertising. Gaines had been influenced by *PM* magazine, which had lambasted advertisers and said that publishers who accepted ads were beholden to them. As a historical antecedent, *MAD* also looked to *Ballyhoo*, a satire magazine that focused on advertisements and had a circulation of 2 million in 1931.[23] The thirties were the decade that saw the establishment of the FDA and heightened regulation of advertising, as well as the founding of the Consumers Union and its publication, *Consumer Reports*. But *MAD* brought debates about commercial culture to a broader, less specialized audience during a decade in which Americans were experiencing greater prosperity and supposed to be consuming more than ever, making up for the deprivations experienced during the depression and Second World War.

Parody of advertising was a fundamental component of *MAD*'s take (or attack) on American culture from the magazine's beginnings, but the ad parodies often took aim at more than a specific product. Fifties culture and consumerism in general were often the target, not the weaknesses of a particular laundry detergent or automobile. The magazine criticized the planned obsolescence of cars, prophesied that advertising slogans would replace everyday conversation, and especially enjoyed taking on the tobacco industry long before the government required health warnings on cigarettes. These ad parodies, along with a broader hostility to commercialism, sometimes conflicted with its status as a commercial enterprise. The early comic book form of *MAD* contained advertising, much as any other comic book. Notable among these were full-page Charles Atlas ads that promised readers he could turn "99-pound weaklings" into bona fide "he-men." The early comic issues also included ads for cigarette cases, elevator shoes, and magazine subscriptions. Though few in number, their presence contrasted with the satirical attitude of *MAD*—a contrast the magazine pointedly drew attention to. The tenth issue of *MAD* in April 1954 included a parody featuring a snake oil salesman who claimed to turn men into the same he-men advertised in the back of the magazine. The artists even cut and pasted the ad into the panels, rather than attempting their own version. The result is a blatant jibe at Charles Atlas's commercial promises to develop the masculinity of *MAD* readers.

The March 1955 issue included parodies of comic book ads, including everything *MAD* had run, from the Atlas ads, to stamps, a hypnotism course, and even guns. Soon thereafter, *MAD* redebuted as a magazine and included no advertisements (save for other EC comic books). This fit the more sophisticated look of the magazine, which also included type rather than handwritten dialogue and more celebrity-written pieces. The redesign worked: the first issue of *MAD* as a magazine completely sold out. In the April 1956 issue, the contents page included a note from editor Kurtzman mentioning the conspicuous absence of regular advertising in the issues since the redebut.

Of course, there has been a reason for this. In the whole history of publishing, it is a well known fact that the mere presence of advertising in a publication has immediately imposed restrictions. Therefore in order to be editorially pure, in the purest sense, one must shun advertising. In other words, *the reason we haven't taken advertising is mainly because we couldn't get any.* On page 7 is our very first real advertisement in *MAD*. Please do what it asks.

This characteristically self-deprecating admission both acknowledged the limitations that ads put on content, then undermined itself by imploring the readers to do what the ad asked. *MAD* used this sarcastic tone to attempt to maintain its critical integrity in the face of "selling out" to advertisers. Readers didn't take kindly to the ad for a home Hi-Fi system. The ad prompted the immediate call of "hypocrisy" by a fan in the next installment of the letters department who wrote "The precipitous rebellion of *MAD* has been utterly obliterated by Real Advertisement."[24] So began *MAD*'s public negotiation between taking potshots at advertisements and commercial culture while being a part of commercial culture and needing advertising revenue to be financially viable. *MAD* ghettoized the sparse ads under a prominent "Real Advertising" banner, where ads for items such as elevator shoes, a pipe set, and Silly Putty appeared.[25] In its February 1957 issue, *MAD* pleaded for more ad dollars with—what else—a parody pitching the magazine as an advertising venue. Charts illustrated how *MAD* came in last place when leading magazines were ordered by length of name, and how the magazine gained distinction by having its zig-zag line go down while those of *Life*, *Post*, and *Look* went up. In the next issue, Al Feldstein, having just taken over editorial duties for Kurtzman, apologized for the presence of the "real" ads, then urged readers to pay close attention to them "so we'll make a good showing."[26] *MAD* wanted—or needed—to have it both ways. As a form of commodity culture, it needed advertising, but such advertising could potentially alienate readers who saw it as undermining the magazine's critical attitude toward commercialism.

Some of the products advertised attempted to capitalize on the particular version of individualism and cultural irreverence fostered by the magazine. A "Registered Critic Kit" including pin, card, and certificate was advertised, as was a "Famous Artists" correspondence art school in which readers could enroll.[27] By the end of the 1950s, however, the "real advertisements" had almost completely disappeared, while the anti-ad rhetoric of *MAD* had escalated. There was one major exception to this: advertisements for *MAD* merchandise. Though *MAD* loved to lambaste Walt Disney for his wanton commercialism and merchandising, *MAD* offered all sorts of supplies for the individual who wanted to advertise his fandom.[28] The first item to be offered was the Alfred E. Neuman wall print, then *MAD* T-shirts, followed by *MAD* tie pins and jewelry, plaster busts of Neuman, and even a *MAD* straightjacket. The ads for these MAD products usually included the staff posing in them, providing the few opportunities fans had to see what the producers of the magazine looked like. Paperback and hardcover *MAD* anthologies were also continually amassed and released.

As the 1950s wound down, the "real advertisements" disappeared, and anti-ad articles such as "TV ads we'd like to see," as well as other TV-oriented features, such as what life would be like if ad slogans replaced everyday conversation, no longer had to compete with "real" invaders from the commercial world. Still, whether ad parodies ever did any harm to a "real" company seems unlikely. One Salem cigarettes marketing wonk wrote the magazine to say that he thought *MAD*'s parody of their ads, which proposed "Sail 'em, Don't inhale 'em" was "a great plus" for their brand. Like the celebrities who embraced their parodic alter egos, advertisers saw a *MAD* parody not as an undermining critique, but as positive publicity. Just as a parody of Jackie Gleason was unlikely to undermine his career, an ad parody was unlikely to undermine a specific product. More important, however, was the production of debate about the nature of advertising and consumption and their roles in American life. While *Consumer Reports* might not have taken ads, *MAD* brought arguments about the deceptive nature of advertising to a broader audience and expanded the conversation to include ways of living and ways of thinking—not just whether a product did what an ad claimed.

In addition to the ad parodies, the early *MAD* chiefly lampooned other comic books, but television was present in the parodies from the very first issue in 1952. Though ostensibly a science-fiction parody, "BLOBS!" featured a man-boy named Alfred (not yet the E. Neuman one) speeding across futuristic roadways in order to find Melvin, "one of the few active brains left." When Alfred finds Melvin, he goes on a tirade about how machines have taken over the lives of men, and how this progressed from the ancient year of 1952, when machines like vacuum cleaners, electric clocks, and air conditioners were beginning to surround humanity. Because Melvin seems to be going down this path, Alfred says, "You're getting like all the rest! Like a kid with a toy! All pleasure! No good hard thinking!" Like the ghost of Christmas past, Alfred shows Melvin how housewives gradually became more and more enveloped by household appliances and men became more and more beholden to automobiles. Melvin sees how men went to friends' houses in cars, then "instead of talking to the friends, they would look at television machines for a few hours, and then they would ride home! Now does that make sense, Melvin?"

Now, says Alfred, instead of attempting to date, men just get a robot woman from a machine, as machines have taken over all of the functions of man. But what would happen if the machine that fixes the machine broke, he wonders? On cue, the machine that fixes the machine promptly breaks, and Melvin and Alfred unceremoniously drop dead. Such technological doomsday-ism is not uncommon material for science fiction; indeed, the domination of mankind by machines has been popular film fare from *Metropolis* all the way up to the *Terminator* and *Matrix* movies, and the *Battlestar Galactica* television series. In "BLOBS!" *MAD* parodies science fiction not to poke fun at narrative clichés or simplistic plotlines and characters, but as a framework for social criticism about consumerism, conformity, and mass culture. These social debates are now framed within a comic format, which means comedy is used to address the issues, as well as including a different audience within the debate. It is no accident that the young Melvin is "one of the few active brains" left, that Alfred is appealing to him not to become like their elders who are completely dominated by technology and, presumably, mass media, like their ancient ancestors in 1952.

Even calling "BLOBS!" a science fiction parody seems a stretch; this is almost as overt (though not as respectable) a work of social criticism as Wertham's *Seduction of the Innocent*. It is difficult not to read the piece as a response to accusations, like Wertham's, that the comics had dangerous, mind-washing powers. Here, in its very first issue, *MAD* responds that mind washing comes not from comics or comedy, but from the socially endorsed pressures to consume products and conform to mainstream tastes.

MAD TAKES ON TV

The third issue of *MAD*, in the spring of 1953, featured a parody of *Dragnet*, called "Dragged Net" which didn't parody television so much as it did the detective genre. Indeed, this was the usual case in the early *MAD*, where parodies of genres were more prevalent than parodies of specific titles. It was not long, however, before the specific properties of the television medium, and the unique programs that the medium created, would bring more specific parodies. In the August 1954 issue, the first "Television Dept." appeared in *MAD*, and featured a parody of *The Continental*, a series with a distinctive first-person address from a suave Latin male welcoming the viewer into his swank apartment to be wined and dined. *The Continental*, with his romantic gaze deep into the lens of the camera in place of the eyes of the viewer, was ripe for parody. Just as the show uniquely constructed a first-person address through the television set, *MAD*'s parody explored the particularities of the new medium. *MAD*'s version of the show, "The Countynental," was immediately visually distinctive from other parodies in the issue. The first panel was framed by a television set, and the rest of the piece applied the horizontal scan lines of a television set across the comic panels, and limited its use of color to grays, punctuated only by the occasional use of red and yellow to connote the sounds of the show, such as a "Slurp!" or a "WOK!"

While the visual design of the parody was specific to television, the piece was structured around the first-person address of *The Continental*, and how this address, though inspired by the supposed intimacy of television, the communion between set and viewer, would ultimately be undermined by the technical limitations of the medium. The Countynental first beckons the reader/viewer into his apartment, "Do not be afraid! Eet is only a man's apartment!" but slams the door shut after the revelation that the viewer had the wrong apartment and was only looking for the janitor. In the next panel, the Countynental determines to try "eet" again, beckoning the viewer into the apartment with a glass of "shomponya." However, he is defeated again; while he is assured that the viewer's children are away at the coal mine, when he asks whether the husband is away, a large boot is thrown at the television set, knocking the Countynental and his program temporarily off the air. When he cautiously returns, he holds up a script, skipping quickly through his routine until the viewer is inside his apartment and he can shut and bolt the doors.

When the free "shomponya" the Countynental has continually offered begins to go to the viewer's head, the panel goes blurry and doubles. The Countynental entreats the viewer to adjust the fine-tuning control knob, but instead the image gets worse when the horizontal hold is adjusted. Next

Figure 2.1 The Countynental" attempts to romance the television audience in *MAD*'s first Television Dept. parody, but fails due to technical glitches and an unreceptive male viewer. E.C. Publications, Inc. All Rights Reserved.

the vertical hold goes haywire and the Countynental gets sick until the image stabilizes, at which point he's had enough. "Look girlie! I've been fooling around with shomponya, cigarettes, flowers, for months now! ... Let's get down to brass tacks! ... Gimme a kiss!" The Countynental's huge lips are met with a "WOK!" as the husband punches the screen again, and the Countynental disappears into the background. The parody continues with "footage" from behind the scenes, however, as an overweight, unattractive woman shows up on the set, distraught that the Countynental wasn't talking to her. Instead, he leaves the set arm-in-arm with his true love, the television camera.

The basic comic device of this parody is illustrating how the first-person address of *The Continental* is ultimately thwarted by the technical realities and limitations of the medium. *The Continental* was a short-lived series, but the first-person address through the television set has been a hallmark of the medium since these early days. "The Countynental" would therefore resonate more broadly through male and female viewers, regardless of whether they had seen this particular show. The program's extreme reliance on the gendered, first-person address made it ripe for parodying both that address and the medium's technical limitations. Many years later, in 1990, actor Christopher Walken would play the Continental in a *Saturday Night Live* skit, making similar jokes about the mildly lascivious Latin's address through the television screen.[29]

In addition to considering the over-the-top first-person address of the original *Continental* as characteristic of romantic fantasy, we might also see its qualities as evocative of the fantasies of immediacy and presence that, as Jeffery Sconce has noted, early television often promoted. Sconce discusses how the television industry encouraged a notion of television as an "ambiguous interactive zone" between the viewer in the home and those beings electronically beamed inside it.[30] *MAD*'s "Countynental" expands both the forms and boundaries of the "ambiguous interaction" of *The Continental*. The liveness of the program not only enables romantic fantasy, but also the ability of the Countynental to tell the viewer how to adjust his set to improve the picture. The broadcast program merges with behind-the-scenes footage as the Countynental reappears onstage rushing through the script, then again when the distraught woman shows up on the set. While the TV industry sought to encourage senses of liveness and ambiguous interaction, *MAD* showed how those could also enable the fantasy of revenge *against* TV. The shoe thrown at the television set, which actually travels through it and hits the (live) Countynental, gets him back not only for his advances upon the lady of the house, but television's intrusion into the home in general. Still, in the end, the liveness of TV enables the parody to give the reader as TV viewer access not just to "The Countynental" as it is broadcasted by camera, but what is going on behind the scenes, at the same time, and even after the broadcast, as well. The interactive zone includes not just that between the viewer and the world inside the television set, but the world around the production of the program, inside the studio.

While *MAD* paid particular attention to *The Continental*'s gendered address, and offered the overweight, unattractive woman showing up on the set as the ultimate dupe of the program, this does not fit into a larger pattern of *MAD* feminizing the television viewer while demeaning the intellect of that viewer. There does not seem to be any simple dichotomy at work such as female television viewer = dupe and male television viewer = active. However, scantily clad women were prevalent in the earliest issues of *MAD*, as they often were in comics, and advertising skewed toward male readers. As noted, Charles Atlas entreated *MAD* readers to become muscular "he-men" in the early issues and the second issue even included an ad for a cigarette case featuring a scenario about a man being one-upped by another due to his bent (limp) cigarettes. Despite this skewing of the early advertisements, the frequent letters from female fans and statistics about the *MAD* readership show that the magazine was popular with female readers as well. This might not be too surprising, since a normalized address to a male reader/viewer was more a benchmark of popular culture than a particular characteristic of *MAD*.

Men and women in the 1950s both faced contradictions over the social roles they were supposed to fill and the satisfactions they were supposed to find at work and in the home. A body of critical work has analyzed the ways in which in the postwar period women were pressed to return to and find satisfaction within the home while men were expected to be productive employees who would return home to domestic bliss and relaxation at the end of the day. Elaine Tyler May has described how this process affected so many American women who joined the workforce during the war then were compelled to leave it.[31] Cultural expectations in the postwar period clashed with personal and cultural realities for both men and women. As Wini Breines writes, "Women had more options than ever before but were discouraged from acting on them, while men were prevented by occupational demands from realizing the domestic intimacy they needed and were supposed to value."[32] It is understandable, then, that *MAD*'s brand of cultural irreverence and constant revelation of the gap between what was *expected* and what *was* found a diverse, at least in terms of gender, audience. *MAD* functioned as a counterpoint to those expectations, even if it didn't necessarily articulate a critique in the same manner recent historians have or contemporary cultural critics did.

Another TV Dept. parody suggests further ways that recognizing the parodic discourse of *MAD* as counterpoint to dominant discourses could mean readjusting our notions about how fifties TV viewers understood television texts. The September 1954 issue featured a parody of the low budget science fiction series *Captain Video*. Again, television scanlines covered the panels and, again, the quality and conditions of television production were chief structuring mechanisms for the parody, titled "Captain TVideo." The story begins with Captain TVideo unable to remove his helmet because the prop men buy them from a nearby five and dime. "When's this show gonna get a decent budget?" he asks, then activates the studio fire hose instead of the stapler that is supposed to be his "Ranger Alerter." No historical distance was necessary to make the production standards of *Captain Video* look cheap to the TV viewer, as this parody shows. Later, the parody tells the viewer that he, too, can conquer Venus with the free Captain TVideo ring, available "absolutely free with $3 for handling and just 200 wrappers from Gooky candy bars." From this integrated commercial with an actor chewing happily on a Gooky bar, the story picks right back up on the Venusian action. Unfortunately, while Captain TVideo has conquered the Venusians in the story, real Venusians have taken over the television actors and studio. The program abruptly goes off the air—an apocalyptic ending that recalls the breakdown at the end of "BLOBS!"

In November 1954, the TV Dept. featured a full-page photo of the Army-McCarthy hearings, then offered "constructive criticism" for how the proceedings could have been made more entertaining. This was the most directly *MAD* had engaged political material, and the fact that the hearings were indeed a popular television spectacle enabled this logical refiguring of them through the established television genre of the panel show. *MAD* could treat politics here because politics had indeed merged with popular, mediated culture. The Army-McCarthy piece probably also resonated with the *MAD* staff and readership because of the similar scrutiny and vilification that Gaines and the comics had suffered at the hands of Kefauver and the anti–juvenile delinquency crusade. During 1954, the tide had turned against Joseph McCarthy. He had been both denounced on the Senate floor and criticized by an Edward R. Murrow television documentary. McCarthy sealed his own doom when it was revealed he had sought preferential treatment from the army for his assistant, David Schine. McCarthy responded by attacking the army. Joseph Welch, the attorney representing the Army, famously rebuffed McCarthy by asking "Have you no sense of decency, sir? At long last, have you left no sense of decency?"

MAD reimagined McCarthy's frightening escapades as a panel show titled "What's My Shine?" featuring "Joseph McCartaway" alongside parodies of other committee members as well as celebrity panelist "Lana Cheesecake." McCartaway produces a photo of mystery guest "Even Steven" (Army Secretary Robert S. Stevens) wearing war paint and clutching a bloody tomahawk, which he says proves Steven is a "Redskin." Steven reveals that the photo is actually doctored, that he was holding a paint roller and the war bonnet appearing on his head was actually a turkey sitting on a fence. McCartaway responds that he realizes that Steven is not "really a redskin but merely a dupe of the redskins," and the two resolve to solve the dispute through "wrassling." The names, accusations, and outrageous fabrications were only slightly embellished and disguised by *MAD*. One of McCarthy's more self-incriminating moments had been the revelation that a photo of Stevens and Schine together had been cropped to look like more of a personal meeting than it had been. Despite the inherent outrageousness of the real-life episode, one reader objected to the piece, writing that the magazine should keep its hands off politics since "Communism is no joke! . . . and neither are the men who fight it."[33] Rather than stifling such objections to its content, *MAD* published them and in so doing encouraged debate about the proper role of comedy in culture.

The characteristic scanlines soon disappeared from the TV Dept.'s panels as television became accepted as its own story world and not as just another piece of furniture or another consumer product dominating human behavior and interaction, as it first was in the "BLOBS!" piece. Still, the primary characteristic discussed in these early *MAD* television parodies continued for some time to be the commercial nature of television and its particular production strategies, rather than the narrative intricacies or simplicities of program content and characters. Even in "What's My Shine?" one of the key moments in the parody is the integration of a coffee ad into the accusations, while committee chairman/moderator "Jay Renkins" sits behind a podium fashioned to look like a jar of "POW" instant coffee.

A particularly strident example of *MAD*'s lambasting of television's commercial nature is "Howdy Dooit," from December 1954. The editors prefaced the parody with an explanation of *MAD*'s recent interest in TV:

> Our constant readers have no doubt noticed our sudden shift to television! We ARE giving special attention to T.V. because we believe it has become an integral part of living . . . A powerful influence in shaping the future . . . But mainly we are giving attention because we just got a new T.V. set!

This characteristically sarcastic introduction pokes fun at taking TV seriously, but the piece is straightforward in depicting the forces driving television production. The narrative trajectory of the sequence follows that of its model, *Howdy Doody*, as Buffalo Bill incites the "Peewee Gallery" to a furor over the impending appearance of Howdy Dooit. When the puppet appears, he says hello to the kids, then immediately takes time out for a commercial and commands the viewer to bring his or her mother into the room to see an ad for "Bupgoo," which makes an ordinary glass of milk look like beer. This commercial routine is repeated a couple of times as Howdy teaches the kids to sneak "Skwushy's" sliced white bread into mom's grocery basket and to throw a tantrum for "Phud" cereal.

The scripting of the broadcast, with its carefully integrated commercial interludes, goes horribly awry after Buffalo Bill queries the Peewee Gallery about what they would like to be when they grow up. One particularly precocious child rebuffs Bill's suggestions of police chief or fireman as juvenile and says it would be much better to get into a white-collar occupation such as investment broker. Finishing his enormous lollipop, the boy, wearing shorts and suspenders, continues: "Of course . . . Advertising and entertainment are lucrative fields if one hits the top brackets . . . Much like Howdy Dooit has! In other words . . . What I want to do when I grow up, is to be a hustler like Howdy Dooit! I want to be where the cash is . . . the green stuff . . . moolah . . . pound notes . . . Get it? MONEY!" Though there was a trend toward addressing a more mature readership in comics of the 1950s, and so many of MAD's readers were high school or college students, this representation of the child viewer as being able to see past the artifice of television is another vindication of the MAD readership as possessing a critical agency in its reception of popular culture. In this manner, the piece echoes "BLOBS!" from the first issue, with the young men-boys Alfred and Melvin the only active minds left on Earth. This focus on the commercial nature of television could go on only so long before the critique simply ceased to be funny. MAD shifted to more specific parodies of program content, which were already at work in "The Countynental" in the first TV Dept. Still, MAD maintained a general hostility to consumerism, present most overtly in its regular parodies of ads, feature articles such as one that explained how planned obsolescence worked to sell automobiles, and in other specific program parodies that deserved special attention. One recurring victim of MAD's wrath was Walt Disney, and when his show *Disneyland* became a quick success, while being so obviously commercial, MAD struck back.

Disneyland was not only popular, but embraced in the press as quality family entertainment. The show recycled old Disney film and cartoon bits and shamelessly promoted the construction of its namesake theme park. Harold Cohen raved in *TV Guide* that the show had "immaculate taste, just as everything Walt Disney had ever done." Even those who pointed out the flagrant promotion going on were quick to endorse the show's quality. *Newsweek* discussed the promotional potential of the series, but only after noting this was true of the program "in addition to being top-notch entertainment." While pointing out that a recent episode was actually a program-long plug for the new Disney film *20,000 Leagues Under the Sea*, the magazine remarked that the program was a "fascinating essay on underwater film techniques." Such sentiment was widespread, as *Variety* marveled that Disney plugs had been so seamlessly integrated into the body of the show that the *20,000 Leagues* episode won an Emmy for best documentary.

"Dizzyland"—MAD's critical antidote—appeared in December 1956. The parodic approach to television meant the magazine got its hands dirtier than the journalists and television critics were willing. MAD had every intention of deflating Disney's wholesome pretension, parodying the show and theme park much as the "total merchandising" ploy television scholar Christopher Anderson has described, where experiencing the park as an "inhabitable text" is structured through consuming all things "Disney."[34] Each week, said the parody, "Dizzyland" opened, promising stories from

What, Me Subversive? 63

the various lands that happened to be different areas of the theme park. There was "Tomorrowsland—a broken promise of things to come," and also "Frontrearsland," which brought "true tales made up from the legendary past." "But mainly," said *MAD*, "each week when this show comes on the air, it really opens this: MONEYLAND." Beneath the Moneyland

Figure 2.2 *MAD*'s parody of *Disneyland*'s supposedly wholesome family entertainment portrayed the show as nothing but a marketing boondoggle. E.C. Publications, Inc. All Rights Reserved.

titles "Dizzyland" merchandise was piled, such as "Darnold Duck Frogman Flippers," and a coonskin "Davy Space Helmet." Here *MAD* is not critiquing the show as boring or otherwise substandard entertainment, but as flagrant commercialism. While the television program ostensibly offers bits and pieces of past Disney material and "behind the scenes" access to new material, *MAD* understands that it is all a commercial pitch, and that the ultimate way to experience Disney is to consume Disney through purchasing all its official goods.

MAD did not spare highbrow programs such as live dramas and documentaries from the sorts of shots it took at middlebrow fare. Live anthology dramas, that staple of early, New York-based television, were extolled by critics then as quality and are wistfully recalled now as TV's "Golden Age." Not so in *MAD*. A short piece on the vaunted *Playhouse 90* offered evidence to substantiate the *MAD* editor's belief that the "90" stood for the number of commercials. The piece featured the cameraman's production schedule for "Payhouse 90" that illustrated how little "live drama" made up the ninety minutes for a broadcast of "Requiem for a Playwright."[35] One minute was set aside for the first act, two and a half minutes for the second act, and two more minutes each for acts three and four. The host not only summarizes the play, but before introducing the trailer for the next week's show, he summarizes all ten commercials that have played. The clear message of this one page TV Dept. was that commercial TV changed "culture" fundamentally, even when supposedly highbrow shows presented supposedly highbrow dramas. The content was minimal and less important than the commercials, station breaks, and trademark graphics and music which continually constructed the respectability of this other example of commercial culture.

As mentioned previously, the targets of *MAD*'s sometimes strident parodies often relished them as positive promotion and status symbols rather than dangerous criticism. This apparent contradiction did not go unnoticed by readers. When Dave Garroway proudly displayed *MAD*'s parody of him on *Today* in 1956, he prompted one *MAD* letter writer to theorize the limitations of the critical function of parody:

> the big fault (in *MAD*) is that this kind of wonder-drug, like streptomycin, soon develops a resistance in the very disease it aims at. So the cynicism gets bigger and better, the germs more virulent, with each shot of *MAD*. As . . . some Television (personality) satirized by *MAD*, featured the satire on his very next program, giving *MAD* and himself a nice plug. The cure and the disease are practically hand-in-glove.

The Letters Department often served as a space where such tensions between lambasting popular, commercial culture and being a part of that culture were discussed. Editor Kurtzman responded to this reader/critic that Garroway needed their plugs like he needed a hole in the head.[36] Fans motivated to write into the magazine engaged in discussions about what the relevance of *MAD*'s comic approach to culture really was. While those who wrote J. Edgar Hoover sought a simple answer to what they assumed was a simple question (Was *MAD* communistic?), these fans engaged more complicated questions about the nature of popular culture. Even for those ardent fans of the magazine, it wasn't clear whether a product of commercial culture could legitimately be critical of that culture or whether that criticism was just hypocritical posturing. *MAD* parodies were producing material for readers to engage in debates as part of their own culture, and about the stakes of criticizing or protecting that culture.

THEORIZING THE USUAL GANG OF IDIOTS

In order to explain the popularity of *MAD*'s critical parodies, and further understand their cultural significance, it is productive to consider Mikhail Bakhtin's work on the carnivalesque. Bakhtin has been particularly useful in the analysis of parody and other cultural forms which are often disparaged as low or trash culture. His formulation of the carnivalesque as subversive textual practices, as well as his concept of dialogism, are helpful in analyzing popular culture, especially parody. The foremost of these subversive textual characteristics include (1) the overturning of social hierarchies, (2) a participatory blurring of the lines between performer and spectator, and (3) the juxtaposition of official language with "unofficial" or common language. While Bakhtin formulates the carnivalesque from an examination of rural folk culture, other theoretical emphases in his work help us employ the concept to analyze popular culture that appears to exhibit carnivalesque characteristics, like *MAD*. When *MAD* made fun of the government, taught readers how to write movie parodies, and rewrote the Army-McCarthy hearings as a panel show, it produced carnivalesque culture.

Bakhtin describes carnival as a time when there is a suspension of hierarchic distinctions and of certain norms and prohibitions of usual life. At the same time as these suspensions and inversions, an ideal type of communication, impossible in ordinary life, is established.[37] Parody, for Bakhtin, is the privileged mode of artistic, carnivalesque communication, and the popular resonance of *MAD* is related to its use of parody as a textual strategy that exercises cultural power. Much of what was considered to be "funny" in the magazine (as reflected in letters to the editor, to the FBI, and its own content) critically engaged American culture. The magazine's comic aesthetic asked the tough questions about American life, and parody in particular was able to critique dominant discourses. Parodies of entertainment texts blended into social satire, such as proclaiming that the suburbs were on their way out and that ranch homes would now be built on high-rise tiers in the city. While exclusively focusing on the failings of the entertainment industry might have been a safer choice, this modus operandi of taking on all aspects of postwar culture prompted one letter to the editor claiming the magazine's general theme was actually "undermining the American way of life."[38]

Parody may or may not be a subversive language in other contexts, but rather than seeing it as the key carnivalesque element that transforms texts, making them essentially subversive, Bakhtin emphasizes the need to ask whether the context is more broadly carnivalesque, featuring or susceptible to other transgressive features. Parody as critical discourse must be considered as part of a broader dialogic context. The parody of television in *MAD* may undermine the generic standards of *Gunsmoke*, but what is more important is how regular exposure to alternative or unofficial ways of reading could influence the reading of not only this, but other texts. These alternative ways of reading texts can be tied to other alternative positions in respect to other discourses; for example, that system of understanding success and happiness through life in the suburban ranch house.

Unquestionably, *MAD* and various television shows that included parody were enormously popular during the emergence of television in the 1950s. They may not have been, however, the most popular type of comedy or programming of the time. The sustained, massive popularity of *I Love Lucy* or even the more middle-of-the-road humor of Jackie Gleason may be more typical of the "average" humor of the time. But long-running popular success is not the key to understanding the cultural significance of *MAD* or someone like Ernie Kovacs, who appeared on various shows on various networks throughout the 1950s. The prevalence of parody that was both critical of popular culture texts and other cultural discourses such as life in the suburbs and the pleasures of consumption signals a symbolic activity counter to more common styles of comedic production and reception, styles which don't run counter to the official systems of language.

Bakhtin's formulation of the carnivalesque and the other literary concepts he developed are useful in discussing today's popular culture because they are fundamentally about language and meaning-making systems. Bakhtin writes:

> The carnivalesque crowd in the marketplace or in the streets is not merely a crowd. It is the people as a whole, but organized *in their own way,* the way of the people. It is outside of and contrary to all existing forms of the coercive socioeconomic and political organization, which is suspended for the time of the festivity.[39]

In applying the carnivalesque to popular culture, we should examine whether producing meaning from the texts enables readers to organize themselves, to articulate their positions in ideology, as Bakhtin stresses here, *in their own way*. The chance for readers/viewers to articulate their own positions may be particularly available when there is an emergence of new cultural forms and audience formations. *MAD* may have helped create reading protocols for portions of the newly forming television audience, but it is important to recognize the existence of these particularly *textual* strategies alongside the more overt attacks on consumer culture and authority. It is the interaction of these—*MAD*'s critical aesthetic—which provides the material of articulation for consumers of the texts.

In its fourth issue, *MAD* published a letter from a mother complaining that "Television programs are bad enough, but one can turn them off and forget it. The ash-heap for *MAD*." This mom was concerned because *MAD*'s unofficial methods of making fun and making meaning had staying power—they couldn't be turned off. The editorial staff of *MAD* seemed to relish this sort of hate mail from people they had never intended to endear as signs that they were doing something right. Issues from the 1950s often included such righteous denunciations, usually likening the magazine to a disease or trash. *MAD* was labeled "rotten literature," "dirt," "filthy-minded," and "imbecilic, moronic, rot." One posited that *MAD* taught children new methods of torture.[40] More articulate critics claimed the magazine was "fit only for the lower classes" and "No more than trash fashioned to degenerate the youth of our country."[41]

These letters proclaimed *MAD*'s utter failure to conform, at least to what was considered to be good taste. They signified that the magazine was successful in developing a countercultural attitude and aesthetic. Though the magazine understandably reveled in such ridicule, the letters department of these issues also included fans praising the magazine as well as embracing the notion of *MAD* indeed being trash. Some rushed to the magazine's defense on higher cultural ground, intellectualizing *MAD*'s content as an antidote to criticism that it (like other comics) was the lowest of low culture. Letters were published by enthusiastic college students, such as one Cornell University fan who called his fellow devoted readers "comrades in the bonds of spoofery," while another wrote "We need a magazine like yours in a nation withering from conformity."[42] In response to one particularly vitriolic, anti-*MAD* mother, a reader wrote "*MAD* is the height of intellectualism" because it "makes its readers stay on their toes to get all the humor."[43]

Another reader wrote "Your *MAD* is satirical, subtle, and sophisticated ... It's actually a 'high-brow' comic, but I hope the public takes to it!" This reader aligned the *MAD* comic-parodic aesthetic with the highbrow taste famously delineated in Russell Lynes's 1949 *Harper's Magazine* article "Highbrow, Lowbrow, Middlebrow." Parody of popular culture would later be a fundamental component of *Playboy* magazine's recipe for masculine sophistication, and Hugh Hefner would draft *MAD* founding editor Harvey Kurtzman to start his own humor magazine.[44] When he did so, Hefner published an article titled "The Little World of Harvey Kurtzman," which included samples from the magazine and discussed the pedigrees and different styles of *MAD*'s artists.[45] *MAD*'s readers could develop such a connoisseur's relationship to the magazine, recognizing nuances of particular artists and comic subtleties that might be missed by the casual reader.

The transformation of low "mass" culture into a high-end cultural product worthy of reflection was not a technique unique to *MAD*. Greg Taylor describes how postwar film critics used both cult and camp readings to apply art-world discourses to the low-end cultural products of Hollywood. In so doing, they sought "to present their criticism of the movies not merely as a consumer guide but as a vehicle for asserting their own creative, artistic response to the challenge of postwar popular art (i.e., middlebrow culture)."[46] Cultism's "radical connoisseurship" involved identifying marginal artworks or qualities of artworks "that (though sorely neglected by others) meet the critic's privileged aesthetic criteria."[47] When *MAD* fans trumpeted the work of one artist over another and proclaimed the need to "stay on their toes to get all the humor," they proposed that one could become a *MAD* connoisseur. In this model of aesthetic appreciation, those who thought the magazine was trash just weren't looking closely enough. On the contrary, those who embraced *MAD* as trash, not art, were more in line with the magazine's own aestheticizing gestures.

An obvious analogy between the film critic's "activation" of the movie text through camp interpretation can be made with *MAD*'s rewriting of television, advertising, and, yes, Hollywood movies. Rather than being the material in need of a camp reading, *MAD* essentially taught lessens in the aestheticizing gestures of camp criticism. The postwar critics Taylor discusses embraced cultism and camp as techniques to transform low culture into high culture. *MAD* encouraged similar methods with more modest aims: to make fun, not make art. But "to make fun" in the *MAD* manner could actually involve cultural criticism and complex decoding strategies.

MAD did get some "official" respect. A principal in Levittown, New York, railing against juvenile delinquency and telling his students they shouldn't read trashy comic books, took time out to specify that he wasn't talking about *MAD*, because he read that himself. English instructors at the University of Kentucky assigned themes on horror comics and *MAD*. An assistant professor at Butler University wrote that *MAD* was "humorous in a wholesome way." When *Reader's Digest* published an article that slighted *MAD*, readers wrote in protest.[48] After actually seeing an issue of *MAD*, the editor and publisher of the *Digest* wrote *MAD* to apologize, saying that the magazine was "not only inoffensive, but positively entertaining."[49] While radio DJs regularly thanked the magazine for providing much-needed content, a church youth activities adviser wrote that he found *MAD* to be an excellent source of humor. Brother John, librarian at Holy Trinity High School in Chicago wrote, "I forward *MAD* to missionaries in heathen lands who sometimes wonder what life is like in the world they left behind. *MAD*'s penetrating portrayal of The American Scene makes them glad they left!" Even Wally Cleaver, in a 1960 episode of *Leave It to*

Beaver, reported that his English teacher read *MAD* in class because he thought it was funny.⁵⁰

Besides sounding off and defending their individual tastes for *MAD*'s parodic approach to culture, readers regularly demonstrated that the magazine had created community—people getting together bound by the pleasure of *MAD*'s cultural decodings. Such subcultural formation was encouraged very early by the magazine, which announced the formation of the EC fan club, a national organization with authorized chapters, in the October/November 1953 issue. Many more unofficial fan groups also formed. The December 1958 letters department included both a photo of the "*MAD* Readers of Plainville, Connecticut," marching in a parade, and the proud members of the Alfred E. Neuman Racing Club of Brentwood, California, alongside their race car. In these cases it would appear that shared activities and backgrounds (flying planes, building a car, living in the same small town) were more important bonding mechanisms for these groups than individual passions for the magazine. Still, their choice of defining themselves through *MAD* signified not just the cultural currency of the magazine, but suggested that they were somehow banded together through a similar humor—not just a comic temperament, but an attitude toward culture.

POTREZEBIE, COMRADES!

The diversity of the magazine's letter-writing fan base begs further questioning to understand what it meant to be "comrades in the bounds of spoofery," to borrow a line from one of the fan letters. What did it mean to define oneself as a *MAD* reader rather than a *Time* reader or a *Boy's Life* reader? Did *Reader's Digest* fans march in parades or form motorcycle gangs? One major difference between *MAD* and other popular magazines was that it could be depended on to provide a jaundiced look at culture. The magazine not only drew upon the shared culture of its readers; it provided a different viewpoint on that culture. The magazine seemed to have the ability not just to express criticism of commercial culture from within that culture, but to manage diverse audiences as well. Rather than being ideologically positioned on the left or right, *MAD*'s cultural irreverence, which meant everything was up for critique, appealed across simplified political boundaries. *MAD* recognized the critical currents channeling through popular culture, and proposed that it was okay to travel them—that didn't make you a communist. The adequate response for those dissatisfied with consumer culture and popular media was to play with the rules of mainstream culture—to invert their intended meanings, or turn them on their sides, anyway.

No doubt some *MAD* readers identified other *MAD* readers as lesser fans, lesser comrades, and especially lesser nonconformists. *Life* published an easy-to-understand guide to Lynes's brow distinctions with an illustrated, taste-level chart in 1949. According to Michael Kammen, pigeonholing one's friends and acquaintances in a particular taste-level became a popular parlor game and topic of conversation.[51] Ten years later, *MAD* published a guide to identifying conformists, nonconformists, and *MAD* nonconformists. While ordinary conformists enjoyed "uninspired Technicolor musicals," "stories with happy endings," and "migraine-provoking Cinemascope," ordinary nonconformists patronized movie houses that showed "experimental films" and "obscure foreign language pictures with the subtitles in pidgin Swahili." *MAD* nonconformists, on the other hand, enjoyed "hand-cranked penny arcade machines which contain film classics like the Dempsey-Firpo fight, Sally Rand's Fan Dance, old Ben Turpin comedies, and Tom Mix pre-adult Westerns." They made other categorical distinctions in music, clothing, reading, pets, and food as well. While ordinary nonconformists played folk songs and Gregorian chant over dance music or rock-n-roll—and played it on their "super-complicated stereo hi-fi sets—*MAD* nonconformists played "bird calls, tap dancing and exercise lessons," and "Senate Committee hearings" on "easy-to-operate hand-wound victrolas." In this article, *MAD* showed that "ordinary non-conformity" was a symbolic system with rules of taste and behavior, just as "conformity" was. One didn't escape consumer culture by becoming a nonconformist. That only meant choosing another set of clothes to wear, movies to watch, or books to read. As the magazine said in its introduction to the piece, "all these Non-Conformists are so busy Conforming to not being Conformists, they all wind up Conforming to their Non-Conformism!" In contrast, the choices made by the *MAD* nonconformist are wildly obscure and willfully anachronistic. The choices aren't those of a connoisseur, which would be carefully selected for consistent quality according to an aesthetic system. Instead, they seem both bizarre and haphazard, except for the fact that they are consumed on antiquated technology—arcade machines and Victrolas. In this *MAD*-ness, they signify not alternative goods to be consumed, but alternative ways of thinking, watching, reading, seeing, etc. One needn't keep up with the march of technology in order to become a *MAD* nonconformist; instead one should abandon it and embrace the hopelessly outdated. Changing practices, not purchases, is the way to really transcend consumer culture.

A look at the other content in the very same issue, June 1959, suggests *MAD* was most influential in formulating identity not through direct prescriptions of alternative, nonconformist, or countercultural characteristics, but through promoting alternative reading and writing practices. *MAD* suggested there was no such thing as conformity and nonconformity, or mainstream culture and alternative culture. There was only consumer culture, everyone was a part of it, and the only alternative, countercultural, oppositional, or nonconformist response was to create your own way of watching, listening, reading, eating—consuming—that culture. In the issue, *MAD* presents "Jack and Jill as Retold by Various Magazines." In

Seventeen the seemingly innocuous nursery rhyme becomes a cautionary tale about being "Old enough to go drinking in the mountains but too young to go steady." *Confidential* asks, "Did they really go up for water?" and promises "The real lowdown on the cutie who made her guy fall . . . in a big way!" The content of the nursery rhyme, which is so consistent and simple when told by Mother Goose, is transformed into the distinct styles and marketing niches of the different magazines. Another article features different movie posters all designed for the same movie, but "for packing in every type of audience." Different portions of the title for the movie, *The Wild Rocking Horse in the Bare Room,* and different characters are emphasized according to the desired audience. For soldiers, Jayne Mansfield and "In the Bare" are emphasized and "The Movie Sexation of the Year" proclaimed. Another poster, for "highbrows" translates the title into French and promises a "motion picture that probes the unfathomable depths of human emotion" with "subtitles in French, German, Italian and Sanskrit." Here *MAD* proposed how a movie could be advertised to appeal to any audience without its actual content being transformed in the process. Again this piece seems to say that the actual content of commodity culture was interchangeable, and all that distinguished one work from another was its marketing.

Sid Caesar was one of parody's foremost practitioners on television, and the issue also featured his character "The Professor" lecturing on space. But perhaps the most significant television/parody crossover in the issue, and the most informative article on alternative methods of consumption, featured "Combined Television Shows." This *MAD* parody constructed hybrid television programs from preexisting shows. "Sea Hunt with a Dragnet" fused the underwater adventure show *Sea Hunt* with the procedural detective show *Dragnet,* for example. "Arthur Murray's Meet the Press Party" merged the variety program The *Arthur Murray Party,* which amounted to a commercial for his chain of dance studios, with the news/talk show *Meet the Press.* The result was an absurd collision of light entertainment and hard news: Eleanor Roosevelt discusses Far East policy as she tangos with a reporter from the *New York Times*. On "I've Got a Secret News Report" members of the television panel attempt to guess the news report secretly delivered by New York Correspondent "Dave Brinkle." Even as individual programs were parodied for their peculiar characteristics, the fact that all these programs were *television* programs made those collisions not completely absurd. One might experience a similar sensation by rapidly switching the channels. *MAD* suggested that these collisions between the programs meant for individual consumption could be both funny and pleasurable.

While a few *MAD* articles explicitly taught how to write television programs or how to write comics (the "DIY" articles discussed previously), the parodic form of others essentially taught the same thing. In fact, parody demands the ability to rewrite, by relying on previous textual (and contextual) knowledge. The difference between the MAD articles that listed "Sure Fire Dialogue" and those that posited "Scenes We'd Like to See" is not so different in this respect: They play on textual experience and expectations in order to produce pleasurable meaning through humor. Rather than see such parodies as producing only a general sense of irony and cynicism, it is important to see these productions of alternative meaning as interventions in systems of representation. A true circuit of meaning is at work: television culture mediated by those writing the parodies and those decoding them.

The "Scenes We'd Like to See" type article serves as an illustrative connection between the overt criticisms of television, mass media, and consumer culture such as that in "Howdy Dooit" or "Dizzyland," and the more purely parodic articles which focus on the content of a particular show or film. These "purer" parodies, rather than abandoning a critical attitude toward their target, are works that have already internalized that critical attitude. Not only is familiarity with the original work necessary to make sense, but this same "nagging hilarity," as MAD was described by fifties critic Robert Warshow, informs the more overt criticisms. More simply, whereas "Dizzyland" spells out the blatant commercial nature of *Disneyland*, these other parodies show what to do with crass, commercial, or just plain tired content. Through reworking, recombining, and rewriting, the always commercial, often shallow nature of television can be made pleasurable and meaningful, if not respectable.

Applying Michel de Certeau's theorization of the resistant politics of "poaching" as cultural production, scholars such as Henry Jenkins and Constance Penley have persuasively shown how TV fans, far from being cultural dupes, take what is pleasurable or useful to them by appropriating and recombining elements from the cultural commodity to create their own narratives.[52] The narrative products of this "slash" culture include comic books, paintings, novels, scripts, and home-edited videos. The key is not the final material product itself but the alternative meaning-making strategies that created them. MAD's enormous popularity points to the possibility of documenting the establishment of alternative reading protocols for television on a large scale, beyond those hardcore fans that actually produce material fan culture. Through parody, MAD armed its readers with protocols for the reading of television texts based on strategies of satire, reappropriation, and recombination. Such poaching tactics, as fan scholars have shown, don't intend to overthrow the system of popular culture producing them; rather, they were a way to exhibit a different way of thinking. While attention paid to the material productions of fan groups provides evidence of viewers resisting the dominant ideology and preferred readings of texts, MAD offers a place to think about the roots of a mainstream, widespread critical viewership. In picking up an issue and engaging MAD's treatment of fifties culture, readers armed themselves with an "unofficial" language of alternative consumption and meaning-making.

While de Certeau may lament that there is a lack of traces left behind by reading practices, *MAD* offers evidence of the production of available reading protocols. Though it may literally be the trace examples of the reception practices of its writers, we should also consider its role—through these practices—in the transformation of the relationships of the readers to other television texts, and media more generally. In addition to the broad critical attitude toward culture expressed in its anti-ad, anticonsumerist parodies, *MAD* specifically encouraged an active participation with media texts. *MAD* showed how to find pleasure in cultural decoding and recycling. Pop culture might not all be good, but there was fun to be made of it. *MAD* involved its readers in the production of meaning. Pleasure produced by inverting, flipping, turning over someone else's meaning is subversive pleasure. It changes the way people use culture. It reminds them of the pleasures of language play (which Freud says is how the joke functions, overcoming social inhibitions and allowing the pleasure of free play with meaning) and reminds them that they are active producers in language systems.[53]

Parody constitutes an intervention in systems of representation; it is then a key intervention in the articulation of political subjects. Postmodern culture has been characterized as preoccupied with surfaces, where individuals experience life, often consciously, as performance. The variety of parodic targets in *MAD*, from sitcom texts to news reporting to the consumer ethos of the times, suggests the extent to which life is experienced and understood textually through representation. These parodies also suggest how meaning-making strategies and alternative modes of pleasure are offered within popular culture as ways of "making do"—not just with what's on TV, but with life away from the set as well.

CONCLUSION

This chapter has sought to show how *MAD* functioned in the articulation of identity through popular culture. It has examined how the magazine intervened in the relationship forming between youth culture and television in particular, and postwar popular culture in general. *MAD* promoted a critical, not just cynical, attitude toward commercial culture. This critical attitude is explicit in many articles, but is also integral to the prevalent rewriting of popular culture in parodies. While in the 1950s concerned readers and parents wrote to J. Edgar Hoover asking whether *MAD* was communistic, there was no easy answer to whether the magazine was subversive. Clearly it called into question assumptions about the infallibility of the American way of life. This, perhaps, explains why many people were alarmed by the magazine's content, even if they weren't sure whether it was made by bona fide "communists."

The production of this fundamentally critical attitude toward the preferred ways of reading popular culture and dominant discourses is *MAD*'s most important "effect." However, there do seem to be some more direct connections between *MAD* readers of the 1950s who would become political subversives of the 1960s. The tactics and political philosophy of the Yippies in particular seem sprung from the *MAD* mindset. How else can one understand Abbie Hoffman's promise that the march on the Pentagon in 1967 would result in the building rising 300 feet in the air, at which point all the evil spirits would fall out, and that marijuana crops, already planted on the Pentagon lawn, would then be ready for harvest?[54] The Yippies' poster announcing their meeting in Chicago during the Democratic Convention of 1968 began "Join us in Chicago in August for an international festival of youth, music, and theater. Rise up and abandon the creeping meatball!" Jerry Rubin's 1968 manifesto *Do It!* countered the popular media explanation that "creeping meatball" was a reference to LBJ. Instead, he said, it was something everyone had: "grades, debts, pimples."[55] Back in 1957, *MAD* had published an interview with radio personality Jean Shepherd titled "The Night People vs 'Creeping Meatballism.'" Shepherd explained that the philosophy of "Creeping Meatballism" is conformity and the rejection of individuality: "The guy who has been taken in by the 'Meatball' philosophy is the guy who really believes that contemporary people are slim, and clean-limbed, and they're so much fun to be with . . . Because they drink Pepsi-Cola." Shepherd contrasted the "Day People" who subscribe to Creeping Meatballism with Night People who don't by describing the effect of watching Betty Furness do a commercial for Westinghouse.

> You know the one where she says "Another new miracle has been wrought! Mankind once again progresses! The new Westinghouse refrigerator for 1957 opens from *both sides!*" Well, a "Day People" sitting there says, "By George, we really *are* getting ahead!" And he feels great. He can see Mankind taking another significant step up that great pyramid of civilization. But a "Night People" watching this thing can't quite figure out what's the advantage of a refrigerator which opens from both sides. All he wants to know is, "Does it keep the stuff cold?"

The cure for Creeping Meatballism, for becoming a Night Person rather than a Day Person, was through thinking and laughing, two things cited as part of the same process by Shepherd. "Once a guy starts *thinking*, once a guy starts *laughing* at the things he once thought were very real . . . he's making the transition from 'Day People' to 'Night People.' And once this happens, he can never go back!" The parodic strategies of *MAD* and the Yippies shared both a derogatory term for their enemies, and an evaluation of how to escape that enemy by being critical of one's culture—asking questions of, or at least laughing at, the assumptions so many others lived by.

Aniko Bodroghkozy has shown how the Yippies and other activists of the 1960s embraced the mass media as a powerful tool for their cause, rather than as an enemy and tool of the state, negotiating a relationship with television and mass media, rather than just ignoring it. This was in contrast to the New Leftists and "countercultural heads and freaks" that "tended to avoid engagement with television to any great extent."[56] When "used" in the right ways, television wasn't an apparatus for the state control, but a powerful tool for changing culture. Rubin was explicit on the issue as well: "You can't be a revolutionary today without a television set—it's as important as a gun!" Rubin describes how television makes demonstrations far more interesting than they actually are, exaggerating them, and making them appealing to those who see them. "TV packs all the action into two minutes—a commercial for the revolution. The mere idea of a 'story' is revolutionary because a 'story' implies disruption of normal life."[57]

The Yippies' embrace of television on their own terms, using it for their own subversive ends, is analogous to *MAD*'s parodic approach to media texts, finding pleasure and producing meaning through and against them. There are, therefore, two clear connections between the tactics of these political radicals and the content of *MAD*: the outlandish, crazy event or "story" that upsets "normal" or mainstream understandings of life and the critical embrace of television culture. This "critical embrace" is better described as both an intervention in mediated representation and the production of culture. In this sense, the Yippies and *MAD* both used television to make cultural interventions—creating counterculture.

Ultimately, then, it didn't matter whether Dave Garroway proudly displayed his *MAD* parody, whether Fred Astaire danced in an Alfred E. Neuman mask, or Pat Boone coveted his *MAD* parody. It also didn't matter whether J. Edgar Hoover could say if the writers, editors, and publisher of *MAD* were communists. What did matter was that in issue after issue the magazine taught an alternative language for making sense and finding pleasure in and through American popular culture. *MAD*'s parodies incorporated discontent with postwar mediated culture into a commodity that could be bought and consumed—but even as its critics hinted, the magazine was not something that would sit well on your stomach. Instead, the urge to parody was bound to strike the *MAD* reader whenever television, the movies, advertising, politicians, the suburbs, or American life in general told a story that just wasn't acceptable "as is."

3 The Parodic Sensibility and the Sophisticated Gaze
Masculinity and Taste in *Playboy's Penthouse*

At 11:30 on a Saturday night sometime in 1959, a television set is switched on. On one channel, an old movie is rerun—for the umpteenth time. The channel switches and stops at the sound of a jazzy piano riff. Onscreen is a Corvette prowling the streets of a city at night. The car pulls up in front of a swanky-looking, high-rise apartment building. The camera cuts to the interior of an elevator as the numbers of the floors light up. When the elevator gets all the way to the top floor, a familiar logo appears—the *Playboy* bunny. When the elevator doors open, the television viewer is greeted by none other than Hugh Hefner himself. Inside the penthouse, a party chock full of celebrities and beautiful women is in full swing . . . and the television viewer is part of the fun.[1]

This swinging penthouse party was actually taking place in a Chicago studio, the set for the short-lived, syndicated series *Playboy's Penthouse*. In the premiere episode, the doors opened to reveal comedian Lenny Bruce, whom Hefner immediately introduced to two of the magazine's "Playmates." Bruce casually walked away, then returned to refill their drinks. Hefner and his production crew worked hard to enforce this informal party air, not just to put his guests at ease and ensure their good time, but to distinguish the show from other variety programs. Guests drank full-power cocktails, hung out around the bar, or chatted on the couches in front of the fireplace. "Hef," as he would come to be known, worked the room, introducing guests to each other and to the Playmates, chatting them up, then casually asking them to perform. The guests were nightclub acts of varying stature, ranging from Ella Fitzgerald to an Ella Fitzgerald impersonator. A guest would saunter over to the piano, or even sing from where he or she was sitting at the bar. Comedians and comedy troupes performed routines and sketches in this format as well. The different performers could make for an eclectic penthouse crowd: Phyllis Diller, Ray Charles, and mime Shai K. Ophir log equal time in one episode.

Such implications of casual drinking, performance, and sex might seem an unusual scene for Eisenhower-era television, but the sensibility was the televisual version of the carefully constructed model of sophisticated taste that *Playboy* magazine had been formulating since its debut in 1953. *Playboy* was an immediate success, nearly selling out its initial run of 70,000 copies and reaching a circulation of 1 million issues a month by 1956.² Editor and publisher Hefner conceived of the magazine as a distinctly urban alternative to the predominant men's magazines of the time, which stressed sports, the outdoors, and hunting as masculine supplements to the ranch house in the suburbs. *Playboy* was also designed to be more sexually frank than the magazine Hefner had formally worked on, *Esquire*.³ In addition to its nude or seminude "Playmates," who occupied only a few pages each issue, *Playboy* included short fiction, interviews, and other features. The magazine also offered recommendations on films, books, and household products, refining the *Playboy* reader's taste in both cultural and consumer goods.

Hefner wanted *Playboy's Penthouse* to be a different kind of television show, as *Playboy* itself had been a different kind of magazine. While the dramatic success of *Playboy* paralleled the meteoric rise of television as both an industry and cultural form during the 1950s, *Playboy's Penthouse* by necessity could not be ordinary TV. Hefner was most explicit about *Playboy*'s attempt to cultivate an alternative masculinity, one frequently at odds with television's dominant presentation of the American male. The magazine cultivated a lifestyle that, while embracing many components of American postwar consumer culture, rejected the notion that happiness could be found by marrying the right woman, starting a family, and

Figure 3.1   Hugh Hefner welcomes the viewer into the television party in *Playboy's Penthouse*.

Figure 3.2 Lenny Bruce and Hefner enjoy champagne with a couple of the magazine's "Playmates" before sitting down for a proper chat.

living a "normal" life in the suburbs. When asked what he was rebelling against, Marlon Brando's famous motorcycling antihero in *The Wild One* responded, "What have you got?" Hefner's *Playboy* constructed a man who was a far cry from the disaffected, aimless youth raising hell in that 1953 movie. Hefner presented an alternative to such proletarian anomie, not to mention the domestic prison of *Father Knows Best* and the rugged sportsmanship of *Field & Stream*. The *Playboy* man was a man of discriminating tastes who chose the indoors over the outside, martinis over beer, and bachelorhood over marriage (at least in theory). The *Playboy* man was expected to actively pursue not only sex, but cultural refinement as well. His sophisticated, urban-oriented tastes would serve to distinguish him from the mainstream American men and ordinary social roles that he defined himself against. Thus, the Playboy was a sort of "refined rebel"—a sexually enlightened sophisticate with specific guidelines for participating in American popular, consumer culture. A parodic sensibility and appreciation of sick comedy would be promoted by the magazine as fundamental to that sophisticated taste.

The alternative or countercultural masculinity broadcast so casually to the viewers of *Playboy*'s *Penthouse* demonstrates, as John Caldwell has argued, how television quite explicitly equates its aesthetic and semiotic strategies with product differentiation and marketing.[4] This televisual formation of masculinity held together the disparate components of the magazine's larger ethos, and provided a reading strategy for that consumer who modeled himself through that identity. Outside of *Playboy*'s own controlled forums, the formulation of a "Playboy subjectivity" involved instilling protocols for the readers/viewers to decode other cultural texts. This "decoding" could be as simple as deciding which fashions were appropriately stylish for the Playboy male, or more complicated, as in deciding whether an album was appropriately alternative to other mass culture offerings: for example, jazz versus rock-n-roll.[5] While men had certainly been instructed in proper taste and consumption before, the *Playboy* sensibility distinguished itself from past guidelines of elitist sophistication that disdained popular arts and pleasures in favor of the rarefied worlds of the country club and symphony. While the cultural tastes of the elites rejected the "common" pleasures of popular culture, *Playboy* endorsed engaging those pleasures in a "discriminating" or "sophisticated" manner. In this respect, the urbane and varied performances of *Playboy's Penthouse* offered a version of sophisticated television production that supplemented the magazine's model of sophisticated television *watching*.

Playboy had always maintained an uneasy, if not unapproving, relationship with television. Though it would become the most significant visual medium of the century, television posed a number of problems for *Playboy*. First, television was derided throughout postwar culture as too commercial to be taken seriously as an aesthetic medium. As discussed in previous chapters, this criticism was sounded by cultural commentators as diverse as Dwight MacDonald and Alfred E. Neuman. Second, according to most of the advertising promoting it, television was fundamentally a domestic (even feminine) medium. The popular image of a family gathered around the television might have sold sets to the suburbs, but it didn't fit the *Playboy* plan for masculine *escape from* domesticity. Third, television was broadly considered aesthetically inferior to other cultural forms. Watching it was considered a simple, passive entertainment. *Playboy* embraced the indoors as a site for seduction, but of women by men, not men *by television*. "Watching" TV simply did not involve the educated taste necessary to enjoy such *Playboy*-endorsed pleasures as listening to jazz or looking at modern art.

Playboy's relationship to television and its joining of the broadcasting ranks functioned as part of a more comprehensive model for masculine, sophisticated "seeing" developed in the magazine. Key to this type of cultural consumption was a parodic sensibility, one that enabled the Playboy sophisticate to enjoy what might seem the clearly *un*sophisticated pleasures of television. This viewing protocol, instilled across the magazine and the series, meant sophisticated pleasures might be had from television, even when no other quality alternatives presented themselves to counter the old movies being rerun. This parodic component of the Playboy sensibility thus helped resolve the contradictions of a man as a sophisticated consumer of mass-produced goods—cultural or otherwise. In this model, the *Playboy* man could gaze with informed appreciation upon the centerfolds in the magazine and abstract modern art on the museum wall, all the while remaining able to reclaim through parodic strategies even the most lowly genre picture on *The Late, Late Show*. This parodic sensibility permeated much of the magazine, and I would argue was as fundamental to the *Playboy* sensibility as its sexual candor.

Of course, *Playboy* was not alone in its embrace of parody as a suitable response to postwar culture. *MAD Magazine*, which relied heavily upon parody of comics, movies, television, and advertising, was also an immediate and colossal success, debuting just prior to *Playboy* in 1952. Parody was also a reliable textual strategy on television, suitable for filling up the large segments of programming occupied by live comedy and variety programs. What is unique to *Playboy*'s parodic sensibility is its articulation within a masculinity preoccupied not only with the pursuit of sex, but also cultural capital and consumer goods. Pierre Bourdieu's work on how the development of cultural tastes constitutes strategies of distinction has shown how, ironically, those cultural products deemed "low culture" can be transformed into cultural capital.[6] *Playboy* would provide its readers with explicit (and not so explicit) instructions to train them in transforming themselves into sophisticated consumers of mass culture.

With its mix of single sophisticates drinking, chatting, performing, and flirting, *Playboy's Penthouse* provides a fascinating and seemingly singular window into the era's sexual and cultural order. Of course, the conservative vision of the 1950s as a decade of prosperity, marriage, monogamy, and suburban domestic bliss has been roundly and effectively critiqued. The best of these correctives point out that this vision obscures economic injustices, racial and gender inequalities, and sexual and political repression.[7] But what is more often cited as a key "problem" of the 1950s, at least in today's popular culture, was the pressure to "conform." In our vernacular sense of fifties America, such conformity meant staying safely within what was deemed acceptable by mainstream America in pursuit of an acceptable American Dream: the kids, the car, the house in the suburbs. Though contemporary conservative and camp sensibilities alike might idealize the 1950s as quaint and innocent, few would go so far as to trumpet "conformity" as a lost virtue.

As the *Playboy* franchise itself suggests, however, the critique of the stifling forces of conformity was already popular during the 1950s. Novels, movies, comics, television, and social scientists alike pointed out the downsides of life in the "'burbs" and bureaucracy in the workplace. William Whyte's term "Organization Man" came to describe the consummate bureaucrat, whose life played out not through his own individualism, but through the organizations he worked for and participated in, from the defense contractor employer to the Parent Teacher Association.[8] On the other end of the social spectrum, Norman Mailer formulated the "White

Negro" as a psychopath, a person so disenchanted with conformity that he sought immediate experience on the margins.⁹ This hipster figure would become a popular—though no less caricatured—antidote to the organization man. While neither of these constructions may have ever been the culturally dominant personality of the time, they both were powerful archetypes for those making sense of their lives through postwar popular culture. Somewhere between Whyte's "Organization Man" and Mailer's "White Negro" lies Hefner's "Playboy." Central to all three modes of identity was the male citizen's relationship to consumption and consumerism. If the organization man was too mindless about his material consumption and the hipster too radical in forgoing the comforts of consumer culture, the Playboy would cultivate a discriminating taste to negotiate between the two. Thus, without fully embracing or renouncing the postwar consumer ethic, the Playboy would seek out only the best clothes and cars, and by a similar logic, would know as well the difference between junk mass culture and quality popular entertainment. Hefner's magazine and television show both offered a compelling model for cultivating a sophisticated gaze, an "aesthetic disposition" in Bourdieu's terms, through which to engage the field of mass culture and negotiate the contradictions inherent to a postwar masculinity grounded in large part in the pleasures of consuming.

Being a sophisticated man and *Playboy* reader went hand and hand with consumption, a point made clear when opening the magazine's premiere issue. On the page facing the table of contents was "The Men's Shop," an advertising section where readers could order items as diverse as ice buckets, a hat rack, a fire alarm, and the "Kan Kup," a device which snapped on top of a beer can to make it "just like drinking from a glass." The men's shop also advertised the Eames rocker, a $40 fiberglass molded chair that, though mass-produced, was even then considered a design masterpiece. This section became "Playboy's Bazaar" in the second volume, and orders went directly to individual advertisers rather than *Playboy*. Even as the advertising continued to center on décor and entertaining, later items like record racks, a "Jolly Bartender Kit," and a composite wood figurine, Miss Zulububu—"chesty wench from the mysterious land of Twanabomba"— established frivolous consumption and kitsch as supplement to the refined urbanity of an Eames rocker. Ads became more and more prevalent throughout *Playboy* in the 1950s, as its success continued, fattening up the magazine substantially by the end of the decade.

Playboy's embrace of consumer culture, frivolous or otherwise, has been cited by scholars as evidence that the magazine was far less subversive than its contemporary critics feared. Though it sought to be frank about sexuality and promoted extended bachelorhood, in key ways *Playboy* conformed to fundamental, mainstream social values. In her examination of male discontent in the postwar period, Barbara Ehrenreich examines *Playboy* as a model for male rebellion, and interrogates why, given the overwhelming popularity of the magazine, the Playboy lifestyle didn't hasten an immediate collapse of the American family. If only a fraction of its readers had acted on the *Playboy* plan for bachelor bliss, she says, hundreds of thousands of women would have been left without breadwinners or stranded in court fighting for alimony.[10] But *Playboy* didn't cause such a cultural revolution, she says, because it offered a guide for pleasurable consumption, channeling male discontent into purchasing. In fact, *Playboy* had sidestepped that most popular of cultural criticisms about male identity, that of the organization man—the much-maligned gray flannel suit only a problem to be replaced by something more fashionable.

According to this critique, *Playboy* was created and shaped in response to conceptions about what it meant to be a "mainstream" postwar man, but because of the embrace of "pleasurable consumption," it never challenged the dominant socioeconomic structures of "the mainstream." While the Playmates offered images to be consumed by the sophisticated, liberated male gaze, consumables to be purchased filled its pages, whether in advertisements or editorially endorsed goods. And yet, I would argue that this very careful and discriminating proconsumption position makes the magazine and television show an interesting case study in how "alternative" or "counterculture" masculinities might function in shaping identities *through* popular culture, rather than simply rebelling against it. Specifically, the magazine proposed alternative ways of seeing mass culture, popular entertainment, and consumer identity. And while the *Playboy* "revolution" did not, as Ehrenreich correctly notes, dismantle centuries of moral, domestic, and familial order, it did dramatically impact how men conceptualized their own identity and desires in the field of mass culture and consumption. Nowhere was this more apparent than in the magazine's ongoing negotiation of television. While looking at art or listening to jazz might align the *Playboy* man with highbrow cultural elites, watching television separated him from them. Watching television "differently" from the low- and middlebrow masses, however, separated him from them as well. Sophisticated viewing, like sophisticated consuming, set the *Playboy* man apart from the mainstream, while still allowing him to enjoy the pleasures produced by postwar prosperity. This applied to both consumer goods and television programming. Thus, *Playboy*'s "sophisticated seeing," a mode of consumption often grounded in parody, was self-consciously a counter- or alternative cultural strategy to produce a hip, masculine identity.

The articulation of this identity took place at a time when many Americans seemed preoccupied with categorizing cultural tastes and mapping shifting cultural hierarchies. American consumer culture boomed as the middle class expanded in the wake of World War II and the GI Bill, which made access to higher education and home loans possible for a greater proportion of the population than ever before. Americans wanted to "catch up" after the lean times of the Great Depression and the war, purchasing homes and filling them with an array of consumer goods. As the middle class expanded, the old social hierarchies no longer applied. A famous salvo

The Parodic Sensibility and the Sophisticated Gaze   83

in this postwar culture skirmish was Russell Lynes's essay, "Highbrow, Lowbrow, Middlebrow," which speculated (as discussed in a previous chapter) that in the postwar period, a stratified system of tastes would be the basis of social and cultural distinction. In this new social structure, the highbrows would be the elites, and their tastes would be formed in opposition to the mass media.

Perhaps the cultural institution that was the most vilified as "middlebrow" was the Book-of-the-Month Club. Janice Radway has described how the club, by providing its subscribers with automated access to books deemed the "best" in particular categories, successfully blended the exercise of cultural authority with mass consumption.[11] This blend was surprisingly controversial because it appeared to undermine those cultural authorities that had previously considered themselves immune or oblivious to market forces. Nonetheless, Radway shows how the Book-of-the-Month Club provided subscribers, beginning in the 1920s, not just reading material, but cultural capital to be displayed in the form of shelves of books. *Playboy* would add lots of record albums to display on readers' shelves, meanwhile eschewing the middlebrow choices assumed to be found in normal homes. The manifestations of the Playboy's sophisticated cultural capital would also extend beyond what was on the shelves, to the interiors of the home itself, and to the strategies of looking and reading what was on them.

THE VIEW FROM THE TOP (OF THE TV)

Playboy's Penthouse was produced for syndication for only two seasons, from 1959 to 1961. It aired late at night, primarily 11:30 on Saturday.[12] An ad from 1960 indicates the show was broadcast in Chicago, New York, Los Angeles, Spokane, Baltimore, Kansas City, Fort Worth, Cleveland, and St. Louis, and was "scheduled to appear in other cities" soon. Several letters to the magazine also indicate viewers in these cities and their outlying regions.[13] Abandoning the usual theater and studio audience format of most variety and talk shows, *Playboy's Penthouse* instead depended on a more intimate studio set designed to replicate a rich and tasteful bachelor's penthouse. This was *Playboy*'s ideal masculine domestic space—a distinct alternative to the ranch home that was considered the mainstream model.[14]

Probably any television program produced by *Playboy* would have been controversial in the days of early TV, but the party's racially integrated setting, in which white party-goers were often hanging out with black performers, caused even more difficulties for nationwide syndication.[15] Hefner has said he knew that the show would never be picked up in the South because of this: "The appearance of black performers on 'Playboy's Penthouse' in a social setting in what appeared to be my apartment assured no syndication in the still-segregated South, but it made me a hero on the

84 Parody and Taste in Postwar American Television Culture

South side."[16] Because of the party format of the show, guests didn't simply appear, perform, and go away or sit quietly on the end of the couch. And, in keeping with Hefner's overall goal of "educating" viewers in sophisticated consumption, much of the show's banter centered on "insider" knowledge and parodic positioning within the entertainment industry itself. In the pilot episode, for example, Nat King Cole talks about his parodies of rock-n-roll during his recent performances with Lenny Bruce, who in turn discusses a comedy bit he wasn't allowed to do on Steve Allen's program. In another episode, Dizzy Gillespie persuades comedian Milt Kamen to dance as he performs, which makes Kamen look like an annoying clown in comparison to the jazz heavyweight. The Kirby Stone Quartet first parodies rock-n-roll in another episode, then parodies Sammy Davis Jr., until he shows up himself.[17]

Interestingly, in a series centered on the politics of popular consumption, this party "commingling" could sometimes reveal rough spots in *Playboy's* patchwork construction of hip masculinity. Before his quartet parodied rock-n-roll, for example, Kirby Stone asked why Hefner's show had been ignoring this growing musical phenomenon. Immediately, contradicting "yeahs" and "boos" arose from the audience/partygoers. At that moment there was no clear consensus whether or not rock-n-roll fit the *Playboy* model for discriminating rebellion, even among the *Penthouse* guests. Jazz

Figure 3.3 Hefner looks on approvingly as Bruce talks about TV standards, sick comedy, and the vagaries of good and bad taste.

was *Playboy*'s music of choice, but rock was difficult to shoo away because much of its appeal, or at least many of the reasons why it was feared and vilified, had to do with its overtly rebellious and sexual qualities. If *Playboy* was against rock-n-roll, it allied itself with the conservative forces deemed its most mainstream, conformist, and unhip of enemies—and yet to fully embrace it meant aligning oneself with the adolescent tastes of undiscriminating teenagers.

The dialogue between *Playboy* as sophisticated alternative to mainstream culture and *Playboy's Penthouse* as a more sophisticated variety show is apparent in the reviews of the show's premiere, which also reveal the challenge being made to traditional senses of good taste by this new cultivation of sophistication. In the premiere, Lenny Bruce does the bit he wasn't allowed to do on Steve Allen's more middlebrow show, then says sick comedy is a writer's device, made up by *Time* magazine, and that all his comedy comes from societal problems and hypocrisy. Later he stops a conversation with Hefner, Nat King Cole, and others to draw attention to himself as he blows his nose—he then says you could label that sick comedy.

"A lot of tastelessness and sophomoric drivel was perpetrated in the name of sophistication," said the *Variety* reviewer, for whom the requisite breaking of taboos consisted of Bruce's nose blowing.[18] Acknowledging the attempt to create a party with effective "realism," since real booze

Figure 3.4 Hefner, Nat King Cole, Bruce, and author Rona Jaffe smoke, drink, and talk showbiz in *Playboy's Penthouse*.

was imbibed, the reviewer also linked this "loose" atmosphere with material that couldn't be performed on a normal variety show. Even if what passed for sophistication on the show was tastelessness for the reviewer, this tastelessness was deemed appropriate to *Playboy*'s cultivation of a sophisticated—but not traditionally highbrow—taste. This negative review signifies that the program successfully broke from the mass-market tastes endorsed by *Variety*, and as a syndicated program independently produced in Chicago, further threatened the Hollywood status quo.

Bourdieu points out that challenges to established taste hierarchies can easily form systems that just put a new hierarchy in place. In the Dizzy Gillespie episode previously mentioned, Gillespie attempts to plug his new album, *The Ebullient Dizzy Gillespie*, but when he holds up the album cover, it is grabbed away by one of the partygoers who is actually a *Playboy's Penthouse* producer. It appears that the producer is trying to avoid a commercial moment which would take away from the casual party atmosphere of the show and instead foreground the fact that this was a promotional appearance, just like one on any other variety or talk show. Much of the rest of the program plays out as a power struggle between Gillespie and the producers. Gillespie manages to fit in quips about jazz musicians not having any money (which stands in sharp contrast to the conspicuous consumption of *Playboy*) and remarks that Hefner "embellishes upon" jazz. Gillespie seems to be referring not to the writing of white jazz critics who tried to explain jazz, but to the white embrace of jazz as part of "hip" culture. As such, Gillespie critiques Hefner's use of jazz to refashion white masculinity. The uneasy exchanges of the episode reveal that the relations between black performers like Gillespie and those in control of the culture industry like Hefner and his producers weren't as cozy as the choreographed party might appear. They also reveal the thin veneer of sophistication covering the commercial reality of (even *Playboy*'s) TV. Gillespie treats the appearance as he would any other TV program—a chance to plug his album—which forces the *Playboy* junta to quickly put down his unrehearsed rebellion and reestablish the easygoing party air. Gillespie's protest on *Playboy's Penthouse* resists the assimilation of jazz to an updated white male taste culture—a new taste hierarchy.[19]

Which is what Hefner's sophisticated urban male culture was, after all: an alternative identity for white men dissatisfied with the prospect of becoming suburban family men and not quite ready to move to Greenwich Village. Thomas Frank describes how the advertising industry in the 1960s used notions of counterculture to successfully market products as well as reinvigorate their own industry, ultimately transforming disgust with consumerism into a reinvigorated consumer society.[20] While advertising of the 1950s touted the pleasures of consumption in terms of conformity and keeping up with the Joneses, the new advertising of the 1960s promised individuality, rebellion, authenticity, and hipness. However, Frank also shows that the advertising industry helped create what "counterculture" meant, not so much co-opting some authentic counterculture, but even further popularizing antiestablishment sentiment. Though *Playboy* didn't hasten a cultural collapse, is it satisfactory to see it only as encouraging consumption rather than potentially offering impetus for a more meaningful countercultural identity?

Just because what constitutes counterculture might be mass-produced doesn't mean "counterculture" is a meaningless term, or that abstract formulations such as the hipster and the organization man didn't have real effects on forging identities outside the mainstream that were countercultural in the sense of political engagement. Andrew Ross notes that Mailer's "White Negro" did indeed have powerful social effects, for white students working in the civil rights campaign, for example.[21] Recognizing the compatibility of the counterculture to corporate culture does help us see how cultural binaries like hip/square are produced and operate through commercial culture. While the sophisticated Playboy might negotiate between the two extremes of that binary, *Playboy's Penthouse* shows how television, comedy, and the variety show could be enlisted in a self-conscious attempt to produce popular counterculture. Whether it succeeded at being "hip," this content would look and sound different, and challenge both highbrow and mainstream notions of good taste.

CONTEMPLATION, NOT CARPENTRY

Playboy is a compelling example to study visual culture because it functions as a nexus for alternative practices of seeing and consuming. When formulating its hip masculinity, *Playboy* interwove the act of seeing with the act of consuming. While the Playmate on the cover created desire, articles and products inside provided the commodities and cultural capital necessary to buy one's way to sophistication. As Bourdieu points out, consumption is also a stage in communication. The act of sophisticated seeing was as important a part of the Playboy masculinity as consuming goods.

Lynn Spigel has shown that while advertising for television in the 1950s portrayed women as active in the home, getting the ironing done, cooking, etc., even with the TV on, men were portrayed as passive, camped out in front of the set. "It could well be concluded," she says, "that the cultural ideals that demanded women be shown as productive workers in the home also had the peculiar side effect of 'feminizing'" the father."[22] While Hefner had chided *Esquire* for being too puritanical, his former employer differed from *Playboy* in ways other than degrees of sexual candor. Spigel notes that *Esquire* (as well as *Popular Science*) suggested males could take an active role in relation to television through building television carts and cabinets.[23] This, of course, was not the *Playboy* way. While it is tempting to simply place *Playboy*'s approach to television within male/female, active/passive gender binaries, *Playboy* plotted a model of seeing that was quite different from these other media outlets. While the gaze upon the pages of *Playboy* models was sexualized and gendered male, it was also carefully constructed as *sophisticated*. This gaze, steeped in cultural capital, would provide the alternative to building a TV cart.

As Ehrenreich points out, Hefner had announced the intention in the very first issue to reclaim the indoors for men. "We don't mind telling you in advance—we plan on spending most of our time inside. WE like our apartment." *Playboy* reclaimed the indoors in large part by showing how masculine social activities usually associated with public spaces could be accessed from within it. The hi-fi, for instance, was a highly coveted consumer good. Articles taught how to choose the correct hi-fi and how to set it up properly in your home. This domestic technology could be used to play jazz records, the favored Playboy music, or comedy albums as well. Jazz records might provide the proper background for a party, or require more active listening to appreciate—an effort owed to the better jazz musicians. Just as jazz records could offer imaginary access to the music's hip performance spaces, the comedy albums could turn the Playboy's pad into a nightclub. The magazine noted the booming success of comedy albums at the end of the decade: "Serving up Nichols and May with cocktails, then Mort Sahl and disc for dinner, followed by Lenny Bruce with the cognac, is the latest cachet of social awareness—a sort of do-it-yourself nightclub with a bill of entertainment that no single club in the country can match."[24] With the addition of the proper technology and the proper taste to know what to play, the apartment could thus be as masculine as a nightclub.

While *Playboy* built an entire lifestyle around masculine consumption, it is worthwhile to restate the obvious: the magazine featured pictures of naked women. Those pictorials may have accounted for only a couple of pages each issue, but were undeniably a large reason for the magazine's success. Hefner has said he founded the magazine because he felt stifled by the lack of sexual candor in *Esquire*. Watching women, seeing women through a privileged gaze was central to the *Playboy* masculinity. This access to a sexualized way of looking was core to the magazine. Visual consumption of women was offered in a few pages. The desire created by those images could be satisfied through consuming the other products, whether cultural goods such as jazz records or consumer goods like the Kan Kup or Eames chair. The centrality of the Playmates to *Playboy*'s success is so obvious that it has contributed to the American idiom that particularly disingenuous phrase, "I read it for the articles."

To fully appreciate the challenge of *Playboy* for television, it is useful to consider how television itself was portrayed within the magazine, as well as how it was imagined to fit in the Playboy's lifestyle. The fit was an uneasy one—indeed, television received little coverage in the magazine, even as it took the rest of 1950s America by storm. During the decade that would end with television receivers in almost 90 percent of American homes, coverage of TV was rare in *Playboy*. The monthly "Playboy After Hours" column that reviewed and recommended books, films, music, and clubs included *zero* mentions of television from 1956 through 1960. What coverage did exist in the magazine had a very specific agenda in relation to promoting parody and satire as sophisticated TV and appropriate material for masculine TV watching.

These notable exceptions included an article in May 1954 that singled out talk show host Steve Allen and praised him for sparking his show with "sophisticated satire." An article on comedian Jonathan Winters later that same year was prefaced by the disclaimer "If you watch TV, and we don't necessarily recommend this as a general thing, you've probably already become acquainted with Jonathan Winters."[25] The December 1958 "On the Scene," a recurring feature on the latest hip performers, writers, etc., included a piece on television director John Frankenheimer, and mentioned his Emmy-winning "The Comedian," produced on the anthology drama series *Playhouse 90*. Another article on television executive Oliver Treyz at ABC focused on his personal drive and success in television *as an industry*.[26] In both of these articles, the inclusion of television had to do with the success of men within the industry: one as a director, the other as an executive. For Frankenheimer, the movie business would provide the next arena for his professional success, for Treyz, a continual climb up the corporate ladder. Neither story suggested either man was producing quality (sophisticated) art on television.

A December 1960 "On the Scene," pointing out currently hip cultural commodities, juxtaposed musician and singer Ray Charles, satirist Paul Krassner, and cartoonists Bill Hanna and Joe Barbera. The pieced lauded the cartoonists as "the thinking man's Disney" whose Huckleberry Hound character was "extremely hip." Hanna-Barbera Productions' immediate preoccupation, the column said, was "exploring the potent satiric possibilities inherent in *The Flintstones*." Here the comic sensibilities of the Hanna & Barbera elevates *The Flintstones,* widely considered a cartoon version of *The Honeymooners*, beyond crass mass media status. While *The Honeymooners* might be expected to epitomize the worst tendencies of mass culture, *The Flintstones* could be expected to satirize those tendencies and indulgences. This would elevate the cartoon from low to sophisticated cultural status. In retrospect, the embrace of Hanna-Barbera as sophisticated television seems particularly significant, since it is *The Honeymooners* that has been enthroned as classic television and the Hanna-Barbera cartoons that have been relegated to a low status because of their supposedly "lazy" animation style. For *Playboy*, however, the style or quality of animation was beside the point.

This endorsement, however, was a rare exception. The unsophisticated, common entertainments of television, watching ordinary programs in ordinary ways, mostly went unacknowledged. One editorial did proffer that comedy was more successful in the medium, while dramas suffered and were destined to be second- or third-rate in comparison to "real" theater.[27]

Playboy deemed such programming pretentious: dramas that attempted to be better than was fit for the low medium. While it might seem counterintuitive for *Playboy* to favor the unpretentious gags of comedy over the dramas, this makes sense in terms of *Playboy*'s new sophisticated taste. Bourdieu points out that "nothing is more distinctive, more distinguished, than the capacity to confer aesthetic status on objects that are banal or even 'common.'"[28] Championed by early television critics as quality culture, the live television dramas were stepchildren of the New York theater, showcases for many of the same producers, directors, and performers working on Broadway. The comedy-variety shows, on the other hand, were descendants of vaudeville. By endorsing what was considered the "lower" culture of the two—in their words, "skits, bits, gags, and wags"—*Playboy* chose the best avenue for return on investments in cultural capital.

In *Playboy's Penthouse*, as in the magazine, overt discussions of the significance of television occasionally found their way into the material. But again, it was in the guise of comic commentary *about* television as a medium rather than any content actually *on* television. Stand-up comedian Bob Newhart did a routine about TV series being replaced by documentaries, a possible new one being "Frontier Accountant," another "Filtration Plant Operator." Talking to Hef, Newhart noted that shows were losing their impact, to which Hef responded "TV is such a terrible medium, it eats up these things. [There's] a continual search for new kinds of concepts."

Figure 3.5 Surprise! Hefner is notified jazz icon Ella Fitzgerald just arrived.

Newhart's merging of documentary, a "quality" television style, with more popular genres pokes fun at the industry's attempt to improve its image with the serious documentaries, and flatters the viewer by assuring him he understands how TV "works." In another episode, legendary folksinger Pete Seeger sat in front of the fireplace and performed a song about the recent quiz show scandals for the couples sitting on the carpet in front of him. While folk songs are supposed to be about the travails of "folk," here the form is used ironically to reframe the woes of the culture industry. Both of these performances exhibit an "intellectual" understanding of television as medium and industry, commenting on the institution's mediocrity, predictability, and corruption.

Television did make one conspicuous appearance in *Playboy*—or rather, *on* the magazine. The March 1956 cover featured a Playmate smiling in front of a television camera inside a studio. In the foreground, the debonair rabbit that was the *Playboy* mascot sat in the studio control room, his hand on a lever, focusing the camera on the woman's face, which appeared in close-up on the monitors in front of him. The cover succinctly aligns the TV camera as a tool for a carefully controlled and constructed male gaze. Inside, the pictorial's title proclaims that Miss March is indeed "Playboy's TV Playmate." Marian Stafford wants to be an actress, reads the copy, and has smiled prettily in commercials, a "walk-on," and a couple of small speaking parts in TV dramas. However, her main gig is as a "human test pattern" for color cameras during rehearsal tests, making her real-life TV role similar to her function in *Playboy*: stand still while the camera/reader adjusts its lens/eyes. The early *Playboy* centerfolds were tame by today's standards, and this one is no different: Miss March smiles at the camera while holding a copy of *TV Guide* below her open night gown. As we might expect, Miss March, in addition to being an aspiring actress and human test pattern, was also a television viewer herself. She poses reading *TV Guide*, no doubt searching for her passive feminine entertainments even as she remains the object for the active male gaze.

Playboy's first TV Playmate met with resounding praise from readers. The next issue's letters department featured the customary "greatest ever" comments, but a number dealt specifically with the television angle of the piece. In fact, the Midwest publisher of *TV Guide* wrote to note how proud the company was that a copy of the magazine was being held in the centerfold. This was a dream product placement for the publisher, who was careful to acknowledge "we and any other male in his right mind would far rather spend our playtime with this Playmate than watch TV or study our magazine." Several other readers responded with parodic praise. Otto Parrish, self-proclaimed member of the "Davy Crockett Assn., University of Cincinnati," joked, "The one thing in your picture that puzzles us is the fact that there seems to be a girl blocking the TV set. What brand is it? (The TV set.)" Another letter, referencing the centerfold, sarcastically began, "I happened to run across your three-page ad on TV decorations and would like to know where I can purchase a similar model for my own drab set." While a television career may be the dream of the TV Playmate, for these readers, television is far more mundane furniture. The role of that furniture in their own lives can only be acknowledged sarcastically, subordinating TV pleasures to the pleasures of fantasizing about possessing the Playmate.

The conflation of discourses of TV and sexuality in *Playboy* inverted or subverted the more careful negotiation and conflation of those discourses in other popular media, particularly advertising. Spigel describes how advertisements and cartoons in *TV Guide* and elsewhere contained the threat of male voyeurism by "circumscribing it within the confines of domestic space and placing it under the auspices of women."[29] In these, men tried to look at women on TV, but their wives changed the channel or blocked the set. In fact, the most common threat from male TV pleasure wasn't this voyeurism, but men's preference for watching sports over all else in the home or on TV. As Spigel notes, "even if the screen image was not literally another woman, the man's visual fascination evoked the structural relations of female competition for male attention." As an example, Spigel notes a 1952 *Esquire* cartoon that featured a newlywed couple in their honeymoon suite, the husband neglecting his wife for the wrestling match on TV.[30] Hefner's attempt to create a sexier alternative to *Esquire* is manifested in a later *Playboy* inversion of this cartoon: in 1960, *Playboy* printed one of a groom carrying his new wife through the threshold of a hotel room. The bride is so addicted to TV that while still in his arms, she reaches down and turns on the TV set.

Understood in this context, *Playboy*'s fixation on developing a male-controlled domestic space is not simply about finding an alternative, sophisticated model of consuming goods, but visual consumption as well. Liberated from traditional domestic space in his bachelor pad or penthouse, the *Playboy* man was also liberated from female control of his gaze. Watching women or TV was not just a desirable mode of viewing, but also the most symbolically powerful revolt against the female-dominated domestic sphere; The man refused to subsume male sexual pleasure to feminine control, or even channel it to more acceptable sports viewing. *Playboy*'s articles on interior decoration, on home appliances, and on hi-fi's, while not explicitly addressing television as technology or cultural medium, nonetheless were fundamentally about creating a masculine space, which could be the only space where a man could really watch what (or how) he wanted.

Playboy did feature another TV Playmate in November 1958—"Shapely Miss Staley," another bit-part TV actress who *Playboy* said could "drop around and be our own private Late Late show any night." But *Playboy*'s relationship to television was most often plotted through parodic or satiric humor. One-panel comics, reminiscent of those in the *New Yorker* and other "sophisticate" magazines, were a *Playboy* mainstay and, predictably, often centered on sexual humor. These comics repeatedly provide insight into

Playboy's assessment of the role and cultural significance of television. An October 1957 issue contained a full-page comic of a TV set broadcasting static, a high heel hanging precariously from each antenna. The entertainments on the set had apparently been abandoned for pursuits elsewhere in the room, without the couple bothering to turn it off. In the June 1960 comic previously mentioned, the groom's impending seduction of his bride is "preempted' by her having already been seduced by television. Another comic played on television's much heralded powers of liveness and intimacy. Two middle-aged men in front of a TV watch a line of chorus girls, one of whom's top has fallen off. "It's these little unrehearsed incidents that make live television interesting," says one of the men. In all of these, the model was clear: Women watched TV, men watched women—especially if there was one in the room. These comics all appeared over the stretch when the "Playboy after Dark" column neglected to recommend any actual television programs as quality entertainment. Indeed, as the comics suggested, television existed primarily as either a prelude or obstacle to sexual seduction.

Scholars have long analyzed film as a mechanism for voyeurism, describing the cinematic apparatus as privileging the male gaze over the female body. When following this model of watching women, looking at women, the Playboy could take pride in his television. But this was very different from being entertained by television programming. Instead, TV was a tool that enabled the Playboy to look at (even more) women, to survey their bodies independently of the medium's mediocre aesthetic ambitions. Second-rate attempts at method acting only got in the way of access to women's bodies. As seen in the *Playboy* comics and the TV Playmate, and as *not* seen in recommended television viewing, *Playboy* made a distinction between normal television viewing and television *watching*. Television thus was useful to the extent that it contributed to *Playboy*'s project of male connoisseurship for the female form, analogous with sophisticated consumption. The TV Playmates most clearly exemplified the magazine's attitude about men's relationship with the medium: Most TV is garbage, but there are at least opportunities to appreciate beauties like the TV Playmates. The magazine dutifully reports Miss March's ambitions in the TV industry—but who cares? She's a test pattern for the camera and should be consumed as such.

Television could also be made into a properly sophisticated, properly male entertainment without necessarily resorting to building the set a new cabinet. *Playboy* rebelled against the mainstream version of fifties masculinity, so an alternative way of making television consumption an active—or at least sophisticated—pursuit was necessary. Parodic readings of television were an alternative and learned decoding strategy, making visual consumption practices a marker of cultural capital. The way to make TV sophisticated according to *Playboy*, then, was not to build a cart for it, but to parody it. Television consumption would thus be made a productive practice through refined aesthetic activities, not brute carpentry.

CONCLUSION

Playboy did embrace the "high culture" of abstract modern art, and this embrace is useful to understand as a component of a consistent model of sophisticated seeing. In his first issue Hefner had placed modern art among the pantheon of *Playboy* interests and seduction tools: "We enjoy mixing up cocktails and an *hors d'oeuvre* or two, putting a little mood music on the phonograph, and inviting in a female acquaintance for a quiet discussion on Picasso, Nietzsche, jazz, sex." *Playboy* embraced modern art not out of some belief that it truly represented the culmination of art history, or even the act of creating art as a manly, intensive chore which allowed for the expression of complex masculine identity, à la Jackson Pollock, whose artistic process was famously featured in *Life* magazine in 1949. Instead, it celebrated the interpretive stages of consuming art, the viewer's process of producing meaning as important as producing the object. Modern art then was "producerly" not because of the work that went into it, but because of the readings that it generated, because with the appropriate cultural capital you could spend hours contemplating it, or at least chat about it for a few minutes with your date.

Perhaps the most salient *Playboy* endorsement of modern art was made in the September 1960 issue. In this issue, the centerfold Playmate was featured in a number of abstract renderings by *Playboy* artists. Aside from the centerfold, all the photos of the Playmate featured an artist or artists gazing at her body *artistically*—as if interpreting her. Here, modern art provided a number of styles that could be accessed to turn—through representation—female nudity into art. Though the artistic renderings take up large sections of the pages, the inclusion of the photos, besides providing the nude for the reader's less artistic needs, celebrate interpretation as a type of masculine, sophisticated looking.

The juxtaposition of humor with art, philosophy, and music was a trademark of the *Playboy* style. In fact, comedy had maintained a privileged presence in the magazine from its beginning. *Playboy* regularly featured satiric essays and comics, in addition to features on comedians and comic actors. Lenny Bruce himself was the subject of a lengthy profile in February 1959. Oscar Levant, the crony of George Gershwin turned actor, comic, television panelist, and professional mental health case was profiled in July 1959. Shepherd Mead's novel *How to Succeed in Business without Really Trying*, made into a successful musical comedy, was published as a series of articles in the magazine, as were a series from another of his books, *How to Succeed with Women without Really Trying*. Other Mead articles included "Selecting Your First Wife," "Training Your First Wife," and "The Dream House and How to Avoid It."

As the titles of these articles hint, satire helped resolve the contradictions inherent to being a *Playboy* man. Not that contradictions were inherent to the swinging bachelor who really did live the *Playboy* lifestyle—the

The Parodic Sensibility and the Sophisticated Gaze   95

contradictions were most prevalent in that portion of *Playboy* readers who were *not* living the lifestyle. During its second volume, the magazine published the results of a subscriber survey. While the average reader was twenty-nine, half of the readers were "free men; the other half are free only in spirit."[31] Articles satirizing mainstream, domestic life like those by Mead assumed some firsthand knowledge of the domestic life, just as a parody requires knowledge of the structures of the original text. That knowledge could come from actually living the domestic life or from the popular criticisms of it prevalent in male culture.

Ironic humor was so integral to *Playboy* that some content could border on self-parody. The November 1959 issue featured plans for the *Playboy* bed. This expansive piece included built-in bookshelves and looked like it was large enough to accommodate the entire swinging party. The feature on the bed—which was to be available soon for purchase—was followed by a topical pictorial: "Beds from Other Times and Places." In this pictorial, Playmates in period costume (or lack thereof) posed on beds in period settings. These ranged from Roman to Venetian nineteenth century to the American 1920s. Today this reads as a supreme example of camp taste; certainly, at first glance, it doesn't seem particularly sophisticated. However, the "historic" pictorial fits in *Playboy* on a number of levels. One, it's an obvious excuse to show more naked women. Two, it relates *Playboy*'s marketing of its own bed to beds in history, thereby making the marketing piece less of an overt ad and more of an introduction or companion to the pictorials. Three, its pseudo-historical tone works as self-parody: Not only is the historical bed piece an obvious excuse for showing more naked women; it's a really lame one, and that's funny. In short, the pictorial must have read as camp even when it was published. Camp content, as Susan Sontag would famously describe it in 1964, proposes itself seriously, but just can't be taken seriously other than as an aesthetic phenomenon.[32] This self-parody creates a critical distance for the *Playboy* reader, who is neither looking at a blatant ad for a bed nor just looking at naked women. The feature on the *Playboy* bed and the Playmates on the beds from other times all work within a parodic sensibility that resolves the contradictions between refined taste and mass culture consumerism.[33]

The culmination of the magazine's embrace of parody and cautious engagement with television was a feature called "Teevee Jeebies" which first appeared at the end of the 1950s then periodically in the magazine for decades. Writer, cartoonist, and future children's book author Shel Silverstein was a long-time *Playboy* contributor and responsible for this popular feature. In "Teevee Jeebies," numerous individual panels shaped like television sets showed photo stills from movies, paired with captions of dialog that rewrote the meaning of the original scene. The content of the dialog ranged from innocuous gags to risqué drug references and, of course, sexual innuendo. A selection of panels from the first installment illustrates the range. In one, a man and woman standing knee-deep in a river recoil in fear as a crocodile lunges at them; the dialog reads, "I told you we should have gone to the public beach!!" In another, a dapper looking man, perhaps a doctor, holds a hypodermic needle as a nurse stands next to him. The caption: "I've never mainlined either, but what the hell . . . " About half the panels feature some type of sexual joke or double entendre. In one of these, a man lies in bed, leaning over a woman, who is wearing glasses and reading from a book: "Here it is—'Frigidity, a state of being abnormally adverse to sexual contact with the male, usually manifesting itself in . . . '." Some of the panels contain no identifiable stars; others featured them prominently. In the November 1960 installment, the first panel featured Fred Astaire in tuxedo, kicking and dancing. "Doggone—I stepped in it again!" he says.

"Teevee Jeebies" provided a course of action for making, according to the second installment's introduction, "TV's continual showing of the same ancient films more bearable by turning the sound down and making up your own dialog." This introduction also noted that the first installment had caused no end of "favorable comment and chuckles" among those who had seen the same films so many times on television that they could recite the lines before they were spoken.[34] But the feature prescribed a method for viewing television, an activity to actually take part in yourself, not just read about in the magazine. "The idea is to turn down the audio on your set and then supply your own scenario to the stirring scenes that move across the video screen," the instructions continued sarcastically.

"Teevee Jeebies" explicitly prescribed parody as a strategy to make television viewing a productive activity, producing both pleasure and alternative meanings. The introductory copy to the third in the series reported that the previous two had been the most popular humor features ever printed in the magazine; this was evidently an "alternative" reading strategy that resonated with the magazine's audience. *Playboy* even published a number of paperback anthologies of "Teevee Jeebies," showing that the series was popular enough to attract buyers on its own—without help from those pesky Playmates. Whether or not the readers actually engaged in this rewriting activity outside of reading the magazines or anthologies, the popularity shows that an alternative, parodic method of reading was both deemed more pleasurable and more sophisticated than the normal, mainstream way of watching the same old movies on TV. "Teevee Jeebies" utilized some of the same countercultural strategies and pleasures exemplified by the parodies of *MAD* magazine and sick comedy of Lenny Bruce—cultural products and personalities endorsed by *Playboy* for the new hip male.

Hefner's taste for parody was so strong that he essentially sought to take over *MAD* magazine and make it his own. Although it began life as a comic book, *MAD* was another great publishing success of the 1950s, and dealt almost exclusively in parody. Every issue featured parody of movies, television, advertising, and American life in general. Hefner was so taken by *MAD* and Harvey Kurtzman, the magazine's original editor, that he hired Kurtzman and much of the *MAD* staff away from EC comics publisher

William Gaines. Hefner and Kurtzman would publish two failed parody magazines, and the artists continued to publish in *Playboy*.[35] In the 1950s, the cultivation of a parodic subjectivity was a form of insurgent cultural capital—an education that changed taste by providing mastery of a code. Hefner both recognized and promoted this. Parody blurred boundaries of taste because it was deemed sophisticated, not just expressing disdain for low culture like TV quiz shows or Westerns, but finding pleasure through them.

Despite being a print magazine, *Playboy* was most influential as visual culture. Yes, there were the "Ribald Stories" recounting mild erotica from the literary past, the lifestyle features, the cultural recommendations in "Playboy after Hours," and the pieces on the latest celebrities in "On the Scene." And, yes, the Playmate pictorials might account for only a couple of pages each issue. But throughout the magazine, the acts of seeing and consuming were ever-present and interwoven. *Playboy* offered a coherent model for sophisticated seeing, resolving the contradictions between masculine independence and the pleasures of participation in material culture. By turning what had been considered low culture into its own version of sophisticated, high culture though parody, the magazine constructed an identity that reconciled counterculture and consumer culture. *Playboy* both provided something to look at and a *way of looking*.

While *Playboy* did not ultimately hasten the collapse of the American family, it did set up an alternative model of tastes. Looking at Mondrian and looking at Miss March could both fit a sophisticated man's way of seeing the postwar world, whether he looked out his penthouse window to see it, into the pages of *Playboy*, or into Hef's studio penthouse on the TV. Perhaps then, to say that one read *Playboy* for the articles wasn't disingenuous, but parodic.

4   Ernie Kovacs and the Logics of Television Parody and Electronic Trickery

Buried deep in the recesses of the UCLA archives lies a fan letter to Ernie Kovacs that serves as a complicated bit of historical evidence for understanding television viewing practices. The letter offers a chance to reconstruct the relationship between a particular viewer's everyday life and Kovacs's television work. In particular, it suggests how prominent the role of parody might be in the dialogue of that relationship.

The letter at first praises Kovacs's stint as guest host on NBC's *Tonight*, as well as his earlier work on daytime television—typical enough for fan mail. In a straightforward manner, the fan mentions that all of her family love his show, kids and adults inclusive. When his show was on in the daytime, she had trouble getting things done because the kids wouldn't leave the house. Now, however, Kovacs actually improves her ability to get her work done. "Seriously, since you are on 'Tonight' I get all my ironing done. With you to watch my friend, a starched shirt becomes a breeze, my iron floats on wings of laughter."[1]

This fan offers not only praise, but autobiographical information about how she *uses* television. From a critical viewpoint, this fan's letter shows how she articulates her everyday life within the popular discourses of the period; she has not only reconciled her television watching and housework, but has so internalized the discourse that she sounds like a television advertisement herself, claiming to have optimized her productivity through her television viewing. But if we pay closer attention to the language of the letter, perhaps the choice of words sounds a bit *too* like those advertisements. This fan borrows her language explicitly from ads, or at least models her fan language on commercial language. "A starched shirt becomes a breeze." Her iron "floats on wings of laughter." If we were to consider this fan a savvy cultural bricoleur, we might instead read her letter ironically, or, in the language of cultural studies, oppositionally. She mocks the language of advertising that suggests household drudgery could be so easily transformed or disguised. In repurposing this language, she applies parody, one of the comic strategies used by Kovacs himself, to address commercial culture.

In order to use the letter to reconstruct television-viewing practices, it is essential to acknowledge this parodic tone. Parody was one of the primary weapons in Ernie Kovacs's comic arsenal, and this fan has employed that weapon to express her own viewing practices. There is an important choice to be made in interpreting this letter: Is it a dominant, hegemonic expression of consumer culture interpellation, an ironic expression of disaffection, or somewhere in between? Examining this letter as a parodic text may help us consider not only how this individual life interacted with television, but how parody may function more broadly in television reading and meaning-making. The letter has implications for how we think about the ways in which parody interacts with other popular discourses on television to produce these aspects of the "practice of everyday life," to use Michel de Certeau's term for how the power relationships that define social life are negotiated by individuals.[2] Through parody, the letter writer portrays herself as conscious of her position within discourses on television and the family. Kovacs's aesthetic may encourage her to position herself parodically or ironically, but not necessarily oppositionally to those discourses. She still has to get the ironing done, regardless what pleasures she might produce from television or parodying commercial rhetoric.

This chapter will seek to understand parody as a textual strategy employed as part of a critical attitude toward television and consumer culture. In order to do this, it is necessary to examine the critical "attitude" of Ernie Kovacs's work itself—an "aesthetic with an attitude" tied to other

Figure 4.1 Ernie Kovacs the TV comic and auteur introduces a segment parodying the Western.

cultural modes which together worked to produce a parodic approach to TV watching. In other words, I will be considering both the reception of television parody as well as contextualizing that parody within the industrial framework that produced it. If we can't label the fan's politics from the letter, for example, we can say that the language she uses is borrowed and repurposed; it is not meant to sell TV sets or persuade other viewers/housewives/mothers to tune in to Kovacs. Instead, it is put in the service of praising Kovacs and expressing the connections between his comic work, her television viewing, and life in the home. This borrowing and repurposing might best be thought of as the fan performing her own parody. She repurposes the commercial rhetoric of advertising in a way that shows her consciousness of articulation within the contemporary discourses. Parody becomes a tool for her to acknowledge that articulation by social forces larger than herself and take some control over that articulation.

That the fan would write this letter to Kovacs, choosing to show him how she can manipulate language, isn't coincidental. Kovacs and the consistently parodic and critical television aesthetic he produced encouraged just this sort of response to television and commercial culture. His work was one of a number of sites—alongside, for instance, those previously discussed in this book—where a popular negotiation of the technology, formats, and content of television was ongoing. The Kovacs aesthetic was a good match for early television production. It was also a good match for early television viewing. By the end of the 1950s, Westerns and domestic situation comedies dominated the television landscape. Television had transformed the way Americans spent their leisure time, and the industry itself had shifted from the standard of live broadcasts originating regionally or from New York to productions taped or filmed in Hollywood. Throughout this period, parody had become a prominent cultural mode through which to make sense (and make fun) of television and other aspects of postwar American life.

This parodic sensibility may be best signified by the success of *MAD Magazine* and the regularity with which Alfred E. Neuman's gap-tooth visage popped up in unsuspecting places during the 1950s. But if any single television personality embodied the eccentric, parodic sensibility of fifties popular culture, it was Ernie Kovacs. Not coincidentally, Kovacs regularly published articles in *MAD*, and was, in fact, more than just a television personality. He appeared in numerous films, and even wrote a novel, *Zoomar*, about the staging of a television beauty contest. On the other hand, Kovacs was a consummate—if itinerate—television personality. From the early 1950s up to his death in 1961, he appeared in local and national programs, as guest host and as host of his own shows, in regular series and in specials, on live and taped programs, and as panelist on a variety of game shows.

A segment from one of Kovacs's final specials serves as an example not only of the importance of parody to Kovacs's aesthetic, but of the complexity of television parody at the end of the 1950s and the beginning of the 1960s.

These characteristics prominently include a critical tone toward television production and the postwar cultural milieu, rather than the specifics of any particular program—its characters or plots, for example. The segment, from a 1961 special, proposes changes to be made to the television Western in order to attract audiences now bored by the preponderance of derivative Westerns then broadcast by the networks.[3] Kovacs begins the segment standing in front of a group of television monitors, smoking his trademark cigar. This positions him not just as an onscreen personality, but a behind-the-scenes creative force. The tools of TV production are at his disposal and he is comfortable among them. His production credentials visually established, Kovacs makes this assessment of the television industry with casual authority: "There's a standard formula for success in the entertainment medium, and that is, beat it to death, if it succeeds." After diagnosing this problem with television content, Kovacs then prescribes numerous remedies for making the content interesting once more. These consist of two key components: (1) more innovative camera work and (2) cross-pollination with other programs, genres, and cultural preoccupations.

After audiences became used to the climactic shoot-out that was always filmed from the same perspective, Kovacs shows more interesting angles to view such duels. These include various close-ups on men, women, and horses witnessing the duel. A hat company even sponsored a shot in which the camera films through a hole shot through a hat, above which "Yucca Hats" is written in large letters. "The only thing we hadn't seen," says Kovacs, "was a gunfight from the perspective of the bullet." Then Kovacs shows us exactly what that would look like: A gun fires and a bullet slowly moves toward an actor, then passes through his body, creating a video "hole" through which we see the opposing gunfighter celebrating. This video manipulation is the sort of "electronic trick" or video sight gag for which Kovacs was renowned at the time.

The rest of the "New Western" segment focuses on the rewriting of this dominant television genre through recombining the Western with other cultural texts. On a new adult-oriented Western, for example, Kovacs introduces the 1950s fascination with psychoanalysis to the old west. In the psychological Western, he tells us, "the emphasis isn't so much *what* happened but *why* it happened." A cowboy lies on an analyst's couch and tries to understand why he killed a man who was always calling him Slim" when his name is "Harold." Kovacs tells us that another Western was being produced "in the Serling-manner" and shows a cowboy walking through a surreal moonscape covered with fog as a theremin plays eerily on the soundtrack. Trees behind him are filled with cattle skulls, and "alien" women with vampire teeth and grotesque fingernails taunt him. He pulls a gun which first fires an umbrella, then turns into a banana. While this "New Western" cites a specific television auteur known for his distinctive, surreal style, the next segment borrows from B-movie science fiction. A cowboy rushes in a ranch house to warn "Miss Cindy" and "Miss Bessie Lou" that a spaceship has landed in the North Forty—"and a there's a mighty big cowboy got out of it." Sure enough, we see a boot and chaps crushing a town underfoot, and the gigantic eye of "The Colossal Cowboy" peers inside the house. Another B-movie–Western hybrid features the incredible shrinking cowboy who, like his cinematic predecessor, is tormented by everyday objects. His foes don't out duel him in gunfights; instead, it is a falling pencil or a maliciously dropped cigar that may bring death.

The combination of the technically advanced video techniques such as the chroma-keying that Kovacs used to show the bullet hole and the decidedly unsophisticated visual gags of the giant pencil dropped on the incredible shrinking cowboy is characteristic of the Kovacs aesthetic. Moments later in the sequence, another "New Western" is introduced that is titled "Rancid the Devil Horse," where the evil gunfighter doesn't ride a horse, but *is* a horse. Kovacs simply shows someone in a cheap horse costume with a huge moustache above the horse's mouth and a toy pistol tied to his hoof. This combination of video tricks and low-rent costume and prop gags is the result of an aesthetic honed in early live—and decidedly low budget—television.

The "New Western" sequence ends with a new "foreign" Western starring Kovacs himself as "Das Einsam Aufseher," a mock-German Lone Ranger. Kovacs and cast sport lederhosen and speak a German/cowboy vernacular. His romancing of a western damsel he calls his "little schnitzel"

Figure 4.2   Frontier psychiatry in the "New Western."

Ernie Kovacs and the Logics of Television Parody   103

Figure 4.3   A TV western in the "Serling Manner."

Figure 4.4   An incredible shrinking cowboy.

is interrupted by "Schwarz Bart." "Du hast gekillen meine mutter!" Kovacs says. In the other portions of the New Western sequence, Kovacs appears before the TV monitors in his behind-the-scenes, creative mastermind role and provides voice-over narration between the segments. In "Das Einsam Aufseher" he is the slapstick comic performer once again, not so far removed from the vaudeville style performance common on much early TV comedy. Even though he's in front of the cameras, the constructed and edited nature of the special's skit is emphasized when the German Tonto slips and falls during his entrance. The scene restarts, and includes footage of the clap of the production slate on which we can read "Kovacs special."

"Das Einsam Aufseher" is similar to the parodic skits on Kovacs's shows throughout the 1950s—including its disclosure of the conditions of the skit's production. It was on these shows, which included both daytime and nighttime formats, where Kovacs learned how suitable parody was for the television medium. Though the "New Western" piece came from a special at the end of his career, it serves as a useful example to examine the Kovacs aesthetic, and especially to understand how the parodic sensibility figured in this aesthetic in combination with the formal innovations and effects that the popular press would call "electronic trickery" and that critics years later would identify as video art.

Figure 4.5 Despite his renowned electronic trickery and elaborate staging, Kovacs maintained an appreciation for simple sight gags and silly costumes. Here, a gunfighter meets his match in "Rancid the Devil Horse."

Prominent among those critics is Robert Rosen, who describes Kovacs's various strategies as creating a "dynamic interactive relationship with the home audience."[4] The "New Western" segment is useful, not just as an illustration of Kovacs's "electronic tricks" but as an illustration of how parody of television and such electronic trickery or manipulation of the video image were part of the same interactive aesthetic. As in this example, they often worked together in one comic bit. The various examples of Kovacs's "New Western" show that his form of TV parody wasn't as concerned with ridiculing specific programs as it was concerned with parody as a model of rewriting and recombining cultural texts. Television parody, in the Kovacs mode, dealt not so much in specific cultural products, but in a broader attitude toward postwar popular culture.

This critical function of parody—its interrogation of cultural texts and discourses—is fundamental to its popularity throughout the 1950s. The "New Western" segment is both characteristic of the Kovacs's aesthetic and useful for thinking about what characteristics of parody (more generally) might not only be labeled "critical" but work to produce a parodic critical sensibility. This sensibility is not only in reference to television programs but other popularly circulated ways of thinking. The popularity of parody in the 1950s should be seen as a symptomatic response to the "textualization" of public and private life. It is not only the lousy Hollywood Western that can be parodied, but also the life in which watching those Westerns is the chosen popular diversion. That life also includes the fascination with mental health and psychoanalysis, B-movies, and other TV shows.

The "New Western" continues narrative strategies Kovacs established in his earliest shows, and can serve as a guide to characteristics to look for elsewhere in his work. What follows, briefly, are what I see as the key characteristics of a Kovacs aesthetic that acknowledges the fundamental role of parody:

1. *A tendency to foreground the conditions of the production of the television text.* Kovacs introduces the segment in front of television monitors inside a studio control room. He then narrates the individual scenes. This negotiates an alternative path between the transparent TV narrative and the vaudeville performance which regularly ignored any notion of a "third wall" between performer and audience. On camera, Kovacs occasionally referred to cameramen by name, even when playing a character such as Percy Dovetonsils, the lisping poet.[5]
2. *The electronic "trick" created through video/electronic manipulation.* For example, the slow-motion bullet traveling through a body, leaving a chroma-keyed hole in the body through which we see the opponent. Kovacs's "trickery," as inventoried by critic Michael Nash, included such techniques as keying, matting, miniaturization, split screens, double exposures, and negative images.[6]

3. *A critique of the redundancy of film and television tropes and narratives.* The entire segment is based on the shared (between Kovacs and his audience) assumption that Westerns tell the same story, the same way, over and over again. As he says, "Beat it to death, if it succeeds." Even when not accompanied by such an explanation, this was a fundamental component of television parodies, from *MAD* to those on television itself.[7]
4. *A rewriting or generation of new texts through the alteration or recombining of existing texts.* As noted earlier, Kovacs tells viewers they can look forward to Westerns done in the "Serling-manner," or sci-fi/Western combinations such as the "Colossal Cowboy." Again, Kovacs's parodies share this hybridization approach to parody with print parodies featured in *MAD* as well as other television shows.

The Kovacs aesthetic offered a model of TV that could change the way viewers looked at television. His electronic trickery was both eye candy and comic content; whether it was self-reflexive art, as Rosen or J. Hoberman would suggest, it certainly expanded conceptions of what TV comedy could look like. But Kovacs was also preeminently concerned with looking at the TV industry. We can consider both his parodies of TV shows and his tendency to show the conditions of production as aspects of this impulse.

Kovacs's television presence across a number of programs and networks in the 1950s makes him an interesting case study for explaining the production of popular criticism of the culture industry within what is most often considered its flagship—network television. By looking at some of his available programs, we can see how prevalent parodic textual strategies were in his work. By examining production documents and correspondence, press coverage, and television histories, we can see how these parodic strategies, which criticized television, were produced within the mainstream TV industry. We can also see how Kovacs's renowned electronic tricks, now revered as forerunners of video art, fit in that industry as well. The Kovacs aesthetic fit a number of different television production "logics." These ranged from the vaudeville aesthetic of early TV comedy to the live, almost free-form, talk format to the fundamental need in commodity culture for product differentiation. Though Kovacs might not have found a consistent home on a network or format, there is consistency to his aesthetic, and a consistent compatibility with the demands of fifties television. Though his work isn't widely seen today, it is cherished by cult TV fans, video artists, and television historians alike.[8] By examining his aesthetic, its production context, as well as its reception, I hope to trace out a better understanding of how parody of television functions in the formation of identity, meanwhile refiguring our understanding of Kovacs's contribution to television culture.[9]

TV ART VS. TV CULTURE

Though the material success of his career was limited, the shows produced by, written by, and starring Kovacs were prolific in lessons on both the creative limitations and possibilities of television. This quality aligned him with other attempts in popular culture to define, explore, and teach television to the audience. Though he may have shared that impulse with others, Kovacs's approach was a unique combination of television production logics.

One of Kovacs's most famous performances was a thirty-minute pantomime work titled "Eugene," which aired in the spring of 1957. The piece was broadcast as an accompaniment to Jerry Lewis's solo television debut following his much publicized split with Dean Martin. "Eugene" includes a number of Kovacs's trademark sight gags, both electronic and prop-oriented. He paints on glass in front of the camera, creating a sort of blue screen. Later, he sits down and attempts to pour from a Thermos, but the liquid mysteriously overshoots the cup by several inches. The piece ends, and reveals that the table was mounted at an angle, and the camera tilted so that Kovacs appeared to be pouring from an upright position.

The contemporary press praised Kovacs's "Eugene" as a more auspicious solo performance than that of Lewis. "Kovacs won the comparison test, hands down," wrote *Time*, "and proved himself TV's most inventive master of pantomime, sight gags and sound effects."[10] In his critical piece written almost thirty years later, Rosen calls the performance "television's first 'no dialogue' masterwork" and "a self-reflexive work which defines the nature of the TV viewing experience while confronting the intrinsic properties of the medium."[11] We can see that though they are separated by thirty years and very different critical methods, both the popular and the academic critic recognized in Kovacs a singular way of producing television based on *seeing* television.

Scholarly work on Kovacs has surveyed his diverse oeuvre, spanning the years of his output across the networks and formats, to find consistent self-reflexive gestures within them. Hoberman places Kovacs high in the pantheon of "vulgar modernism," "a popular, ironic, somewhat dehumanized mode reflexively concerned with the specific properties of its medium or the conditions of its making."[12] Though he privileges the work of Kovacs and others such as Frank Taschlin and Harvey Kurtzman over other parodic practitioners, he acknowledges that these grew somewhat organically out of the production context of early TV. "Some of Kovacs' gags—misprompting or inflicting off-screen pranks upon the show's news-reader, yanking the cameraman in front of the lens, taking an ax and destroying the set of a cancelled program—were founded on the improvisational quality of live television."[13] Rosen, long-time director of the UCLA film and television archive, was an early critical champion of Kovacs, publishing his short essay on him in an anthology in 1985. In a couple of pages, he succinctly outlined the self-reflexive techniques seen in much of Kovacs's work and marveled at their appearance on commercial television. "Kovacs managed—against all odds—to use television as a vehicle for exploring the outer limits of video as an aesthetic and creative medium. His style was distinctly postmodernist: a fusion of the avant-gardist's concern with the formal aspects of video space and the showman's instinct for accessible mass entertainment."[14]

Rosen and Hoberman thus set the terms of discussing Kovacs's techniques as modernist gestures made on that most popular of popular arts, commercial television. This critical self-reflexivity at home on a medium that was not only accessible but popular made Kovacs an antielitist modernist, and retroactively deemed him the first video artist. Bruce Ferguson, in a more in-depth consideration of the Kovacs body of work, addresses the contradictions between the self-reflexivity of Kovacs's work and its fit within the fundamentally conservative, commercial medium of television in the very years the industry's primary production practices and commercial structure formed. If Kovacs's gestures were truly self-reflexive in the modernist, critical sense of undermining transparent narratives, how is it they didn't have more effect on early television style and content? This question is suggested by Rosen's choice to describe Kovacs not as a modernist, but as a *post*modernist. The idea that he made modernism popular makes him postmodern. Does it therefore divorce him from the politics of modernism? Or is Kovacs a key individual in the blurring between high/low culture in the twentieth century like, say, Andy Warhol? Ferguson suggests the term "radical conservatism" to describe this tension between the self-reflexive, critical qualities of Kovacs's work and its ability to fit seemingly so well on television. The term "is meant to suggest a tension or polyvalence that could be called a Kovacs aesthetic, or discursive practice, which was noticed at the time of production and which has been continually reinterpreted as radical or transgressive of conventional ideas of the codes of network TV."[15]

There is a body of critical work that identifies characteristics of art, literature, film, and even television as "self-reflexive" and embraces that art as not only aesthetically but politically or socially subversive. TV scholars writing about Kovacs have repeatedly identified self-reflexive characteristics of his work, but they have been pressed to explain its existence on commercial television—that dreaded flagship of the culture industry. As Dana Polan discusses, self-reflexivity is a formal device that isn't inherently "subversive" in the social sense. It is necessary to reconstruct and analyze the "attitude" that the artwork adopts toward the material world and the dynamics of history.[16] It is not enough to just identify self-reflexivity, but necessary to examine the historical context, and how the work addresses that context. Such criticism should be twofold: on the one hand, identifying those self-reflexive characteristics and tendencies, then connecting that particular aesthetic world to the political or historical world. In addition to such necessary dialogic contextualization, a more complete description of Kovacs's aesthetic and its production logics is required to understand his contribution to TV culture.

Though scholarly work has praised Kovacs as a video artist before there was such a thing as video art, it has failed to acknowledge the fundamental role of parody in the Kovacs aesthetic. This may be because television parody is considered commonplace TV content, a derivative style, or even a parasitic genre. By comparison video art is, well, "art." However, acknowledging the fundamental role of parody in the Kovacs aesthetic helps us understand the popularity of Kovacs both to the television industry and to his fans—historical, academic, and cult. It also helps explain how those electronic tricks/self-reflexive gestures ever made it onscreen.

Discussions about whether or not aesthetic styles such as self-reflexivity "matter" culturally are not limited to the academic world, and as discussed in chapter one, there was much popular discussion in the fifties about just how *serious* comedy and the American sense of humor really were. In April 1957, Kovacs graced the cover of *Life* magazine. Inside, an article praised him as the possible savior in a "national drought of mirth."[17] "Kovacs uses the tools of television for his own comic ends," said the magazine, concentrating attention on Kovacs's manipulation of video technology, explaining the special effects "trickery" of his peering through the hole in an actress's head, or he and Tony Bennett appearing from only the legs down on *The Perry Como Show*. This attention paid to Kovacs's "trickery" is typical of the popular writing about Kovacs's TV work. However, the *Life* piece is interesting because it doesn't stop at describing Kovacs's electronic or video sight gags. "Taking advantage of the enormous flexibility of the TV camera, he puts together gags and situations so outrageous yet so skillfully done that his nonsense takes on its own logic." Lacking any literal explanation of what that logic is, it appears to be Kovacs's careful balance of camera tricks, television parody, and vaudeville humor. The *Life* article describes Kovacs's approach to television comedy as a dialogue between the innovations enabled by the television camera and the more traditional, vaudeville-style approach of comic presentation.

The piece gives Kovacs a chance to trace out his comic philosophy by showing how the same skit could be ruined by too much camera work or too much slapstick. "Kovacs teams with the camera . . . but has learned, through his own mistakes as much as anything, that the camera can intrude on comedy too, cutting much of the wit out of a comedian's work."[18] This reiterates the importance of the Kovacs aesthetic being at least as much about performance as electronic tricks or camera work. The scene used to explain Kovacs's creative approach is an especially salient choice because it parodies the TV viewing practices of the housewife. In the scene, a woman deals with all sorts of diversions as she scrubs the floor, comforts a crying baby, and pays the milkman. All these harassments she can manage, except for the droning poet (Kovacs) on the television. While still scrubbing, she pulls a pistol and shoots the poet, who falls halfway out the television screen.

Kovacs presents his favored framing of the scene, with a stationary camera, never altering focus, and never drawing too much attention to unessential parts of the scene. This style he compares with alternates which would use too much camera, making the scrubber overly dramatic with close-ups and lots of shadows, or too much slapstick, making the "overgagged" version equally unfit for TV. The particularly televisual Kovacs aesthetic is shown as the middle road between film theatricality and vaudeville slapstick. TV becomes the perfect medium for such a comic aesthetic.

Elsewhere in the same issue, *Life* explored the "crisis in comedy" on American television as audiences, sponsors, and prime programming slots were being lost by comics. The magazine asked prominent TV comics to comment on the causes and future of the crisis. George Gobel lamented that making TV comedy was simply too tough and had to be done too often without enough chances to try out new material. Milton "Mr. Television" Berle was working in Vegas and claimed not to have even watched television for a year. Even worse, Sid Caesar was getting fewer viewers than his competition, Lawrence Welk. One reason suggested for the crisis was that there was no longer a training ground or farm club like vaudeville for which comics could test and refine material, then jump to TV. The article also posed that the crisis in comedy had as much to do with the TV audience as the comic performers.

> As an audience they cannot be counted upon to be either attentive or receptive because they have been assembled not so much by design as by default. A man who removes himself from a comfortable chair in his home to occupy a less comfortable one in a crowded theater becomes predisposed to laugh in a way he would never do if he stayed home.

The author's generalization about the receptiveness of the TV audience to comedy is offered as an excuse for the lapse in popularity of TV comedy. It can also be seen as an example of why Kovacs was considered a possible remedy for this crisis in comedy. Kovacs's techniques—his "electronic trickery" in the parlance of the popular press or "interactive relationship" in Rosen's—was expected to snap the TV viewer from his sedentary state of disinterest. In this sense, Kovacs was working against the grain of television as passive entertainment. However, that "going against the grain" was the very thing needed by the industry: formal innovation in a period of stagnation in television comedy. If Kovacs's sometimes-self-reflexive aesthetic wouldn't undermine TV, could it actually do the opposite, shoring up TV comedy as a stable of network fare?

The alternative view was that comedy—especially parody—could be too challenging for audiences and was therefore a key reason for the genre's decline. In February 1958, *The New York Times* magazine commented on Sid Caesar's return to television after his own "crisis in comedy" occasioned a hiatus. His return came at a time when other comedians were still dropping like flies.[19]

> In the minds of several million people, probably best stigmatized as intellectuals, it [Caesar's return] represents the triumph, however isolated or transitory, of art over Westerns, of comedy over Trendex and of the American Broadcasting Company over the National Broadcasting Company. In the minds of most professionals, however . . . it represents the last magnificent throe of the stand-up or sketch comedian in an ill-matched struggle to be seen weekly.[20]

Perhaps what is most interesting about this quote is the "stigmatized as intellectuals" statement about who most lamenting the loss of the variety comics. Could parody be too highbrow for television? Was Kovacs challenging not because of his televisual tricks, but because of his parodic tone? An ABC vice president, commenting on Caesar's and partner Imogene Coca's chances of success said that the two would prosper "just so long as they don't get egghead and do stuff that gets esoteric—I mean takeoffs on Japanese movies nobody has even been to an art theatre in New York to see."[21] Parody could become esoteric if it veered too far from everyday experience and shared television culture.

But such esoteric parody alone couldn't be blamed for the current crisis. The conventional wisdom within the TV industry, according to the piece, was that the business was having difficulty finding new comic talent, though the reasons cited for that difficulty ranged from overexposure of performers to exhaustion of comedians and material, a sharpening of the public taste, the ignoring of public taste, natural trends and ratings, bad time-slotting, and the whimsical behavior of advertising agencies and sponsors.[22] The success of Westerns and situation comedies could be explained, at least in part according to the author, by the lowered demands those genres placed on the television viewer. "The higher the demands made on the attention of the viewer over a long period, the more rapidly does he become (a) bored and (b) critical, and very few forms of entertainment call for as much attention as comedy."[23]

"Eugene" had, in fact, been the only television program displayed by the United States at the Brussels World's Fair in 1957.[24] But Kovacs was more often portrayed as a zany eccentric than an egghead. A *Holiday* magazine piece emphasized the Kovacs aesthetic as very much a personal, individual artistic voice. The writer quoted an NBC executive: "There's something elemental about Kovacs. He can't be formatted. He's his own format, and that's a crime these days. He's the last spontaneous man."[25]

The article did not mean just the last "in television," but alluded to his improvisational style as being an antidote to the same cultural malaise fueling the popularity of the Beat writers. In fact, Kovacs's creative methods bore resemblance to the methods of the Beat writers, such as "automatic" or stream of consciousness writing. Jack Kerouac famously railed against editing, as did Kovacs, who claimed to have written his novel about the television industry, *Zoomar*, in just thirteen days. "I don't change a thing. I figure the first things a man says are his spontaneous things."[26] "Spontaneous" was a very loaded term at the time, and it is worth noting its use in these two separate articles. By using it, the author of "The Last Spontaneous Man," the NBC executive providing the quote, and Kovacs himself construct his aesthetic as the antithesis of the gray-flannel, conformist blues popularly understood to be plaguing fifties culture. On the one hand, these statements seem typical of the narratives of originality or genius often used to describe the singular vision of an artist. But because Kovacs was so identified with a particular television aesthetic (both visual and parodic), it is important to recognize that this praise isn't just about Kovacs the singular artistic genius, but a particular way of both seeing and making television.

NBC president Pat Weaver is considered a preeminent figure in the history of American television for a number of reasons. He helped popularize the use of the multisponsor magazine format, and his development of "spectaculars" also broke with the radio-patterned model of television programming that dominated TV. Christopher Anderson discusses how these one-off or irregularly programmed specials were an attempt to restore novelty to television, which Weaver feared was already stagnating in the mid-1950s.[27] Kovacs's "Eugene" was part of just such a spectacular on Weaver's NBC—an example of the Kovacs aesthetic as an alternative programming strategy. While Westerns were the bread and butter of network TV at the time, especially ABC, Kovacs's electronic tricks and parodies offered product differentiation—an antidote to other television programming trends. But parody as "industrial antidote" is not enough to explain the evolution of the Kovacs aesthetic. Nor can it tell us much about how viewers "used" the aesthetic, how they made sense of it, or used it to make sense of other TV texts, or the textual nature of their lives outside the tube. That requires further reconstructing the "attitude" of the Kovacs aesthetic (both its production and reception) by further examining the history of Kovacs's work.

A BRIEF KOVACS HISTORY

Perhaps it is something of an injustice to apply the word "typical" to any of that work. Viewed today, everything from his guest host appearances on NBC's *Tonight* to the monthly television specials he did immediately prior to his death seem atypical. His unpredictability and his distinctly visual approach to the medium cemented his reputation as an eccentric TV genius/ artist. Still, outside the parallel universes of cult TV fans and academic television critics, Kovacs is lesser known than many of his comic contemporaries. Perhaps this is because he never enjoyed much time in the same time slot or even on the same network. Regardless of his lack of presence today,

Kovacs appeared all over television in the 1950s. He began by making the jump from radio host and newspaper columnist in Trenton, New Jersey, to local television on the NBC affiliate in Philadelphia. There his first gig was as host of a daytime cooking show, *Deadline for Dinner*. A daytime fashion/quiz show followed, as well as a wake-up show, a daytime comedy show, and another cooking show—all this between 1950 and 1952, with a good deal of overlap between shows. In these, the earliest years of television, Kovacs was already a very busy man. NBC briefly gave him national exposure with a prime-time comedy-variety show in 1951 and a daytime show in 1952. This New York-produced talk show, titled *Kovacs Unlimited*, featured many television parodies, and has been described as a forerunner of the *Saturday Night Live* style.

Kovacs's jump to a national nighttime show in 1953 (on CBS Tuesdays opposite Milton Berle and Bishop Fulton J. Sheen) was noted by *Newsweek* as "one of television's most unheralded debuts."[28] The piece emphasized Kovacs's ability to get low-cost laughs, explaining that since the show did not have a sponsor, his budget was still about the same as for his daytime show. The principal difference, it seemed, was Kovacs now had an orchestra at his disposal. The main ingredient in the production of low-cost laughs was, according to this early national press, television parody. "As before, the most successful part of the show is his spoofing of TV programs and commercials. Last week Kovacs . . . took good care of Ted Malone, *What's My Line?*, the Gillette commercials, and those interminable spiels for silver and dinnerware that punctuate so many old movies."

This, the earliest of popular press attention to Kovacs, shows how integral parody was to the appeal of his productions. Though much attention deserves to be paid to Kovacs's televisual tricks, they must be considered as part of a larger Kovacs aesthetic. When looked at from a broader aesthetic standpoint, these techniques cease to be acts of inspired genius, but are one strategy among a broader aesthetic developed not for one-off specials such as "Eugene," itself part of a network spectacular, but as the natural extension of the daily grind of local television production.

In his discussion of early television comedy, Barry Putterman notes how local television producers turned to radio personalities as one strategy to meet the demand for round-the-clock programming when the networks and syndication could not fill the schedule. Many radio personalities were called upon to hold together "hastily constructed" cooking, interview, quiz, and kid shows, especially. Putterman says the hosts of the "kiddie" shows filled hours of live programming each day by "kibitzing with puppets, enacting skits that featured the comic adventures of their own character creations, inventing schtick with dimestore props, and exploring whatever meager studio equipment was used to broadcast their shows."[29] He points out that when Pat Weaver introduced NBC's daily, long-form talk shows *Today*, *Tonight*, and *Home* for the morning, late night, and midday time slots, he was nationalizing these local television concepts. This meant adopting the casual—if not free-form—talk style that relied on the host's manner for linking disparate subjects and filling large blocks of programming with limited means or content.

This is precisely the environment in which Kovacs's early work was produced, and a viewing of what remains of his early daytime programs reveals the strategies Putterman notes were indeed used to fill the hours. Kovacs's work has been described as "grandiloquent" gestures rather than gags, and Jack Lemmon, at the beginning of a *Best of Ernie Kovacs* collection that originally aired on public television, implores viewers to "Relax. It was a slower time," presumably so we don't become annoyed at the drawn-out pacing of many of the segments. TV critic Jack Gould actually objected to that pacing originally, when he called Kovacs an exponent of the shaggy dog school of television. But this drawn-out nature is inextricably tied to the production demands Kovacs was working to fill. The format of his comedy-variety shows was developed first on local TV to fill up large pieces of the programming schedule every single day. This was the case again when the networks looked to expand nationwide programming beyond the prime-time hours.

Kovacs moved to the CBS affiliate in New York where he bounced from local daytime comedy-variety to primetime comedy-variety to quiz shows. This game of "network roulette," as Kovacs biographer Diana Rico terms it, continued when he moved to the struggling Dumont Network in the mid-1950s, where he had more late night comedy shows and daytime quizzes.[30] It was then back to NBC for more daytime and prime-time comedy-variety. During this stint, in 1956, Kovacs garnered national attention as guest host on Monday and Tuesday of *Tonight* for Steve Allen. In the late 1950s, Kovacs had a number of specials on NBC and ABC, as well as time spent on another quiz show, *Take a Good Look*. Ultimately, he is probably best known for (and the *Best of Ernie Kovacs* collection draws heavily from) his monthly primetime specials on ABC in 1961 and early 1962. Through these many programs we can chart not a linear development of the Kovacs aesthetic, but the ways in which his aesthetic was shaped in response to production demands at particular points in his career, as well as how his aesthetic "fit" the needs of different networks and formats along the way.

Ultimately, we know how the "nuts and bolts" history of Kovacs and his television productions end. Leaving a poker party early one morning, he wrecks his car on a wet Santa Monica Boulevard while attempting to light a cigar and is killed. His final special airs on ABC and is nominated (but does not win) a Peabody Award. Filmed or taped sitcoms, many with canned laughter, dominated television comedy. Following his tragic and all too abrupt disappearance from TV screens, nothing resembling the Kovacs aesthetic ever became the dominant style on television.

Because Kovacs was writer/producer/star of his programs, much of his correspondence with cast members and the networks that is available in his papers makes the role of structural constraints on shaping content explicit. In his memos to casts, crews, and network executives, he discusses strategies that will lead to "habitual viewing" as well as the need for added effort during "sweeps." For example, in order to develop habitual viewing, he suggests that it was less important to have well-developed scripts than a "family set-up" that viewers would want to tune into. Daytime slots, according to Kovacs, needed a "generalized honest" address to the viewers: "both in presentation and in personal feeling . . . In other words, a kind of happy family."[31] Kovacs's emphasis on the importance of this "happy family" anticipates how essential that technique would become to the format of news programming when the news became more and more expected to be profitable entertainment rather than a public service.

In an outline for the format of his 7 to 9 A.M. show, *Kovacs Unlimited*, he refers to the production of earlier live shows saying that "the ostensible lack of a rigid format was the solution" for filling such a large segment of programming every day.[32] The lack of a rigid format instead relied on tried and true strategies such as parody, prop gags, and character skits. In another memo to the cast and other producers, Kovacs outlines the daily segments of *Kovacs Unlimited*. These include the "Nevada Saga," presumably a Western spoof, for which scripts will be available a day in advance, as well as "Ignorance Unlimited," a parody of panel shows. This shows that parodic sketches or spoofs weren't free-form improvisations that simply materialized on the spot. Rather, the dependable structure of parody provided the bare bones on which scripts could be easily generated, and sketches stretched and improvised as necessary to fill those shifting requirements.

True to those who would later label him an electronic comic or video artist, this same memo proposes "Experimental camera work using full facilities of electronic matting amplifier, prisms, etc." But, the memo also calls for "at least in hypothesis, a baby elephant as a regular cast member weighed daily, etc." This combination of parody, experimental camera work, and a hypothetical baby elephant should remind us that this was, after all, a daytime show with a mixed audience that included a large proportion of children. Kovacs was as much a savvy TV producer as he was a video artist or a television comic: "I don't think there is any question as to who govern the station selection at that hour," reasons Kovacs in the memo. "Any youngster would fore-go an 'all-news' program," he says, alluding to his main competition, Dave Garroway's *Today*.[32]

This memo both outlines a new Kovacs program and the essential ingredients of a Kovacs television aesthetic, showing the structural mixture of parody (lightly scripted, improvisational, cheap) and electronic camera work (meticulously planned and often expensive). There were other bifurcated approaches to producing the program that had to do with the mixed daytime audience. Because much of Kovacs's work ran during the day, a double address or coding of the content was a necessary strategy to appeal to both the older and younger viewers. We can see this double address at work in his aesthetic years later in a daytime incarnation of *The Ernie Kovacs Show* on NBC in 1956. The episode begins by revealing a studio audience including many children. Over the course of the show, there are a number of coded (and probably homophobic) references to sexuality. Kovacs parodies Rock Hudson as "Rock Mississippi," wearing fake eyelashes and speaking with an exaggerated lisp. In another segment, a behind-the-scenes Hollywood reporter mentions a compromising photo of Lassie and Rin Tin Tin together, but reports that they were "just old fraternity brothers." This subtext of homosexuality reveals the dual address of the Kovacs aesthetic to the kids at home as well as their caregivers. The reliance on audio cues as well as exaggerated voices between characters also fits the mode of daytime TV addressing distracted viewers—those moms doing their ironing on wings of laughter.

There is aesthetic continuity not just among Kovacs's live daytime programming, but also his taped specials at the end of his career. Viewing shows that fell between these establishes that neither the parodic nor the electronic textual manipulations of the "New Western" were anomalies. Instead, they were common tactics used in his shows across the 1950s, across the networks, and across the programming segments of the day.[34] These examples are valuable not because they constitute a representative sampling with an indexical relationship to "X" number of other episodes with similar content, but because they help us think about how compatible this parodic and electronic textual manipulation was with early television style and programming requirements.

On an episode of *Tonight* from 1956, *Candid Camera* host Alan Funt appears as a guest and is the subject of a skit titled "Rancid Camera," where the supposedly impromptu scenario of the show is remade in a skit where the camera and microphone are clearly visible and imposing. Kovacs as host "Short Bunt" repeatedly interrupts the allegedly candid gag to adjust blocking and costumes. The joke is, in essence, how uncandid and scripted *Candid Camera* might actually be. The primary tool here is the obtrusive presence of the camera and constant interruption of the host, as Kovacs plays with the production techniques and formulas of television. This is similar to the clip of the "New Western" that shows Kovacs literally at the studio controls in order to frame his sketches and discussions about the shortcomings of TV. But while the special is clearly a "canned" program, produced ahead of time, the live nature of the early Kovacs daytime work occasioned moments of more spontaneous, to again use the modernist term, "self-reflexivity." For example, an episode of his NBC daytime show in 1956 opens with Kovacs explaining that the show is being kinescoped because everyone is going on vacation. Later, a bit where Ernie and his collaborator and wife Edie Adams provide the voices to two swimming fish is completely derailed after a missed close-up cut by one of the cameras. Back at his desk, Ernie explains how to edit out the mistake, and then walk on the excised footage to destroy it.

A late night show on CBS in 1952 had similar moments of exposing and drawing attention to the TV production apparatus. The show ostensibly started midprogram before Kovacs stops and says that it will be started over for the benefit of those tuning in late. Later there is a "shaggy dog" parody of a panel show in which a completely uninteresting railroad engineer is interviewed, and a train whistle blows repeatedly and without reason, save to grab our attention through annoyance in lieu of interesting content. This annoying whistle may be thought of as the forerunner of both the technically impressive visual gags such as the video bullet hole and such low-rent carry-overs as "Rancid the Devil Horse." The flagrant technical manipulation of sound in the kid shows is early evidence of Kovacs's reliance on technical gags, as well as an establishment of the aesthetic of technical manipulation that viewers would come to expect from his work.

THE CIGAR-SMOKING ACTOR/AUTEUR

Kovacs was considered a television innovator by the press and his contemporaries, and his parodies and electronic tricks were about exploring the depths of television, if they themselves weren't "deep." This book's reconstruction of television production and reception builds, among other things, on television studies work done on fan cultures. These have shown that fans, far from being cultural dupes, "poach" for pleasures without regard for the autonomy or intentions of the original TV text. Though I do consider a number of items of fan mail, one of my purposes is to broaden such discussions of viewer agency to a broader viewing public. Kovacs's work belongs to that sort of parody that equips viewers with alternative reading protocols—models for producing alternative meanings and pleasures from television texts. As has become increasingly clear from their incorporation into official program "overflow" and other ancillary materials proliferating online, these strategies aren't strictly limited to the hardcore or "cult" fans producing slash fiction or fan web pages.

Seen today, Kovacs's work seems simultaneously disorienting and familiar: disorienting because of the alternation between short sight gags or "blackouts" and the longer, parodic sketches that try our attention spans; familiar because much of his simultaneously critical and comical, often self-deprecating shtick has been borrowed by others, from the writers of Steve Allen's *Tonight*, which he guest-hosted, to all incarnations of *Saturday Night Live*, to David Letterman's shows, and, most recently, *The Daily Show with Jon Stewart*. Way back in 1957, *Newsweek* checked in with Kovacs and reported on his sponsorless status. Again commenting on Kovacs's inability to ensconce himself in a prime evening slot, the piece noted this was ironic, since a number of Kovacs innovations and aspects of his aesthetic had been adopted by other programs and performers. These included his "teaser openings" or "black-outs" as Kovacs called them, his "lavish use of electronic tricks," and an "exaggeratedly offhand approach to the TV audience."[35] Kovacs spun his situation as favorable—as if he was enjoying a break after working all over the place for the past eight years. Privately, however, Kovacs revealed that he was somewhat bitter about these comic "borrowings" at his expense. In one document in his papers, a vociferous memo apparently written in a rage at another comic being credited for a black-out Kovacs had originated years earlier, he rails against the widespread borrowing of his material which is treated, he says, like "public domain." "One of the honest and nicest of these people," he says, is Harvey Kurtzman, editor of *MAD Magazine*, in which a number of Kovacs pieces appeared during the 1950s. "Harvey wrote me, after an issue or two, and said, 'We are stealing freely from you, please feel free to steal from us.' Now THAT is my kind of a guy."[36]

This is worthy of mention because it makes a direct (and friendly) connection between two places (Kovacs and *MAD*) where we can see parody functioning to produce alternative reading strategies. The note helps reconstruct the dialogue between Kovacs's work and the early television audience, and points to a Kovacs aesthetic being more than just electronic trickery if not only other TV comics, but the nonelectronic *MAD* could steal from him. This aesthetic was being deployed across media, not just across comics or networks. Kovacs's own parodies were accessible from television, his writings in *MAD*, his novel about the television industry, and his various guest appearances on other people's shows. Kovacs's own work is multiplied by all the other comics employing such a critical/comic aesthetic, a practice so pervasive as to make Kovacs see it as having been transformed from being associated with an individual to being "public domain."

Kovacs, on several occasions, also expressed his desire to work primarily behind the camera rather than in front of it. Articles in the popular press noted that he not only performed on his programs, but wrote, produced, and directed them. Those behind-the-scenes duties were what Kovacs claimed to be most interested in. He told *Newsweek* that he didn't care whether he appeared in the skits or not. "After the gags are set up and timed, it doesn't matter who delivers them. What I do before a show is more important than what I do while I'm on."[37] This attitude must have been partially to blame for his struggles, as his contradictory status as commercial television auteur may have actually worked against his success in the industry. Because of his star image, sponsors wanted Kovacs in front of the camera as much as possible. Kovacs explained to one writer that his commercial overseer (from a cigar company) really liked the content of the work Kovacs produced, but needed him to be the star as well. "His only complaint is that I'm not in it enough. I get up there in the control room and I write myself out of the show. My real interest is in timing it."[38]

While creating his electronic tricks entailed large amounts of effort at all stages of production, the sponsor demanded that Kovacs appear in front of the camera. Though his star persona and reputation for producing elaborate TV tricks enabled him to pour effort and money into them, rather than on big-time guests, that star persona demanded he appear on camera. He was the famous cigar smoker, after all, not his TV tricks, even if those tricks might cause smoke to rise mysteriously from someone's head or ears. Other comics "burnt out" because they were on the air so much; but there simply wasn't enough of Kovacs to go around, even when his production schedule was limited.

Things became especially hard for the TV comics at the end of 1957, when a "contractual massacre," in the words of the *Saturday Evening Post*, took place. Kovacs was still busy, piecing together work, but explained his predicament to the *Post*, who asked if the networks could afford people with ideas like his. "Frankly . . . they can't. I was offered a couple of regular shows, but in each case the below-the-line budget—that's the part which includes the sets—was so small I knew that I couldn't build the things I wanted to build."[39] Kovacs explained his frustrations about not having steady work in terms of not fitting the production schedule as a "regular" show. Instead it was the specials that afforded him the resources to produce his hybrid style that filled the network's (whichever one at the time) need for product differentiation. The monthly specials may have been the perfect outlet for Kovacs. It is doubtful that his style of comedy would ever have become the norm on television. At a time when the networks were consolidating control over content, the idiosyncratic work of Kovacs was best displayed in these intermittent specials. For the grind of the weekly series, the domestic situation comedy and the Western were more *predictably* dependable.

In the 1970s, highlights of Kovacs's shows were pieced together for a public television series. In the mid-1980s, there was a bit of an Ernie Kovacs boom, as his widow and collaborator Edie Adams allowed access to her private collection of his taped performances, a Museum of Television and Radio retrospective was shown, and a TV movie about his sometimes tumultuous life aired on the pay-cable channel Showtime. Much of this activity constructed Kovacs as a somewhat-forgotten television auteur. As the *Life* article from 1957 shows, Kovacs was credited with a singular vision in the popular press early on. His reputation as a hard-living, cigar-smoking, and potentially gambling-addicted celebrity who didn't pay his taxes has no doubt added to his cult status. Though these latter characteristics make great material for TV movies, the range of Kovacs's television work deserves the attention he gets today from both cult TV fans and academics.

In his analysis of the Kovacs aesthetic, Bruce Ferguson (like Rosen and Hoberman) shows how Kovacs's work on early TV utilized the same sort of defamiliarizing techniques video artists would begin to use decades later. His productions presented "the technology and its complementary techniques revealed and adapted as new creative strategies for the production of signs and, significantly, the production of a critical audience."[40] While Ferguson and other writers have been understandably interested in Kovacs's formal techniques, he also points to how these video tricks/art are integrated into more general narrative strategies. "Another reason for identifying these productions so singularly, in tandem with the structural disclosures they perform, is that Kovacs took on television; that is, he interrogated its content, its genres, its mundanity, and its reductive entertainment narratives."[41]

All of this he did in great part through parody. Those fans who bothered to write letters to Kovacs appear to have paid more attention to his parodic narratives of television and popular culture than they did his video tricks. Many wrote in to suggest possible targets for his parodies. One, a Mrs. A. Maddaloni, actually sent Kovacs a prioritized list of what she believed to be the contributions to his success, circa 1954. Sight gags, electronic effects, or anything that might have meant his video tricks are nowhere on the list. Instead, the contributing characteristics mostly describe the show as "informal," "unconventional," and "diversified." In terms of specific program content she mentions his guest interviews and her belief that his treatment of advertisements is "not too frequent or aggressive." She also cites "skits," especially those in which Kovacs "pokes fun" at other programs. Her final reason is that she believes the show ends too soon, and this leads viewers to "wait for the next installment like a comic strip."[42] In the case of this fan, at least, Kovacs's plans for creating "habitual viewing" succeeded, even if the show wasn't technically a serial.

Though fans and academics agree that Kovacs "took on television," that in no sense made him an elitist. He relished the popular form of television, and the interaction with a large public it made possible.[43] His parodies of television genres, tropes, and specific shows were part of a broader critical aesthetic which included his elaborate electronic and prop tricks. The rub is that this combination was so compatible with the industry needs of his time. So perhaps it is not surprising that some of his viewers saw no contradiction in adopting a parodic position within, rather than against, television discourse.

In one document in his files in particular, Kovacs explicitly states that he doesn't believe viewers are dupes.

> I don't believe the much-touted statistic which exposed the average (key word, that) viewer has a twelve-year-old mentality. . . . I don't believe these people whom I have gotten to know and genuinely like believe the announcer when he says that he's peddling a perfect loaf of bread . . . I think that these people whom I've come to know as friends and who are little numbers on pieces of paper to statisticians, might be more inclined to buy the Little Jiffy Eight . . . [if the commercial were to say it is a] stinker on gas and the upholstery didn't quite come out like we planned.[44]

In this letter, Kovacs expresses his faith in the intelligence and critical capacity of his viewers. He also shows that he doesn't believe that critical capacity is incompatible with the commercial function of television. His comment that viewers would be more likely to buy an automobile if the commercials were more honest about its short-fallings is a shrewd anticipation of the famous Volkswagen "Lemon" ads by Bill Bernbach. Instead of dwelling on small improvements or fabricating a sense of "newness," Bernbach emphasized continuity in a simple style that capitalized on the growing public distaste for the relentless promises of commercial pitches that so often failed to deliver the goods.

Though the fan who writes that her iron floats on wings of laughter seems to be parodying commercial rhetoric, other fans do show that the commercial pitches work more simply—perhaps in the "preferred" ideological manner. One writes that "The Admiral 'Big 10' is truly all you say—and more," referring to the TV sets advertised on *Tonight*.[45] Another, Mrs. Art Treadwell, wrote that "[i]f the worth of a television program is, as some critics claim, measurable by how thought provoking it is, your program should be considered a great artistic success, at least around our house." However, the motivating powers of Kovacs's appeal do have their limits. Mrs. Treadwell continued that "they have not moved me to take up smoking cigars, as I am too inhibited by the mores of modern society for that to ever happen."[46]

The popularity and prevalence of Kovacs's parodic strategies produced critical, negotiated subjectivities while peacefully coexisting within the commercial structure of the television industry and within discourses on television. Rather than reasoning that this ambivalent position means parody doesn't matter, that it doesn't create critical subjectivity in any meaningful sense, the fan mail—as well as the Kovacs material as daytime fare—shows how prevalent critical viewing positions can be, and how compatible they are with "normal" production practices. Parody is a strategy of negotiation: both in the production practices of the television industry and the meaning-making practices of the viewer. The pervasiveness of these techniques, and how transportable they were across networks, day segments, and audiences, points to the availability and receptivity of parodic reading practices to a broad audience.

CONCLUSION

Ernie Kovacs appeared all over television in the 1950s—the decade of the medium's emergence, as well as a period when "postmodernism" as a culturally dominant mode of representation is considered to have taken hold. Television has also been considered the preeminent postmodern art form. On the one hand, the format-jumping of Kovacs's work—from daytime variety programs to quiz shows to late-night talk shows to his own specials—seems typical of the postmodern artist—jumping from medium to medium, genre to genre. Though he worked primarily in television, his work jumped from one format, network, or sponsor to another, depending on economics and the whims of the industry. Still, we can describe a Kovacs television aesthetic, one that remained somewhat consistent over the decade. This individual style, as well as an emphasis on self-reflexivity, might suggest that Kovacs could be considered a "modernist" television artist. But, as Rosen points out, Kovacs's instinct for accessible entertainment made him distinctly postmodernist.

Rosen's comment that Kovacs succeeded "against all odds" is perhaps not emblematic of the resistance of early television (whether technologically or industrially) to Kovacs's "artistic" acts, but reflects how Kovacs could appeal across brows, using the same gestures that were the hallmarks of "difficult" modernist art. "Against all odds," the work of Ernie Kovacs would have broad, popular appeal for a time, then both a cult following and an avant-garde audience. One would embrace his work as that of an oddball, the other as that of an artist. Like all the "vulgar modernism" Hoberman canonizes, such as the Frank Tashlin directed films of Martin and Lewis, Tex Avery cartoons, and *MAD Magazine*, Kovacs's work—even his most self-reflexive—fit well within the political economy of his medium. His particular television aesthetic was shaped on early local live television—a format that relied upon filling large expanses of live programming.

That environment, in Kovacs's case, bred an approach to TV comedy that was both mainstream and available to other performers (parody) and a unique artistic approach to the TV image (electronic tricks). Though we can talk about a Kovacs aesthetic, we must recognize his work as existing in different production contexts: live and taped. These two different production contexts were distinctive materials and brushes and could have resulted in two very different types of television content. Instead, they worked in tandem to construct a consistent aesthetic based on both parodic and electronic textual manipulation. Whereas one was live, broadcast over the air and disappearing forever unless kinescoped, the other was produced on tape, painstakingly edited, then rebroadcast. The taped programs allowed for a reliance on image/video manipulation far beyond what Kovacs could do on his early shows, most of which were made before videotape had been developed for television use. Kovacs's use of television parodies didn't cease on these later productions; they just became more technically complex. "Rancid the Devil Horse" shows that "low" production worked alongside electronic tricks because both were fundamentally parodic gestures. Though TV parody had its earliest roots on daytime, kid-friendly TV, it had the potential to be both technically complex and too esoteric to find a broad audience.

Susan Murray discusses how early television commentators assumed that stage comics trained in vaudeville and nightclubs would be best suited to television work particularly because of their ability to "maximize the visual immediacy of television."[47] Kovacs was not trained as a comic performer, but instead made the quick jump from radio to television. Still, we could assume that, as a producer of electronic tricks, he "maximized the visual immediacy of television" in ways unlike other television performers trained in interacting with a live theater audience. When we add his use of parody as another critical aesthetic tool to his formal gestures that endear him to critics, we have a more complete picture of the characteristics that made Kovacs a valuable property on early television and that also give him "cult TV" status today. While Kovacs's contribution to television comedy (and video art) is singular, it is also important to understand how his work fit within—rather than against—the logics of early television. Rather than treating his work as an avant-garde fetish object, we can actually see how his style fit well within the production demands of early television—even if it was sometimes as only the occasional network product differentiation. We also ought to understand the audience's relation to television texts not as dominant or oppositional, but as articulated through the alternative avenue of parody. This is what a "negotiated" reading aesthetic is about: an aesthetic route that weaves in and out of the dominant discourses of reading and production structures. Parody works alongside, matching or fitting industry requirements at times, then becoming an oppositional strategy for expressing disaffection at others. Pat Weaver conceived of specials as events to spice up the television schedule and the experience of television viewing. Parody provided similar anomalies on a more readily available basis.

Though Kovacs was one individual performer producing a particular brand of television comedy that included a great deal of parody, television parody ought to be thought of more broadly as a cultural mode: a mode at once of production and reception, a commonly accepted method of producing television content *and* producing pleasure from watching television. The value of parody as a textual strategy ultimately supersedes differences in format or genre as a common encoding and decoding strategy. Parody of a TV Western has much in common with the textual strategies of parodying a sci-fi movie, for example. Parody as textual strategy is a cultural mode that applies across formats and genres.

In the case of Kovacs, parody was another technique of creating television content while meditating on television form. Not only did Kovacs share some parodic techniques with his contemporaries, but his work was one of the many sites where a popular negotiation of television technology, form, and content was ongoing in the early years of the industry. While it may be true that his electronic tricks were unique experimentations with video, these too fit in this popular negotiation over the "uses" of television. In Kovacs's hands, self-reflexivity was not just about the process of an author telling a story and creating a novel. Kovacs's self-reflexivity involved the production techniques and commercialism of the television industry, as well as the meaning-making strategies of the viewing public. Thus, the "attitude" of the Ernie Kovacs aesthetic integrated the formal styles of self-reflexive art with parody, creating an innovative comic style that was valuable to television networks because it was distinct from other comedy of the time. This distinction can also be seen as producing both the video art and cult TV status of Kovacs today. Both Kovacs's tricks and parodies (or when they were one and the same) demanded viewers look at television differently. Kovacs didn't just tap existing discontent in his audience, but produced an attitude toward television and consumer culture that found in parody an acceptable language for making discontent with television or culture look and sound different—and funny.

5 Black Tie, Straightjacket
Oscar Levant's Sick Life on TV

> Funny the way things work out in television. Take Oscar Levant. Here he spends years studying and practicing so he can become a great concert pianist and he practices being a sharp wit and suddenly he winds up on television—so an all-night fry cook in Downey can shake his head and say, "He's sick!"
>
> Mort Sahl[1]

In 1958, Oscar Levant hosted his own popular Los Angeles television talk show and seemed poised to do one of two things: 1) become a national sensation as a network talk show host or 2) suffer a debilitating mental and emotional breakdown that would finally end his long, varied, and unpredictable career. Today he is almost forgotten, but in the late fifties Levant was truly a "sick" star. As discussed throughout this book, the American culture of the late 1950s was a culture preoccupied with distinguishing between the normal and the sick. Social scientists wrote bestsellers diagnosing the suburbs and the corporation as cultural structures producing profound psychological changes in Americans. Vice President Richard Nixon declared mental health the number one problem facing the nation. In movies and television dramas, characters struggled with mental health and fought to keep their personal demons at bay. Perhaps the area of popular culture best remembered as part of this preoccupation was that form of humor termed "sick comedy." Lenny Bruce, Shelley Berman, and others turned comedy not into a diversion away from normal life, but a diagnosis of the standards of normalcy themselves as sick. In this culture where everyday Americans were asking themselves whether or not they or their culture were sick, the pianist, composer, actor, and radio and TV personality Oscar Levant was the real, sick thing. Levant wasn't just sick in some metaphorical or "bad taste" way. He was sick in the clinical sense. Levant had done time both on the couch and in mental institutions, and though some called him a hypochondriac, he suffered throughout his life from depression, a variety of neuroses, and prescription drug addiction.

Rather than a dark, personal side kept from the public, Levant's sickness was a foremost component of his star persona in the 1950s. Levant embodied the critical attitude toward postwar culture that was articulated in the various cases examined in this book—from *MAD*'s parodies of television and advertising, to *Playboy*'s prescription for sophisticated taste, to Shelley Berman's neurotic stand-up routines and Ernie Kovacs's eccentric skits.

Because of this conflation between the sick things Levant said and the sick person he proclaimed to be, contemporary viewers often found watching Levant both thrilling and discomforting. In the pre-cable era of early TV, the taste for those alternating feelings did not translate into national broadcast success. Instead, Levant's career offers a conclusion of this book's examination of the trajectory of parody and sick comedy in early television culture, and a prehistory of television narrowcasting as it existed in local television.

Levant didn't directly parody television culture in the sense that *MAD* or Ernie Kovacs did, but his guest appearances on national shows and hosting his own local show in Los Angeles subverted all standards of conventional television performance. Reconsider Levant's appearance on *The Jack Paar Show* in 1963, discussed in an earlier chapter as a sick spectacle buffered by Shelley Berman's standard performance as relevant—but ultimately safe—sick comedy. Everything about Levant is antithetical to what a talk show guest is supposed to look like and say. His hair and clothing are disheveled, his bare legs visible above his fallen socks. He sweats and wiggles uncomfortably in his chair. He is a has-been, with nothing to promote, "who was," in Paar's words, "one of our most gifted artists." Though he goes along with the Q&A and even plays the piano, Levant undermines his host because despite Paar's suggestion that he is only a hypochondriac, his physical appearance and speech show he clearly isn't well. He regales the audience not with boasts of professional success or personal stories of domestic bliss, but of being institutionalized and, in his own terms, unconscious for six months. Even though at the time he was a well-known celebrity, the audience has to be told how to make sense of his appearance, because it is so counter to what Paar's "normal" guests look, sound, and behave like. This appearance occurred a couple of years after Levant's own show in Los Angeles had ended, and well after it was clear he would never host his own network show. Though the easiest way to explain Levant's failure to make the big jump to network success is to blame his worsening mental and emotional state, the truth is that his instability was key to what had made him a promising TV commodity to begin with—as an antidote to normal TV.

Another network example, from a few years before his local show, testifies to Levant's sick credibility, as well as to the ways in which his star persona could shake the content, if not form, of early television. In 1955, Levant appeared on *Tonight with Steve Allen* to promote an earlier reemergence from drug addiction and institutionalization in a piano performance at the Hollywood Bowl, and more importantly, a film role in *The Cobweb*—a movie set, not coincidentally, in a sanitarium. Although Levant is introduced in terms of that upcoming performance and as having already appeared in a great number of movies over the years, the interview immediately turns toward Oscar's neuroses, and only secondarily his role in *The Cobweb*.

ALLEN: What have you been doing lately besides playing the piano?
LEVANT: Lately I've been doing research in neuroses.
ALLEN: Neuroses? How'd you get interested in that?
LEVANT: Well, I was unemployed for about 15 years and my doctor suggested I cultivate a hobby. So I started to acquire a taste for sleeplessness, and nervousness, and fear . . . I'm in a catatonic state now . . . before you know it, my hobby became a lot of fun.
ALLEN: That's a very nice way to look at it. You've just finished a movie, now does that tie in? What kind of a role did you play in this picture, *Cobweb*?
LEVANT: I play a neurotic.[2]

Allen sets Levant up nicely for his punch lines like your typical talk show, with the distinction that the recent personal history Levant relates isn't typical star banter. Levant plainly states that his longtime friend and the director of *The Cobweb*, Vincente Minelli, got him the job. Allen asks Levant if he's ever seen a sanitarium; Oscar says he's been committed twice, but never saw the outside of one. If this is a set-up joke, the next segment transcends its staged framing to become truly sick TV. Oscar says that during the period he was committed he thought of a new educational and cultural program called "Name this Pill." The two play the game: Allen tells Levant a color, and Levant tells Allen which name brand pharmaceutical that is. Though the introduction and scenario might have been created for him, Oscar's responses to Allen appear ad-libbed and genuine.

ALLEN: What's red?
LEVANT: Red's Seconol.
ALLEN: What's Seconol do for you?
LEVANT: Seconol is a very light sedation. It's supposed to put you to sleep very quickly and have no residual toxic effects, but it doesn't put you to sleep quickly and it has residual toxic effects.
ALLEN: What's red and blue?
LEVANT: Tuenol, made by same company, Eli B. Lilly, Indianapolis.
ALLEN: You've done a lot of research into this.
LEVANT: Frankly I'm under the effect of a lot of these pills now. I hope I remember these pills.
ALLEN: What's dark blue?
LEVANT: Chloralhydrate—that's supposed to be a tranquilizer. That means you're supposed to be quieted down if you have a propensity for palpitation. I always am palpitating.

Oscar puts his hand on Allen's shoulder as if to reassure him that his palpitations aren't the host's fault, then the two run through blue (Sodium amathol), green (Dexamyl), orange (Thorazine), and on and on. A couple of years later, when Levant had his show in Los Angeles, he reprised the pill game on Allen's new, eponymous show, proving it was indeed a comedy routine, if one with legitimate, firsthand credibility. Seen today, the routine of the game seems anachronistic in its casual treatment of drugs, especially when one of the interlocutors not only has firsthand knowledge of their effects, but visibly manifests them. In these appearances on both Paar and Allen, Oscar's sickness disrupts normal television, requiring whispered assurances from both hosts that it is "okay" to watch and laugh at Oscar.

Thus, while some comics might make jokes about the rage of diagnosing neuroses, Levant visibly manifested the symptoms of a whole host of them. His credibility as a sick star was rock solid. According to an interview with former producer Al Burton in Levant's *A&E Biography*, for a while during the time his local show was on the air between 1958 and 1960, Burton would check Levant out of the psych ward at Mount Sinai Hospital, take precisely the same route to the TV studio (as per Oscar's instructions), do the program live, then drive Levant back to the hospital and check him back in. The television Levant made under such extraordinary circumstances resonated with the L.A. audience and garnered national attention as being a sort of "antitelevision" that broke the rules of ordinary TV, even if ultimately it wasn't suited to mainstream, mass audience tastes that governed network television programming.

Throughout his showbiz career, Levant had never been thought of as being quite normal. As Sam Kashner and Nancy Schoenberger chronicle in their biography of Levant, *A Talent for Genius*, during the 1930s, 1940s, and 1950s, Levant maintained a peculiar sort of stardom.[3] He was known because of the various entertainment media he performed on, and particularly because of his caustic sense of humor, which he frequently turned on celebrities, but most often himself. That humor was integrated into all of his performance venues; at one point in his career, his classical piano tour was promoted as a "concert with comments." Levant's career in the popular limelight shifted from the concert stage to the radio quiz show *Information, Please!* to Hollywood, where he composed film music and appeared in a number of musicals, and finally to television. This ultimate stage of Levant's celebrity, his TV career, had two distinct branches: first, his guest appearances on national telecasts including variety and talk shows like Paar and Allen, as well as the sitcom *The Joey Bishop Show* and the celebrity panel show *What's My Line?*; second, his own local show, sporadically produced in Los Angeles over several years in the late fifties and early sixties, *The Oscar Levant Show*.

In his 1965 book, *Memoirs of an Amnesiac*, Levant succinctly summed up his sick, sophisticated appeal in terms of attire: "black tie, straightjacket." Though that book would become a bestseller, the liveness and presence of

Black Tie, Straightjacket 129

television provided the most direct access to Levant as sick, sophisticated celebrity. The dynamics of the television industry in the 1950s can help us understand what Levant "meant" in the different contexts of national, network TV and local, Los Angeles television. The history of Oscar Levant on television is helpful for understanding how the early television industry, in both local and national contexts, produced content in order to connect with the sometimes contradictory sensibilities of contemporary audiences. What Levant's sickness signified was distinctly framed on the national, network stage versus on his local program. The signifying discourses Oscar as a star performer brought to television were met by different production standards and sponsor and audience expectations. This chapter will examine his star persona through television programs themselves, promotional and publicity materials from those appearances and his show, and critical reviews from both the popular and industrial press.[4]

BUILDING AN INCOMPARABLE PRESENCE

One way to understand the significance of Oscar Levant's star persona in television culture is to recognize his function as a mediating connection between audience members and the culture of the late 1950s—both the mass, network audience, and the limited, local L.A. audience. Both these provided access to Oscar, and Oscar provided an acerbic model for making sense of postwar culture—particularly commercial media culture. Oscar appealed to a narrow segment of the Los Angeles television audience because his peculiar wit resonated with that audience. But this wit was not just what Oscar said; it was who Oscar was and how much Oscar differed from other television celebrities. Very little of Oscar's televisual presence remains, though his impact can be traced through his papers and what was written about him and preserved by fans and television critics. The different production and reception contexts of Levant's television appearances structured the possible meanings of what could in passing (or in retrospect), like his 1963 Paar appearance, too easily be dismissed as a sick spectacle.

Oscar was a figure whose symbolic presence in Los Angeles television culture far outweighed his actual production output. In Hollywood, a landscape rife with glitter and polish, Oscar stood out as quite a mess. His dissipation went hand-in-hand with a cynical, somewhat contradictory attitude toward commercial culture that resonated with his fans. A measure of how much Oscar "stood out" can be gained by examining a case of his physical presence on the L.A. landscape: a billboard that stood on the corner of Wilshire Boulevard and Western Avenue in 1959.[5] The billboard features at center Levant, from waist up, wearing a suit, staring down, oblivious to being the subject of a photograph, much less a billboard. On the left side is a quote from *TV Guide* stating "Most talked-about show on TV" and the station channel and name, KHJ-TV, Channel 9. On the right side, "The

Incomparable Oscar Levant" and the broadcast times, Tuesday and Friday at 7:30 P.M. As most ads do, this billboard seeks to distinguish its product from its competitors. This is accomplished in small part by the phrase "most talked-about" and the modifier "incomparable." Such phrases are commonly used ones that the billboard may share with not only other TV billboards but ads for soap, shoes, etc. The image of Levant, however, does work to differentiate the show from other TV programming. Rather than flashing a smile and a mouthful of gleaming whites to the cars passing by, Oscar is looking down, lighting a cigarette. His pose suggests that he is poised to offer a quick dose of his wit, but first, he is most interested in lighting a cigarette. He is not performing, but thinking, and having a smoke. Though his eyes don't engage the passersby, his body language and presence suggest a private engagement. Oscar doesn't care enough to look up and put on a big smile for the masses driving by—that's not his style, and not his audience's taste, either. Making sense of what Oscar Levant "meant" on TV means examining the collisions between his signifying practices as a performer and the TV audiences making sense of him, like the drivers going by, some "getting" Oscar, some gawking at his awkwardness, some not bothering to look. The shifting programming strategies of early television enabled these collisions, and worked to control their effects in different ways.

Levant embodied the tensions between the discursive structures of what distinguished culture with a capital "C" from bad "Masscult"—his career straddled boundaries between popular entertainment and legitimate culture. Promotional materials for Levant's television appearances commonly foregrounded his classical training and concert career, despite the fact that he was best known as the surly music expert on the radio panel show *Information, Please!* Though Levant had left home in his teens to study with the world-renowned classical pianist Sigismund Stojowski, he couldn't make a living as a classical concert pianist, and got by "taking jobs with small dance bands, playing in speak-easy cabarets, smart hotels and in Japanese restaurants" as NBC promotional material for his Steve Allen appearance noted.[6] This distinction between classical music as what Levant aspired to perform and popular music (and later, film, radio, and TV) as what he performed in order to get by remained a structuring binary throughout his career. When Levant moved to Hollywood to write film scores, biographical reports never failed to note that he also studied with modernist composer Arnold Schoenberg on the side.

Still, it was broadcast media and the radio program *Information, Please!* that made Oscar Levant a household name. Joan Shelley Rubin describes *Information, Please!* as the epitome of "middlebrow" culture, as an intermediary link between book and educational programs and the quiz shows that would follow. Rubin writes that the program, particularly its host Clifton Fadiman, "alternately touted and sabotaged the contestants' credentials, typically mixing respectfulness and satire" and foregrounded the display of personality, not just intellect, as a way to allay sponsor fear that the program would be too highbrow.[7] Levant was the resident music expert on the panel, who would attempt to answer questions submitted by the public. Levant became known as a "wit"—a sophisticated intellectual who could undercut pretentiousness through humor. His undercutting of intellectualism in favor of a humor that bowed to a populist sensibility was typical of *Information, Please!* and later would be particularly suited to exploiting the midcentury obsession with taste wrought by and propagated through mass culture. Rubin writes that *Information, Please!* delivered not just a quiz show, but the "opportunity to declare one's home a center of refinement and distinctiveness" because of the intellectual mannerisms and posturing of the host. Levant's posturing, however, was more subversive. His refinement was a popular one, which used humor to deflate highbrow pretension, even as he showed mastery of arcane knowledge. Later, Levant's wit was the enabling "sophisticated" element cited by fans and critics that distinguished him from being merely middlebrow. Much as *Playboy* prescribed parody to render television quality entertainment, Oscar's fans would proclaim that his sick wit subverted and transformed radio and TV talk.

If *Information, Please!* did much to secure Levant's stardom, it also nurtured his physiological sickness. Levant first began to rely more on eccentric "habits" in order to deal with the anxiety of producing the program. Today these habits would be understood as obsessive compulsions. Though he subsequently developed a semisuccessful career as a film actor, notably in several MGM, Arthur Freed unit musicals in the 1940s, Levant's health began a steady decline. A brief bright spot was 1951, when he had a celebrated role as the piano-playing sidekick to Gene Kelly in *An American in Paris*. During the early 1950s his health turned particularly bad, he became addicted to various prescription drugs, and he spent time in and out of mental institutions and hospital psych wards.

During these early years of network television, Oscar also made a number of tentative forays into the new medium. Most likely these were attempts to mine the popular persona created by *Information, Please!* and maintained through his film roles.[8] In 1951, *Variety* reviewed Oscar's appearance as emcee of *General Electric Guest House* on CBS, a program that blended panel quiz and variety elements. Oscar introduced guests who would first present questions to the panelists, then perform a variety act. Like many early television reviews, this one paid particular attention to the production standards ("ragged"), but also the question of how Oscar, a radio wit and concert pianist, would translate as TV emcee. The review found fault with his reading too much, and especially how he seemed "not too certain about how consistently he should stick to his bad boy act."[9] The program was short-lived, apparently, as no mention of it exists in Levant's biography, or in Brooks and Marsh's *The Complete Guide to Primetime Television*, which charts prime-time network programs back to 1946.[10]

In May 1955, Levant reemerged with mental and physical sickness as foremost components of his "bad boy act"/star persona. The catalyst was his role in *The Cobweb*, and in addition to the *Tonight* appearance discussed earlier, Levant also appeared on a nostalgia show, NBC's *Remember . . . 1938* alongside Groucho Marx and Ethel Barrymore. Levant was there to re-create his performance at a 1938 memorial to George Gershwin. In the thirties, perhaps second only to his role on *Information, Please!*, Levant was known as a sidekick to Gershwin, and he had reprised the role of sidekick in a number of film performances over the years, perhaps most notably opposite Kelly in *An American in Paris*.[11] But the Levant of 1955 was not the Levant of 1938 or even of 1951. His star persona had become less the irascible sidekick and more the sick wit—perhaps a distinction symptomatic of the profound differences between 1930s and 1950s American culture.

In *The Cobweb*, Levant plays a patient for whom all hope of a normal life seems lost. In contrast to Stevie, a young, promising artist who is a fellow patient, Levant serves as an example of what can go wrong if creative but unstable individuals can't keep it together. Like his sidekick character in the earlier musicals (a number of whom were named "Oscar"), Levant's character is again drawn closely from himself. However, it is Stevie who shows promise as an artist, not Levant's character, whom we have little diegetic information about, but who nonetheless warns Stevie of the precarious life of the artist, thereby alluding to that experienced by the real-life Levant. "Ah, the Cezanne of the psychos," he calls Stevie, "You're on the assembly line of success. From now on you'll hover between exhilaration and despair. I pity you. For a few moments of elation, a mass of inflamed nerve ends." Levant reappears in the film a couple of times in various dissipated states, but there is no happy ending for him. He ultimately is led back to bed after one outburst and is never heard from again. Levant's presence seems calculated to heighten the otherwise melodramatic film's realism: The inability to cure his "real" neuroses and mental collapse is displaced upon the more easily solved narrative enigma of whether Stevie will get well/grow up and leave the hospital.

If *The Cobweb* marked the reemergence and rewriting of Levant as sick star, the *Tonight* appearance following the film's release is fairly typical of what Levant's network television persona would remain in the coming years. He would continue to make appearances over the next decade on national television, most notably with Paar, who would be criticized for putting Levant on the air in what was, even by Levant's standards, a disheveled state. In these network appearances, Levant's neuroses and unstable mental health in general are portrayed as curiosities, and his willingness to joke about these problems a genuinely unique, genuinely sick comedy. This model of Levant as sick wit continued through the 1950s and into the early 1960s, including the second rendition of the pill game, and sunk to its lowest point in a 1964 episode of *The Joey Bishop Show* in which Levant plays himself as a houseguest from hell—complete with an entire suitcase full of pills. But even in earlier appearances that were contemporaneous with his local program in Los Angeles, the difference in framing, in what Levant talks about and how he is introduced and treated, is significantly different from how he was talked about in the L.A. press or by his L.A. fans and critics.

THE LOCAL LEVANT

Levant got his first extensive shot at a local television program in 1956, on KNXT's *Words about Music*. The program soon migrated to KCOP, making it Levant's first program on that channel, and the first produced by Al Burton, who would produce his later shows as well. The KNXT version was moderated by Frank DeVol, and Levant presided as the prominent "anchor panelist." The format of the show featured a well-known composer or performer who would play a new song and the panel would talk about whether the song would be "a pop or a flop." An episode of the program, presumably the premiere, is available at the UCLA archive, and it features well-known composer Sammy Cahn. Predictably, Oscar dominates the program, even though he isn't host and even though there's a slew of other panelists, including Natalie Wood. At the beginning of the program, DeVol asks Oscar how he feels about being on the television show, and Oscar says "utterly degraded"—anticipating, perhaps, what Mort Sahl would say about Oscar being on TV years later. This doesn't slow the opening banter however, and DeVol asks where Levant has been.

> *LEVANT:* I've been escaping reality.
> *DEVOL:* No one can escape reality.
> *LEVANT:* I can. I have character. And I have a drugstore, too.[12]

The neurotic and pharmaceutical references are there, but it's an anticommercial attitude that becomes the edge of Levant's television persona. *Words about Music* was sponsored by Chevrolet, and featured a long commercial for the new Chevy Station Wagon. When the program ends, DeVol tells Oscar he looks like he had something to say. Levant refers to Chevrolet, "You get the feeling they're ashamed to offer you the car for nothing, as if they'll offend you." Up to this point, the rest of the panel hasn't said a word. This exchange is interesting because it shows how Levant's anti-TV wit could fit soundly within the commercial format, that there was no fear that Levant's negative jibes could hurt the sponsor. *Words about Music* is (with Oscar's irreverence excepted) a straightforward paean to the culture industry. There is really no guise of music education at all. The show is not about quality but about potential popular success. After Sammy has sung his new tune, the panel gets to evaluate whether they think the song could be a hit on today's market. Levant comments, "Well, I think the title 'If you can dream' presents a psychiatric problem which I think I can solve. I have a pill that induces nightmares and lowers blood pressure. As a matter of fact, I have no blood pressure left, all I have is nightmares. Sammy Cahn's record is so offensively successful that I would have to go along with him."

Levant again knows that it isn't his job to critically engage the material, but to make a joke about himself. When DeVol counts the panelists' votes, he stops and reads Levant's: "I couldn't be less interested, Oscar Levant." Such comments were even used in a promotional document for the program, Oscar's "wit" combining cultural snobbery with self-deprecation, yielding an ironic populism that allows—as we have seen repeatedly with postwar parody—an engagement and consumption of television and popular, commercial culture more broadly. Out of nine quotes included in a promotional release for the show, seven are from Levant. In response to a panelist's comment that "mankind is only one of God's creatures who suffer from boredom," he is reported as having said, "You mean this show?" Again, these comments are featured in *promotional materials* for the show, not criticism. We see here a model for producing and promoting ironic television comedy, formed around Oscar's high/middle/lowbrow-crossing as a concert pianist turned radio/TV celebrity and his volatile mental health, the combination of which allows him to say things others can't or don't but that people—some people, at least—want or need to hear. Levant's status as revered pianist and wit allowed him to create humor from the contrast between that status and his "degraded" television persona. In this way, he found himself in a position similar to that on *Information, Please!* He was an intellectual making fun of intellectuals, a popular icon making fun of popular icons. His dismissive comments about TV are laughed off not just because of his caustic or even sick wit, but because of this ease with demeaning television and himself at the same time—in essence eroding the cultural hierarchy which Levant's comments seem to uphold, but which his very presence and persona undermine.

Words about Music didn't last for long, but in March 1958, Levant subbed for talk show host Tom Duggan on his program that was also broadcast on Channel 13, KCOP. Levant's appearance inspired an immediate response from fans and the press. Particularly popular with both was his badgering of the program's sponsor, a fur salesman. *Los Angeles Times* critic Cecil Smith wrote, "The entire sequence should have been filmed to put in a cornerstone where the moon men might find it one day to prove that wit still existed in the 20th century."[13] Levant's sick status was as much on display as his wit. Though Smith praised the program, he ended by saying how terrible Levant looked. "Earlier, I almost described Levant as the 'immortal' Oscar, but he never looked more mortal—a bag of bones in an unpressed suit supporting a weary and wasted face that looked as if it had been drawn by Charles Addams." Still, it was a winning combination of wit and sickness: the next week, Levant was given his own weekly show on KCOP, with the same fur salesman as sponsor. This badgering of the

Black Tie, Straightjacket 135

sponsors would become one of Levant's trademarks, both endearing and infuriating his sponsors. The show soon expanded to two ninety-minute programs a week, and in May of 1958, featured Fred Astaire in what was billed as Astaire's first talk show appearance. The event was considered significant enough to be preserved on kinescope, and this program is the only complete episode of *The Oscar Levant Show* that still exists.[14]

Even though Astaire's appearance on TV might have been atypical, the episode can be used as an example of the show's televisual style, as well as Oscar's approach as host. The program begins with a shot of Oscar's hands playing the piano, then tracks out to reveal his wife, June, sitting beside him. Oscar continues playing the piece, then stands up, stares at the floor, and awkwardly begins a standardized introduction, which he immediately wrecks. The first words he uses to recover from his misstep are to admit that he's worn out and can't think, talk, or breathe. "This is Oscar Levant, the irreligious Billy Graham of Los Angeles." Oscar looks unkempt, and though he acknowledges his sick disposition, he also offers himself as a celebrity of a different proselytizing appeal, particular to Los Angeles. He then describes the episode as a momentous occasion because of Astaire's pending appearance, then launches into the song "I Married an Angel" in honor of June. Oscar awkwardly introduces Astaire, who sits on a stool next to him and appears something of an uncomfortable bystander to the festivities. The show continues with Levant at piano, reminiscing with Astaire, who will occasionally sing a few lines of a song suggested by Oscar. The production style of the episode is simple, with two cameras:

Figure 5.1 Frame grab from opening of *The Oscar Levant Show*.

one medium shot of the three which pans and tracks, and another camera which maintains a close-up on Levant. They reminisce about films and different times Oscar can manage to remember. Astaire talks about Gershwin. All through the episode, Astaire looks impatient, as if he is only tolerating the experience as a favor to Levant.[15]

The show is interrupted by ads for Standard Car Leasing, Executive Toilet Water, Anacin, and the Riviera Convertible Sofa, and also deviates from reminiscing for an extended period when June reads an article about Oscar that appeared in *Time* magazine. Astaire gets up and takes a break, leaving the stage. Oscar paces and responds to the article's discussion of his various struggles, saying that contrary to what the article states, he was never a drinker. Levant gets most animated at the magazine's remark that he repels some of the audience but appeals to most. "Be honest," he yells to those crammed in the studio, "Who do I repel?" None of these faithful, apparently, but Levant continues to make a point that it isn't meaningful to appeal to everyone. "If you do please everybody you're nothing. You have to have some point of view." The audience applauds this; they are a part of the select few, the Oscar faithful, and he again jokes and reaffirms his quasi-spiritual appeal by saying he doesn't get paid by his sponsor—he's a religious leader. When June reads *Time*'s note that he often turns his wit on his sponsors, Oscar sarcastically protests, "I'm supine in my adoration for my sponsors." It's a tongue-in-cheek acknowledgment that his show

Figure 5.2 Oscar Levant introduces himself as the "irreligious Billy Graham of Los Angeles" while wife and co-host, June, looks on.

is indeed commercial culture preoccupied with its status as commercial culture, but unique because it is commercial culture with a narrowcasted cultural taste: in Oscar's words "a point of view."

Though the show contains lots of attempted performances, they are almost all aborted, and the appeal of Astaire's appearance (apparent in newspaper and fan accounts) really seems to be the casual, impromptu interaction of Levant with Astaire, with June, and with the *Time* article. As a showcase for musical performance, the show is a miserable failure. But as access to unpredictability, as access to Astaire, who is not simply performing but chatting and reminiscing with Levant, the show works. It works, perhaps, by connecting audiences with another type of television culture through its unique treatment of stardom—both Levant's and Astaire's.[16]

In late June 1958, Levant left KCOP after an on-air spat over his negative comments about his sponsor, Philco televisions. Levant apparently crossed a line when he didn't just give the sponsor a good-natured hard time but literally told the audience, "Don't buy Philco." Though KCOP tried to make up with Levant, he jumped to KHJ, Channel 9. Cecil Smith reported in his column that several sponsors declared on the air that they would follow Oscar wherever he went.[17] *Variety* gave the KHJ premiere a positive review, noting that the new show was much like the old one, "which was unlike any other show on television," and admittedly not for all audiences.

Figure 5.3 Oscar squirms while June reads a *Time* magazine article about his show. "Who do I repel?" he asks his audience.

138 *Parody and Taste in Postwar American Television Culture*

If the show wasn't a success, according to this *Variety* reviewer, the problem wasn't Levant's, it was TV's: "Levant's program may be too grownup for a medium that holds suspect performers who can correctly dispatch words of more than three syllables. But some 300 people showed up in the studio and 15 sponsors participated, so apparently a lot of folks dig words and thoughts of intellectual substance."[18]

Between August 1958 and the fall of 1959, Oscar remained on KHJ, but took at least two extended absences before going off the air in the winter of 1959. During that time, he published a series of columns in the *Los Angeles Mirror News* that echoed his television persona as sick celebrity with privileged access to Hollywood culture and a jaundiced way of presenting and commenting upon that culture. Of reuniting with Judy Garland, whom decades earlier he had had a close friendship with, he wrote: "When she and I embraced each other, I felt this was the getting together of the two greatest pill repositories since the Maginot Line met the German army in 1940. Our embrace was the peak of pharmaceutical history. Everybody else gave Judy flowers, but I sent her a secret bottle of tranquilizers."[19]

In the spring of 1960, Levant began a taped, syndicated version of the show also scheduled to be shown in New York. The guests for the first episode were Christopher Isherwood and Tennessee Williams. In October 1960, Levant and June received local Emmy nominations and awards for outstanding male and female personalities and most outstanding

Figure 5.4 Oscar's modestly sized in-studio audience offers reassurance.

achievement in music and/or variety. By mid-1961, however, Oscar had returned to bed, seemingly for good. TV critic Hal Humphrey was already reminiscing about the Levant show that once had been: "Oscar's tete-a-tetes on TV with friends like Fred Astaire, Sammy Davis Jr., Groucho Marx and Christopher Isherwood were frequently as contemporarily 'hip' as anything you might hear in Beatnikville." Reporter Joe Hyams visited Oscar and mentioned that a parade of entertainers and cultural luminaries had paraded through the house in attempts to revive him.[20] "How does Levant pass his time? He doctors himself constantly by taking pills, potions, capsules and other forms of medicine. He indulges his sickness with the happiness of a hypochondriac left overnight in a well-stocked pharmacy."[21] As for his television presence, there were only the scattered guest appearances on Paar, the houseguest episode of *The Joey Bishop Show*, and *The Celebrity Game*, a panel show à la *Hollywood Squares*. In 1965, Levant published the biography, *Memoirs of an Amnesiac*, and its success brought a couple more TV appearances, including an episode of *What's My Line?* in which Milton Berle and the other guests look truly disturbed at Levant's state, and Levant can't even make eye contact with any of them, the host, or the camera. Also in 1965, *Variety* noted Levant's precarious appearance on ABC's *Nightlife*, a program in which the host and guests spent the night on a raft in the pool of the Beverly-Wilshire Hotel. "Physically a shambles, Levant still had virtually all of the old wit—the devastating audacity that reflects a brilliant imagination."[22]

Figure 5.5 "They LOVE you!" June tells Oscar.

INGREDIENTS OF A TV ANTIDOTE

Thus ends Levant's life on television. Levant the man died in 1972. What that life meant, despite its brief existence on the national scene, isn't so easily explained. On the one hand, Levant's TV life was so limited that understanding it seems a particularly academic exercise, an attempt to resurrect from obscurity a figure and program that are in themselves merely blips in TV history. However, the appearances and programs do seem significantly "different" from other TV. Even in his own time the reaction to Levant, in the local and national press, and from fans both obscure and notable, was way out of proportion to his limited TV output. Screenwriter Ben Hecht, who published an article on Levant and his local show in *Esquire* magazine in 1958, described Levant as "more antidote than entertainment" and "a relief from the relentless sycophancy of other talk shows."[23] Levant created a ruckus not just because of his willingness to air his neuroses, his acerbic wit, or his ability to attract big-name stars to local TV. Instead, it was how different his program and his approach as TV host was from his mainstream contemporaries. What Levant signified as a local television host in Los Angeles seems to have been very different not just from other people's television shows, but from *himself* on other people's television shows. Though the persona and his performances were still in many ways tied to his neuroticism and willingness to discuss his tumultuous personal life, these were more a means-to-an-ends in the local context. On local TV, these served (along with other unconventional aspects of his show) to distinguish Levant from network fare. These marked him, his show, even his sponsors, as a peculiar form of sophistication that made sense only when contrasted with "normal" television programming. As such, Levant's TV life is an important precursor to our current era of narrowcasted television comedy.

Whatever Levant's high/middle/lowbrow credentials, whatever the brow classifications of his guests or audience, the format of Levant's show, and his performance style, created what were considered at the time to be a sort of antitelevision. In the words of his station manager at KCOP, Al Flanagan, (and quoted in the pages of *TV Guide*) "this show is for people who hate TV."[24] Flanagan's quote reinforces the suggestions of critics and fans that Levant appealed to a particular audience not just because of his legendary caustic wit, but because that wit was part of a broader televisual structure that incorporated a popular form of mass culture critique. There are a variety of characteristics that we can identify as making *The Oscar Levant Show* television for people who hate television. The shorthand way to refer to these characteristics in the popular press was to say that it was "Oscar being Oscar"; but what Oscar meant and how he performed changed throughout his career. It was the local L.A. television version of Oscar that bore the distinctive characteristics referred to by TV critics, fan letters, promotional materials (and even fan-written promotional materials sent to TV critics) as evidence that Oscar undermined and transcended normal TV. Judging by these textual materials, Levant's program succeeded in connecting to viewers not because it provided unfiltered access to a sick spectacle, but because Oscar served as, in Hecht's term, an antidote. Who Oscar was and how he performed his show broke with the standard television talk prototypes and connected with audiences critical of those tropes. The key characteristics of "Oscar" repeatedly mentioned by fans were (1) his antagonism for his sponsors, (2) the improvisational performance style (which often took precedence over his guests), (3) "intelligent" talk, (4) guests from various "brow" levels in combination, and 5) Oscar's confessions about his neuroses and other aspects of his personal life. Taken together, all these created not just a self-consciousness about Oscar, but a critique of TV programming that appealed to viewers. It was the sum of all these that made Levant television for people who hate television.[25]

As Astaire's appearance evidenced (and for which he was paid the minimum union rate of $82.50), Levant's show featured guests—often his personal friends—from across entertainment media as well as what were popularly understood as different distinctions of taste. Besides the Astaire episode, his guests included Aldous Huxley, Sammy Davis, Jr., Hedda Hopper, Christopher Isherwood, Dean Martin, Jerry Lewis, and Red Skelton, to name just a few. Because of his position straddling taste cultures, Levant mocked the middlebrow aspirations of so-called quality TV. Even on the momentous occasion of Astaire's appearance on his program, Levant distinguished between his show and the anthology dramas deemed his contemporaneous quality TV. In the midst of his conversation with Astaire, he took a swipe at middlebrow TV: "I am not a member of *Playhouse 90* where they think they're O'Neill and GBS [George Bernard Shaw] and they're really not." Levant was making something different, and genuine, for what ought to be an unpretentious medium, television.

One of the most storied episodes in *The Oscar Levant Show*'s short history involved Levant making a plea for assistance after his scheduled guests failed to appear. Oscar reportedly told the audience he didn't know what to do, played the piano a while, showed a filmed interview with Supreme Court Justice William O. Douglas, and then Red Skelton showed up, supposedly having heard Levant's plea at home while watching the show. Whether this was true, the episode speaks to the unique possibilities of a local television show produced in Hollywood as much as Levant's chumminess with celebrities. That it was Skelton who showed up on what was considered a sophisticated show is particularly interesting for understanding Levant's transformative appeal. *The Red Skelton Show* would years later, in 1971, become one of the victims of CBS's famous housecleaning in order to improve the demographic profile of its audience. Red Skelton did not suddenly cease being hip in 1971. He wasn't particularly hip or sophisticated in 1958, either. Nor, presumably, was he inspired to sophisticated comedy and intellectual discourse when he showed up in the studio for Levant. Instead, it's the impromptu nature of the unscheduled appearance, its unpredictability, its liveness—dependent upon the show's status as local television and Levant's practices as host—that made this a significant event in Levant lore, much noted in articles written about the show locally and in the national press. Skelton's appearance becomes quality entertainment because its impromptu nature is counter to "normal" television content. The great variety of guests, then, was important, but it was also inextricably tied to the format in which Oscar interviewed them, and the improvised, even erratic nature of their conversations. The liveness of the program was fundamental to that unique celebrity appeal. Oscar's show was often lauded as quality because of how well its liveness connected with local audiences. Humphrey wrote that an episode with Sammy Davis, Jr., might "just as well have been working out in Oscar's living room. On TV this impromptu quality frequently is much more effective than many produced and directed shows."[26]

When Oscar began a taped, syndicated version of the show in 1960, *Variety* publicly wondered whether the relative lack of liveness in the taped format would lessen Oscar's appeal.

> Fact that the show is taped will be a relief to executives, but it's apt to wear down Levant's viewers, presumed to be cultured and on the qui vive, since a major part of the pianist-comedian's appeal depends on his saying something unsayable from time to time—thus interest will depend on how frustrating tv's enfant terrible finds tape and how judiciously the stations etc. use the medium.[27]

Oscar's on- and off-air disputes with sponsors, improvised or staged, were yet another element ingratiating him with his fans. During an episode when he was supposed to demonstrate an "unbreakable" transistor radio, Levant smashed the thing to pieces by throwing it on the floor. "Why should everything be unbreakable, anyway?" he responded. Whether belittling the fur salesman on Tom Duggan or imploring his fans not to buy Philco sets, Oscar's anticommercial comments fit within his caustic wit that was so often turned on the generalized tastelessness of commercial media and the culture industry. As a wit, Oscar was famous for cutting celebrities down to size. Making fun of Philco was not so different from making fun of Zsa Zsa or Marilyn Monroe. His on-air smashing of the radio was as significant a piece of what *The Oscar Levant Show* was "about" as intellectual conversation or the airing of neuroses.

While Oscar crossed the line by explicitly telling viewers not to buy Philco, it is important to note that the television industry had for some time already considered a little humor directed at the sponsor to be a positive thing. In 1953, the industry trade journal *Television Magazine* reported that irreverence toward the sponsor could work in the sponsor's benefit, noting that "quasi-testimonials" of performers were more effective than "canned" testimonials because these were more integrated into the relationship between the program, the viewers, and the performers.[28] While a few stars like Sid Caesar refused to do commercial endorsements, Susan Murray also describes how Arthur Godfrey ad-libbed during his commercial spots, often joking about the claims made about products. "This strategy, although occasionally off-putting to agencies and sponsors," says Murray, "enabled Godfrey to appear more believable to consumers than someone willing to just mouth scripted endorsements."[29] How better, then, to appeal to Oscar's audience than to have him make fun of you? This meant that audiences could gripe about the commercials (just like Oscar did) and the sponsors would remain happy. No surprise, then, that far from flinching from Oscar's jibes, sponsors announced on the air that they would follow Levant wherever he went. Indeed, this would allow even sponsors to transcend the constraints of normal TV by rebelling against the demands to tame Oscar.

The seamless nature with which Oscar integrated anticommercial sentiment with TV talk in order to produce "quality" commercial culture was noted by Humphrey in one of his columns: "Where else on TV can the viewer listener hear poetry delivered by Christopher Isherwood, then be treated to a sales dissertation by furrier Eddie Gevirtz? . . . When Oscar has to break up conversation with Isherwood for a Fizrin commercial, he blends it into his neurotic persona by calling it the only panacea in life."[30] Here Humphrey draws attention to how Oscar's sickness bridges commercial culture and "Culture" with a capital "C." Oscar's comment combines the desirability for sponsors to have spokespersons refer to their products "in character" and the newly developed tendency to categorize life itself as sick.

Indeed, Oscar did openly air his neuroses on his program; it wasn't just the network TV hosts that were interested in exploiting them. For Oscar, however, these seemed to not only get laughs, but serve as grounds for commenting upon human experience. Though he was clearly upset by *Time*'s exaggeration of his bout with alcoholism, in the Astaire episode Levant gets even more worked up about the word "success," passionately telling his audience that success doesn't matter, that it is fleeting, and that the only thing that matters is "to function."

The local show also gave special access to Levant family feuds, and when covering *The Oscar Levant Show*, Cecil Smith's column was part television criticism, part gossip.

> Whenever the Levants have troubles, Southlanders by the thousands are aware of it. Because the couple's difficulties are freely discussed on Oscar's thrice-weekly TV show on Channel 13 . . . The latest row came to light Monday night when Mrs. Levant failed to appear to take

her accustomed place at her husband's side on the show. Oscar wept openly. He asked the audience to frame a telegram to ask June to come back. He fretted and fumed and felt sorry for himself.[31]

Following the Levants' feuds was thus an aspect of his content's appeal, not just its intellectual or cultural content. Smith later wrote that his column had been criticized for giving so much space to the Levants' antics, "but they are a wild pair and in a season when television has played it safe to the extent of utter dullness, it is a natural impulse to fasten onto its one unpredictable and original note."[32] The Levants, then, weren't just a talk show—they were a prototypical docusoap. Levant's fans cited the redeeming social qualities of his confessions of marital strife as well. A promotional letter sent by "The Official Oscar Levant Fan Club" to Humphrey offered the view that Oscar "uses his own tragic experiences to benefit others."[33]

Levant's popularity seems to have crested for a period of about six months in 1958. As *Time* reported, some (particularly Levant himself) thought he was poised to become the next big network talk host. That never happened, and the standard explanation is that Levant was too difficult a personality—too unwell—to pull it off. Levant's personal history is a series of "what might have beens," his history on TV the last among them. Just as Levant might have become a preeminent composer if he hadn't fallen under the spell of Gershwin, Levant "might have" become a big network talk host, if he could have only kept his sickness in check—or, if only the local sponsors and stations had been more supportive. But the truth is Levant was not the stuff of network TV hosts—at least not in the late 1950s. The entertainment industries, after all, have always worked hard to accommodate difficult personalities. What made Levant a sensation in Los Angeles simply wouldn't appeal to the less urban, and less urbane, network audience. Even at the height of his powers, it must have truly seemed unlikely that Levant would get his own network show, given the mainstream tastes of network audiences. During the six-month period in 1958, while doing his own show and rehearsing for a performance of the new Shostakovich piano concerto in UCLA's Royce Hall, Levant appeared on *The Eddie Fisher Show*. *Variety*'s review of the episode noted that although Levant certainly was popular in LA, it wasn't clear how his style would translate across the nation.

> Across the broad expanse of our land and away from the cultural centers of high literacy and low regard for the normalcies of TV, there must've been quizzical acceptance of Oscar Levant, making his return to the networks in a role unfamiliar to them . . . .On a local Hollywood station, where he has a peculiar appeal for the "smart crowd," he is an idol of sorts but the by-and-large citizenry may not have dug him at all. To them his self-inflation of his own importance may have rankled them after a weekly helping of the Comos, Gobels and Tennessee Ernies.[34]

The reviewer could just as well have thrown in "Skeltons" among the list of unsophisticated network fare. What gets left out of the traditional biographies that chart his missed opportunities is how what Levant "meant" changed throughout his career. TV was one popular medium providing access to Levant. On both network and local stages, Levant connected TV to audiences. Not only does Levant's story illuminate the different programming strategies between local and network TV, but how these connections between programming and audiences were forged is a history of television as culture. On Los Angeles television, Levant's sickness ("Oscar being Oscar") qualified as distinctly sophisticated. Rather than being watered-down legitimate culture, Levant was seen by fans and critics as bringing sophistication to television—not sophistication in a highbrow cultural sense, but in the very complicated sense of sophistication that emerged in the postwar era to distinguish quality popular media culture from bad Masscult. Call it "ironic populism": His existence on the boundaries separating good and bad taste, and high and low culture, made Levant a personality that resonated with audiences adjusting to those shifting boundaries. Though undoubtedly some local viewers did tune into Levant for a sick spectacle, Sahl's "fry cook" comment that opens this chapter refers to how TV transformed performance and personality, whatever the performer's prior successes. But beneath that surface, the comment is really a symptom of the blurring of taste boundaries that were inevitable when a fry cook from the suburb of Downey could tune into the neurotic ramblings of a Beverly Hills sophisticate like Levant.

Conclusion
Television for People Who Hate Television?

By the end of the 1950s, parody had become one of the preeminent ways in which Americans both made fun and made sense of their culture. Though parody in television culture might not always be "about" TV, the entrenchment of parodic strategies in both the industrial and popular economies of television had gone hand in hand with the new medium's incredible growth during the decade. Television was the foremost communication technology and entertainment forum in American culture. Parody had simultaneously emerged as a "way of looking" not only at television, but at "American life in general" as one critic of *MAD* noted. Deliberately crossing boundaries of what was considered to be in good taste had gone hand-in-hand with this, the by-product of a shifting cultural landscape where questioning what was considered normal was increasingly a sign of sophistication. To know the rules, and then break them, was a sign of distinction. This applied to parody, where one knew how a sitcom or a western TV narrative was supposed to play out, and anticipated and undermined it. And it applied to the broader social realm, where one knew how one was supposed to behave at parties, and yet drew attention to oneself when he blew his nose, or knew one was supposed to revere authority figures like the president or the pope, but mocked them.

While mass culture was critiqued as a homogenizing force by cultural elites, the boom in parody at the same time television first gripped the nation alerts us to how television actually served as a catalyst for reflection not only on its own content, but the forces (commercial, creative, socioeconomic) shaping that content in both its production and reception contexts. With the simultaneous boom in comedy LPs, new audiences gained access to controversial humor as those ideas found their way far outside the clubs and concert halls they had previously been relegated to. As parody and sick comedy boomed in popular culture, so too did critical discourses on the American scene that were widely watched and read by the American people.

This project was first inspired by a vintage *MAD* parody that stripped away the family-friendly pretenses of the watershed fifties television program *Disneyland* via a parodic critique of the program's blatant commercialism. Christopher Anderson has written persuasively about how participation within Disney narratives is ultimately experienced through purchasing Disney products, and he details how *Disneyland* established that standard. When I first encountered that *MAD* parody, it seemed to me that deep from within fifties popular culture, *MAD* had presciently anticipated these criticisms of a television scholar published many years later. That particular parody suggested many questions about whether such popular forms of cultural criticism "mattered" to early television viewers. I believe that the cases examined in this work demonstrate that parody can potentially be a powerful cultural force, shaping how individuals decode television texts as well as other popularly circulated discourses.

This book is not just about parody, however. It has sought to understand a certain kind of laughter produced in television culture by writers, performers, producers, artists, and their audiences that self-consciously ran against the dominant currents of postwar culture. This humor was in its time considered by many to be socially transgressive, even dangerous, while others viewed it as little more than lowest common denominator comedy. It should be clear that I believe there is a fundamental distinction between subverting the political and subverting the cultural, and what we have seen here are largely cases of subverting dominant cultural tastes resulting in the production of new cultural products and new taste cultures to consume them.

This is not to say that humor can't serve as a potent tool to address the overtly political. Indeed, *MAD*'s lampooning of the Army-McCarthy hearings is a brilliant political satire that no doubt resonated with its readers not just as entertainment but as political and cultural critique. Certainly we can see in the Yippies and the countercultural press of the 1960s examples where parody was employed in political acts. While none of the parodic texts examined in this book hastened revolution, they did subvert cultural boundaries and senses of quality and taste, taught decoding strategies, and served as potent identity markers. The new, socially relevant comedy of Lenny Bruce, Shelley Berman, and others was labeled "sick" because it suggested that American culture was not nearly as "well" as many assumed. Like television parody, sick comedy articulated and popularized criticisms of postwar life and demonstrated how such criticisms could be propagated through corporate-controlled media. African-American comedians, in particular Dick Gregory and, later, Richard Pryor, would go further, using stand-up comedy and LP records to enunciate specific political disaffections that went far beyond the middle-class aggravations typical of Berman or Bob Newhart. *MAD* was not a comic front for the Communist Party, but it did use parody to take on many facets of American life. *MAD*'s (and *Playboy*'s and Ernie Kovacs's) parodies of television and movies didn't just temporarily undermine the integrity of specific, targeted texts, but taught alternative strategies for producing meaning and pleasure from the products and discourses produced by the culture industry. This shows that although parody might not undermine the industrial economy of the culture industry, by teaching alternative strategies it can have profound effects on the popular economy—the ways in which viewers produce pleasures from those products and make them meaningful. These cases in the cultural history of television underscore the need to look at the identity formation and decoding practices of consumers in order to think, talk, and write about how popular culture can function "subversively."

Playboy magazine provides a somewhat contradictory example where parody was quite consciously employed as an alternative method for engaging dreaded "Masscult." Though Hugh Hefner envisioned *Playboy* as a (sexual) revolutionary force, a parodic sensibility was another marker of sophistication and cultural capital for the *Playboy*-man. According to *Playboy*, men *needed* parody in order to engage television actively, in contrast to the passive pleasures women were assumed to get from it. Consequently, *Playboy*'s appropriation of parody was an inherently sexist project bound up with Hefner's refashioning of postwar masculinity.

Inside the industrial economy of television production, we can see how parody, as employed by Ernie Kovacs, could interrogate the plots, formats, characters, and production practices of early television without undermining their continued use. Kovacs's aesthetic, of which parody was a fundamental component, fit well within a number of the production logics of early television. Though he is better known now for his elaborate "electronic tricks," he also used parody to create television that was far from routine.

The Oscar Levant Show, like *Playboy's Penthouse* and Ernie Kovacs's various television incarnations, offers another example of the parodic sensibility translated into television production. The program shows how a critical approach to mass culture need not only comment upon that culture, but create something new that appeals to a particular segment of the television audience. The fact that *Playboy's Penthouse* and *The Oscar Levant Show* didn't survive for long shouldn't be too surprising. Both programs embraced an alternative approach to making TV, rather than just incorporating parodic skits into preexisting formats. In the broadcast era of TV, these shows weren't going to appeal to everybody. To paraphrase Levant's producer Al Burton, they were, after all, "television for people who hate television." On the fringes of the local and national scenes, however, they could connect with audiences desperate for something different—not just to distract them from everyday life, but to engage it. The parodic sensibility was not merely parasitic. By breaking with normal ways of making sense of television, parody could lead to new ways of making television.

In the postnetwork era, the rules are different. The success of satiric programs like *The Daily Show with Jon Stewart* and *South Park*, both of which integrate parodic elements with deliberate bad taste in order to produce satire, are not the results of profound changes in American cultural tastes. Rather, they are symptomatic of the fact that today's television programs succeed by connecting to select audiences, like those cult audiences that "found" Kovacs or Levant but weren't enough to make them network stars. What we see in the history of parody and sick comedy in postwar television culture is the prehistory not just of a broad comedic sensibility, but of current television satire specifically. The sense of ironic populism produced by *MAD*, Shelley Berman, Ernie Kovacs, or even Oscar Levant was the result of a fusion between parody and the deliberate crossing of taste boundaries described at the time as "sick comedy." Despite *MAD*'s success, what Hugh Hefner found with his failed satire magazines was that satire was a minority taste—at least too minor for mass culture success. It would take a different media environment for a figure like Kovacs or Levant to be commercially viable.

Fast-forward to the late 1980s and the end of the network era. The forerunner of current TV satire and arguably the first major success of this fusion between parody and sick comedy was *The Simpsons*, which helped "make" the FOX network by clearly showing it offered something different from the big three. That "different" has been analyzed and explicated to contain many components, but prominently includes an all-permeating sense of irreverence and indifference to social decorum that would make Lenny Bruce proud, a self-consciousness about the form of both the sitcom and animation on par with *MAD* and Kovacs, and an abrasive intellect given to erudite references that might stump Oscar Levant. *The Simpsons* has, of course, gone on to influence satires in many different forms: animated sitcoms (*King of the Hill, South Park*), news parody (*The Daily Show, The Colbert Report*), sketch comedy (*Chappelle's Show*), and genre-busters like *The Sarah Silverman Program*.

Just as it had in the fifties, parody today continues to offer alternative strategies for making sense of the world and one's place within it. Not surprisingly, as evidenced by the success of shows like *Family Guy* and *South Park*, the impulse to offend, to refuse to abide by commonly accepted senses of good taste, remains a reliable way to find an audience. The title of one of the chapters in this book, "What, Me Subversive?", echoes Alfred E. Neuman's famous catchphrase, "What, me worry?" It is meant to echo a self-conscious ambivalence about the revolutionary potential of humor that I believe many of the texts and performers discussed in this book exhibit. Does comedy actually have the power to change culture? Certainly individuals can articulate oppositional attitudes through humor, and this book has sought to understand what happens when those attitudes are popularly reproduced, packaged, and sold through industrialized culture. Those oppositional attitudes, however mass-produced, remain subversive in the sense that they are symptomatic of—and often explicitly express—a refusal to accept the status quo. But it is only what people do with the rebellious impulses and identities that comedy nourishes and sometimes articulates that ultimately can be socially or politically subversive.

Still, a look around the media landscape at the beginning of the twenty-first century confirms that if you've got something critical to say about culture, the best way to say it and insure a lot of people hear it is through comedy. Satire is booming on television, though it is usually tucked away on cable channels, and earns ratings that pale in comparison to the networks' reality competitions and forensic dramas, and even their "real" news and talk shows. The one primetime network show that regularly veers into satire, *30 Rock*, wins critical raves, but has only a fraction of the audience of the retrograde *Two and a Half Men*. Despite the attention it attracts, comedy that is critical of culture remains a minority taste. In the postnetwork era, the payoffs for acquiring that taste are better than ever, in large part because the television industry does a better job of marketing to that taste than it did, or could do, in the network era. That will continue only as long as advertisers believe the demographic profile of fans of satiric comedy makes up for what they lack in numbers.

But the pleasure of being a fan of critical comedy like those examined in this book isn't just that you can find a television show or magazine that makes you laugh. It's having a sense of community and being in on the joke—knowing that you are not the one being laughed "at." To borrow a phrase from a letter to *MAD*, it is far better to be "comrades in the bonds of spoofery"—to be in the minority doing the spoofing—than to be spoofed. The most important and popular arena for satire and parody these days is probably the online video, shared and consumed via social networks both formal and informal, commercial and noncommercial. Just as people passed around copies of *MAD* in the 1950s, now they forward hypertext links to one another via e-mail or post a video to Facebook for their friends to see. The Internet technically enables the distribution, but these communities of fans and friends are the real networks.

Luckily, there's no longer a "Red Menace" to cast a shadow over comedy and make people wonder whether laughing at something is un-American. By the end of George W. Bush's second term, FOX News might have been the only place a person could go too far making fun of the president. But we would do well to remember that there were indeed some shaky moments after 9/11 when irony was proclaimed dead, and that in the 2000s it became obligatory for comedians—not just politicians—to voice support for the troops before pointing out absurdities of the wars in Iraq and Afghanistan. It may be, though, that along with the more democratized media distribution that the Internet has enabled, social networks have replaced the singular authority figure (à la J. Edgar Hoover) that can be called upon to judge the appropriateness of comedy. Instead, the social network constitutes a jury of one's self-selected peers, and posting a satiric video draws a response directly in proportion to their political sentiments. Whether those responses are treated as opportunities to engage and exchange ideas, or to "unfriend" and make one's network more ideologically homogenous, is a matter of individual taste.

Either way, social networks and online videos certainly make talking about parody and satire more convenient. A worn-out copy of *MAD* makes nice material evidence of shared cultural attitudes and tastes, but waiting around for each of one's friends to read it—much less to see what the letters say in the next issue—surely lessens the urgency one might feel to talk about it. So while it's hard not to romanticize the sense of camaraderie that must have accompanied passing *MAD* from friend to friend in the 1950s, or staying up late to watch a different kind of TV on *Playboy's Penthouse,* or "getting" Ernie Kovacs, or laughing "with" rather than "at" Oscar Levant, we ought not complain. Satire and parody that critically take on culture are everywhere, and the opportunities to engage them immediate. In that respect, such newly formed public dispatches may be the most subversive yet.

Notes

NOTES TO THE INTRODUCTION

1. "The Quiz Show Scandal," *The American Experience*, PBS.org, *http://www.pbs.org/wgbh/amex/quizshow/peopleevents/pande02.html*. (Accessed 21 September 2010).
2. William Boddy, *Fifties Television: The Industry and Its Critics* (Urbana: University of Illinois Press, 1993), 223.
3. Jeffrey Sconce, *Haunted Media: Electronic Presence from Telegraphy to Television* (Durham, N.C.: Duke University Press, 2000), 129.
4. Raymond Williams, *Television: Technology and Cultural Form* (New York: Schocken Books, 1975).
5. *Life*, February 15, 1960, 106.
6. For an in-depth consideration of the historical evolution of television satire, see Jonathan Gray, Jeffrey P. Jones, and Ethan Thompson, "The State of Satire, The Satire of State," in *Satire TV: Politics and Comedy in the Post-Network Era*, ed. Gray, Jones, and Thompson (New York: New York University Press, 2009).
7. Boddy, 21.
8. Dwight MacDonald, "A Theory of Mass Culture," in *Mass Culture: The Popular Arts in America*, ed. Bernard Rosenberg and David Manning White (Glencoe, Ill.: Free Press, 1957), 60.
9. Michel de Certeau, *The Practice of Everyday Life* (Berkeley and Los Angeles: University of California Press, 1984), 169.
10. Margaret A. Rose, *Parody: Ancient, Modern, and Post-Modern* (New York: Cambridge University Press, 1993), 52.
11. For example, see Steve Neale and Frank Krutnick, *Popular Film and Television Comedy* (London: Routledge, 1995), 19.
12. Max Horkheimer and Theodor W. Adorno, *Dialectic of Enlightenment*, trans. John Cumming (New York: Seabury Press, 1972), 129.
13. J. Hoberman, *Vulgar Modernism: Writing on Movies and Other Media* (Philadelphia: Temple University Press, 1991), 32–33.
14. Roland Barthes, *The Pleasure of the Text*, trans. Richard Miller (New York: Hill and Wang, 1975), 11–12.
15. Dwight MacDonald, *Against the American Grain* (New York: Random House, 1962), 74.

NOTES TO CHAPTER 1

1. *Peter Gunn*, "The Comic," NBC, 1959.

2. Kenneth Jackson, *Crabgrass Frontier: The Suburbanization of the United States* (New York: Oxford University Press, 1985), 241.
3. Richard Armour, "A Good Joke Book Might Soften the Reds," *Saturday Evening Post*, December 12 ,1953: 12.
4. Richard Hanser, "Wit as a Weapon," *The Saturday Review*, November 8, 1952: 13.
5. Ibid, 14.
6. Hanser, who had written for television and film, had also made psychological warfare broadcasts to German soldiers over Allied radio transmitters during the war. Humor was considered in some ways a more effective propaganda tool, apparently, because it functioned subversively on a more discrete psychological level. These broadcasts consisted, he said, of an earthy, "man to man" language designed in contrast to the more formal, "high-flown" generalities of most American propaganda. These daily psychological broadcasts included the telling of an anti-Nazi joke, a steady supply of which had been gathered from German prisoners.
7. William Whyte, *The Organization Man* (New York: Simon and Schuster, 1956).
8. David Riesman, *The Lonely Crowd: A Study of the Changing American Character* (New Haven: Yale University Press, 1950).
9. Whyte, 453.
10. For an overview of advertising practices in postwar America, see Juliann Sivulka, *Soap, Sex, and Cigarettes: A Cultural History of American Advertising* (Belmont, Calif.: Wadsworth, 1998).
11. Sloan Wilson, *The Man in the Gray Flannel Suit*, (New York: Simon & Schuster, 1955).
12. Hanser, 13
13. "State of the Nation's Humor," *The New York Times Magazine*, December 7, 1958.
14. This chapter began as a survey of articles about humor in popular publications in the 1950s, drawn from the *Reader's Guide to Periodical Literature*. I looked up the generic terms "humor" and "comedy" from 1950 through 1962, as well as the names of specific performers. I was particularly interested in finding discussions about broad changes in humor or the changing significance of humor during the emergence of television. The majority of the articles did indeed focus on television comedy. Most simply discussed specific television performers through the beginning and middle of the decade, but by the end of the 1950s, more attention began to be paid to the social significance of a certain number of comedians.
15. "Crisis in Comedy," *Life*, April 15, 1957.
16. Arthur Frank Wertheim, "The Rise and Fall of Milton Berle," in *American History/American Television: Interpreting the Video Past*, ed. John E. O'Connor, (New York: Frederick Ungar Publishing Co., 1983), 69.
17. Ibid., 74.
18. "The Wit in the Mirror," *Newsweek*, January 12, 1961: 62.
19. Walter Blair and Hamlin Hill, *America's Humor: From Poor Richard to Doonesbury* (New York: Oxford University Press, 1978), 499.
20. Ibid., 489.
21. "The Sickniks," *Time*, July 13, 1959: 42.
22. Russell Lynes, "Highbrow, Lowbrow, Middlebrow," *Harper's Magazine*, February 1949.
23. *Life*, April 11, 1949.
24. Michael Kammen, *American Culture, American Tastes: Social Change and the 20th Century* (New York: Basic Books, 1999), 100.

25. Lynes, 20.
26. Martin Williams, "The Comedy of Lenny Bruce," *The Saturday Review*, November 24, 1962: 60.
27. Marshall Scott, "The New Sense of Humor," *Cosmopolitan*, November 1958: 16.
28. Scott, 16.
29. Sahl himself said that sick comics were "juvenile rebels, at best" who didn't "jab specific targets, just anything that will bleed." "State of the Nation's Humor," 25.
30. In a 1962 *Newsweek* article, Berman mentions people having objected to the piece when he performed it on *The Ed Sullivan Show*: "My God, is it pro-Semitic! It's true, it's about my *father*!" "Seeing Shelley Plain," Newsweek, August 13, 1962: 56.
31. Original air date: May 12, 1961, CBS.
32. Original air date: June 12, 1962, CBS.
33. Sahl later gained notoriety for becoming an outspoken supportor of New Orleans District Attorney Jim Garrison's inquiry into the Kennedy assassination. Sahl was actually deputized by Garrison, and appears in Oliver Stone's 1991 film, *JFK*.
34. This is echoed by Jules Feiffer in the program, who notes that the role of satire primarily is to be subversive.
35. Lenny Bruce supposedly opened his first post–JFK assassination show with a long sigh and the pithy comment "Vaghn Meader is screwed." Elizabeth McCracken, "The Temporary Kennedy," *New York Times Magazine*, December 26, 2004.
36. Stephen E. Kercher, *Revel with a Cause: Liberal Satire in Postwar America* (Chicago: University of Chicago Press, 2006), 194.
37. Nixon's declaration can be seen in the documentary *Atomic Café*.
38. Allen Ginsberg, *Howl and Other Poems* (San Francisco: City Lights Books, 1996).
39. Gerald Grob, *Mental Illness and American Society, 1875–1940* (Princeton: Princeton University Press, 1983), 317.
40. Ibid.
41. Roy Porter, *Madness: A Brief History* (New York: Oxford University Press, 2002), 196.
42. Ibid., 199.
43. Porter, 95.
44. Jacob Levine, "Responses to Humor," *Scientific American*, February 1956: 31.
45. Sigmund Freud, *Jokes and Their Relation to the Unconscious*, ed. and trans. James Strachey (New York: Norton, 1960), 164, 283.
46. Ibid., 208–210.
47. Levine, 35.
48. John E. Gibson, "How's Your Sense of Humor?" *Today's Health*, March 1960: 8.
49. Ibid., 9.
50. Ed Sikov, *Laughing Hysterically: American Screen Comedy of the 1950s* (New York: Columbia University Press, 1994).
51. Ibid., 22.
52. Glen O. Gabbard and Krin Gabbard, *Psychiatry and the Cinema*. 2nd. ed. (Washington, D.C.: American Psychiatric Press, 1999), 76.
53. Sikov, 19.
54. Original air date: October 11, 1963, NBC.
55. Freud, 122.

56. Porter, 190.
57. "Show Business," *Time*, July 13, 1959: 44.

NOTES TO CHAPTER 2

1. Letter to J. Edgar Hoover dated February 17, 1963. The letters in the FBI's files on the question of whether or not *MAD* was communistic continue until 1971, but sparingly. The FBI files are available at http://www.collectmad.com/fbi/FBI-MAD-Bufiles.htm. (Accessed September 27, 2010).
2. *MAD*, October/November 1956.
3. *MAD*, July 1956.
4. *MAD*, September 1958.
5. *MAD*, March 1959.
6. Lynn Spigel, *Make Room for TV: Television and the Family Ideal in Postwar America* (Chicago: University of Chicago Press, 1992).
7. Maria Reidelbach, *Completely Mad: A History of the Comic Book and Magazine* (Boston: Little, Brown and Co., 1991), 188.
8. Ibid.
9. *MAD*, November 1954.
10. *MAD*, September 1956.
11. *MAD*, September 1958.
12. *MAD*, March 1958.
13. Letter dated May 1955, FBI files.
14. Letter dated May 17, 1961, FBI files.
15. Letter dated March 8, 1962, FBI files.
16. Letter from Hoover dated June 6, 1955, FBI files.
17. Note attached to file dated June 6, 1955, FBI files.
18. Fredric Wertham, *Seduction of the Innocent* (New York: Rinehart and Company, 1953), 355.
19. James Gilbert, *A Cycle of Outrage: America's Reaction to the Juvenile Delinquent in the 1950s* (New York: Oxford University Press, 1986), 104.
20. Roger Sabin, *Adult Comics: An Introduction* (London: Routledge, 1993), 147.
21. Reidelbach, 28.
22. Ibid., 34.
23. Ibid., 53.
24. *MAD*, July 1956.
25. In the next issue (September 1956) a reader sarcastically asked, "After sending for a Davy Crockett Gatling Gun, do you think I'd be dumb enough to send for a glob of Silly Putty?"
26. *MAD*, February 1957.
27. Ibid.
28. The most sought after of memorabilia are from an ad in the March 1959 issue for genuine 14 karat goldbrick cufflinks "for rich kids who weren't afraid to let everyone know they are rich." According to fan site collectmad.com, the cufflinks were owned by Bill Gaines and one reader purchased them for $66 in 1959. http://collectmad/collectibles/faq.htm. (Accessed September 26, 2010).
29. Indeed, Walken has reprised the role during a number of later appearances over the years.
30. Jeffrey Sconce, *Haunted Media: Electronic Presence from Telegraphy to Television* (Durham, N.C.: Duke University Press, 2000), 129.
31. Elaine Tyler May, *Homeward Bound: American Families in the Cold War Era* (New York: Basic Books, 1999).

32. Wini Breines, *Young, White, Miserable: Growing up Female in the Fifties* (Chicago: University of Chicago Press, 2001), 41.
33. *MAD*, March 1955.
34. Christopher Anderson, "Disneyland," in *Television: The Critical View*. 6th ed., ed. Horace Newcomb (New York: Oxford University Press, 2000).
35. *MAD*, December 1958.
36. *MAD*, April 1956.
37. Mikhail Bakhtin, *Rabelais and His World*, trans. Helene Iswolsky (Bloomington: Indiana University Press, 1984), 16.
38. *MAD*, April 1957.
39. Bakhtin, 255.
40. *MAD*, May 1954.
41. *MAD*, February 1955.
42. *MAD*, September 1956.
43. *MAD*, November 1954.
44. This embrace of parody as masculine sophistication is explored in detail in my *Playboy* chapter.
45. *Playboy*, December 1957.
46. Greg Taylor, *Artists in the Audience: Cults, Camp, and American Film Criticism* (Princeton: Princeton University Press, 1999), 8.
47. Ibid., 15.
48. "Progress in Cleaning Up the Comics," *Reader's Digest*, February 1956.
49. *MAD*, July 1956.
50. In 1956, my own father wrote a college English paper on a *MAD* article parodying bullfighting by likening it to the sport of puppy dog kicking.
51. Michael Kammen, *American Culture, American Tastes: Social Change and the 20th Century* (New York: Basic Books, 1999), 96.
52. See Henry Jenkins, *Textual Poachers* (New York: Routledge, 1992); and Constance Penley, "Brownian Motion: Women, Tactics, and Technology," in *Technoculture*, ed. Constance Penley and Andrew Ross (Minneapolis: University of Minnesota Press, 1991).
53. *MAD* also explicitly gave readers "alternative" dictionaries. In 1953, *MAD* published a Bop dictionary, providing translations of hip or jazz-scene-oriented language. The Bop dictionary prompted a number of letters suggesting additions. An expanded Bop dictionary was later printed, as well as a Bop version of the Gettysburg Address. This latter piece drew an exceptional number of negative responses.
54. Jerry Rubin, *Do It! Scenarios of the Revolution* (New York: Ballantine Books, 1970), 70.
55. Ibid., 84.
56. Aniko Bodroghkozy, *The Groove Tube: Sixties Television and the Youth Rebellion* (Durham, N.C.: Duke University Press, 2001), 59.
57. Rubin, 106–108.

NOTES TO CHAPTER 3

1. An earlier version of this chapter was published under the same title in *Television and New Media*, 9(4) July 2008: 284–304 (Sage Publications).
2. Barbara Ehrenreich, *The Hearts of Men: American Dreams and the Flight from Commitment* (New York: Anchor Books, 1984), 42.
3. Thomas Weyr. *Reaching for Paradise: The Playboy Vision of America* (New York: New York Times Books, 1978).

Notes

4. John Thornton Caldwell, *Televisuality: Style, Crisis, and Authority in American Television* (New Brunswick, N.J.: Rutgers University Press, 1995).
5. When referring to "Playboy" as a lifestyle or masculine identity, I have merely capitalized the term. When referring to the magazine or television show, it is italicized.
6. Pierre Bourdieu, *Distinction: A Social Critique of the Judgment of Taste*, trans. Richard Nice, (London: Routledge, 1984).
7. See, for example, Kenneth Jackson, *CrabgrassFrontier: The Suburbanization of the United States* (New York: Oxford University Press, 1985); George Lipsitz, *A Rainbow at Midnight: Labor and Culture in the 1940s* (Urbana: University of Illinois Press, 1984); James Gilbert, *A Cycle of Outrage: America's Reaction to the Juvenile Delinquent in the 1950s* (New York: Oxford University Press, 1986); Wini Breines, *Young, White, Miserable: Growing Up Female in the Fifties*, (Chicago: University of Chicago Press, 2001); Elaine Tyler May, *Homeward Bound: American Families in the Cold War Era* (New York: Basic Books, 1999).
8. William Whyte, *The Organization Man* (New York: Simon and Schuster, 1956).
9. Norman Mailer, *The White Negro* (San Francisco: City Lights Books, 1957).
10. Ehrenreich, 50.
11. Janice Radway, *A Feeling for Books: The Book-of-the-Month Club, Literary Taste, and Middle-Class Desire* (Chapel Hill: University of North Carolina Press, 1997).
12. The primary reason for the production of the show seems to have been to promote the magazine and *Playboy* corporate identity, perhaps as a "loss leader" of sorts, driving more potential readers to the magazine.
13. The shows are difficult to get ahold of now, but the Museum of Television in Beverly Hills has eight episodes of the show on tape, spanning the two seasons and including the pilot. A recent DVD release of *Playboy After Dark* also includes two episodes of *Playboy's Penthouse* (ZYX Music, 2007).
14. It is interesting to note, however, that the introduction and first-person address of *Playboy's Penthouse* was similar to that of *The Continental*, the often parodied, first-person perspective program that featured the suave "continental" Renzo Cesana, who welcomed the female viewer into his apartment to be romanced through the television set.
15. For a history of how black performers were systematically censored on TV stations in Jackson, Mississippi, see Steve Classen, *Watching Jim Crow: The Struggles over Mississippi TV, 1955–1969* (Durham, N.C.: Duke University Press, 2004).
16. Hugh M. Hefner, "TV Tests Our Attitudes," *Chicago Sun-Times*, November 21, 1999, http://www.suntimes.com/century/m1960.html. (access no longer available).
17. In the second year, however, the show looked more like a traditional variety show if only because of the trimming of Hefner's chatting. Also cut were features on products discriminating bachelors should have in their own pads (*Variety*, September 21, 1960). This transformation is clear from watching just the eight programs available at the Museum of Television. While in the pilot much time is spent lounging on couches, the later programs barely break between acts.
18. *Variety*, November 4, 1959.
19. For additional discussion of Gillespie's appearance on the program, see Robert McMichael, "We insist—freedom now! Black Moral Authority, Jazz, and

the Changeable Shape of Whiteness," *American Music* 16(4) 1998: 375–416.
20. Thomas Frank, *The Conquest of Cool: Business Culture, Counterculture, and the Rise of Hip Consumerism* (Chicago: University of Chicago Press, 1997).
21. Andrew Ross, *No Respect: Intellectuals and Popular Culture* (New York: Routledge, 1989), 68.
22. Lynn Spigel, *Make Room for TV: Television and the Family Ideal in Postwar America* (Chicago: University of Chicago Press, 1992), 96.
23. Ibid., 97.
24. *Playboy,* September 1960.
25. *Playboy,* November 1955.
26. *Playboy,* April 1959.
27. Here *Playboy* anticipates Horace Newcomb, *TV: The Most Popular Art* (Garden City, N.Y.: Anchor, 1974) in which he proposes that television programs are most aesthetically successful when they don't try to replicate other media like film or theater on the small screen.
28. Bourdieu, 5.
29. Spigel, 123.
30. Ibid., 120.
31. *Playboy,* September 1955.
32. Susan Sontag, "Notes on Camp," in *Against Interpretation and Other Essays* (New York: Anchor Books, 1990), 284.
33. The parodic sensibility could rewrite history as well. In the August 1958 issue, "History Revisited" reexplained historical events in terms of illicit affairs, such as Leif Erikson discovering America but having to leave after teaching Swedish massage to the local Indian chief's daughter.
34. Coincidentally, it was the late, late shows of old movies that *Playboy's Penthouse* was up against in many markets.
35. In December 1957, *Playboy* published an extensive article on Kurtzman and many of the *MAD* artists, including many pages of reprinted *MAD* parodies. The "Little World of Harvey Kurtzman" primarily sought to associate the *MAD* parodic sensibility with Kurtzman, who was then editing *Humbug* for Hefner, the second failed attempt (after *Trump*) by the two to re-create the success of *MAD*.

NOTES TO CHAPTER 4

1. Letter dated October 16, 1956. box 61, folder 5, Ernie Kovacs Papers (Collection 1105). Department of Special Collections, Charles E. Young Research Library, University of California, Los Angeles.
2. Michel De Certeau, *The Practice of Everyday Life*, trans. Steven Rendall (Berkeley and Los Angeles: University of California Press, 1984).
3. On the derivative nature of TV westerns, see Christopher Anderson's discussion of the literal recycling of other program scripts into westerns through minimal script changes. Christopher Anderson, *Hollywood TV: The Studio System in the Fifties* (Austin: University of Texas Press, 1994) 183.
4. Robert Rosen, "Ernie Kovacs: Video Artist," in *Transmission: Theory and Practice for a New Television Aesthetics,* ed. Peter A'Gostino (New York: Tanam Press, 1985), 144.
5. It is important to note that this particularly outlandish Kovacs character was in some sense a caricature of the worst stereotypes of gay men. However, it is also important to note that Percy's original poetry was published on a

number of occasions in *MAD Magazine*. I believe this suggests that Percy's appeal had more to do with the language play of his poems than of the caricature of homosexuality.
6. Michael Nash, "In the Beginning," 9, cited in Bruce Ferguson, "The Importance of Being Ernie: Taking a Close Look (and Listen)," *Illuminating Video: An Essential Guide to Video Art*, ed. Doug Hall and Sally Jo Fifer (Aperture, 1990) 356.
7. See, for example, Hugh Hefner's comment to Bob Newhart: "TV is such a terrible medium, it eats up these things. [There's] a continual search for new kinds of concepts." Discussed in my *Playboy* chapter.
8. A "best of" series was released on VHS in the 1990s, and on DVD in 2003. The Trio television network also aired episodes of *The Ernie Kovacs Show* intermittently in 2003–2004 as part of their *Brilliant but Cancelled* series.
9. Whether we choose to call that identity modern or postmodern is not the subject of this chapter, though I do believe this examination certainly has ramifications for distinguishing between modernist and postmodernist art and identity.
10. "Utility Expert," *Time*, January 28, 1957: 66.
11. Rosen, 144.
12. J. Hoberman, *Vulgar Modernism: Writings on Movies and Other Media* (Philadelphia: Temple University Press, 1991), 33.
13. Ibid., 38.
14. Rosen, 143.
15. Ferguson, 362.
16. Dana Polan, "A Brechtian Cinema? Towards a Politics of Self-Reflexive Film," in *Movies and Methods*, vol. 2, ed. Bill Nichols (Berkeley and Los Angeles: University of California Press, 1985).
17. "An Electronic Comic and His TV Tricks," *Life*, April 15, 1957.
18. Ibid., 169.
19. "Milton Berle, Red Buttons, Jackie Gleason, Buddy Hackett, Wally Cox, Martha Raye, and Sam Levenson lost their programs. Eddie Cantor is in retirement. Jack Benny, Bob Hope, Jimmy Durante and Jerry Lewis are seen either irregularly or at limited intervals. Bert Lahr and Ed Wynn are not only seen irregularly, but sometimes as dramatic actors." Gilbert Millstein, "TV's Comics Went Thataway," *New York Times Magazine*, February 2, 1958.
20. Ibid.
21. Ibid.
22. Ibid.
23. Ibid.
24. Frederic Morton, "Ernie Kovacs: The Last Spontaneous Man," *Holiday*, October 1958.
25. Ibid., 155.
26. Peter Martin, "I Call on Edie Adams and Ernie Kovacs," *Saturday Evening Post*, December 28, 1957.
27. Anderson, 86.
28. "'Uncle Ernie' Kovacs," *Newsweek*, January 12, 1953: 70.
29. Barry Putterman, *On Television and Comedy: Essays on Style, Theme, Performer and Writer* (Jefferson, N.C.: McFarland and Co., 1995), 137.
30. Diana Rico, *Kovacsland* (San Diego: Harcourt, Brace, Jovanovich, 1990).
31. Memo dated April 29, 1953. box 55, folder 7, Ernie Kovacs Papers.
32. Ernie Kovacs to Dr. Frank Stanton, CBS, October 19, 1953, box 63, folder 16, Ernie Kovacs Papers.
33. Ernie Kovacs to Lawrence, Hough, et al. October 19, 1953, box 63, folder 16, Ernie Kovacs Papers.

34. Shows discussed and air dates:
    Tonight. Originally aired December 11, 1956, NBC.
    The Ernie Kovacs Show. Originally aired January 26, 1956, NBC, 10:30 A.M.
    Kovacs Unlimited. Originally aired May 28, 1952, CBS, 8:30 P.M.
    The Ernie Kovacs Show. Originally aired May 25, 1956, NBC, 10:30 A.M.
    The Best of Ernie Kovacs, Volume 1. Originally aired as *The Ernie Kovacs Show* on ABC, 1961.
35. "This Is No Gag," *Newsweek*, June 3, 1957: 56.
36. Letter on stationery titled "From the desk of Caligula...et al." box 58, folder 7, Ernie Kovacs Papers.
37. *Newsweek*, June 3, 1957: 56.
38. "King Leer," *Newsweek*, September 18, 1961: 64.
39. Martin, 39.
40. Ferguson, 355.
41. Ibid., 357.
42. Letter from Mrs. A. Maddaloni, April 24, 1954, box 58, folder 4, Ernie Kovacs Papers.
43. One disgruntled viewer wrote to complain about Kovacs habit of "ridiculing all forms of higher culture." Letter from Vick Alexakis. May 23, 1959, box 58, folder 3, Ernie Kovacs Papers.
44. Document titled "The Driest Beer, The Wettest Soap, and Thou Beside Me," box 55, folder 3, Ernie Kovacs Papers.
45. Letter dated October 18, 1956. box 61, folder 5, Ernie Kovacs Papers.
46. Letter dated December 11, 1959 from Mrs. Art Treadwell, box 58, folder 3, Ernie Kovacs Papers.
47. Susan Murray, *Hitch Your Antenna to the Stars: Early Television and Broadcast Stardom* (New York: Routledge, 2005), 41–42.

NOTES TO CHAPTER 5

1. "Oscar Levant's Allergy: Oscar," *Los Angeles Mirror-News,* June 27, 1958: 1.
2. *Tonight.* January 28, 1956, KNXT.
3. Sam Kashner and Nancy Schoenberger, *A Talent for Genius: The Life and Times of Oscar Levant* (New York: Villard, 1994).
4. A small number of fan materials also exist, thanks to *Los Angeles Mirror-News* critic Hal Humphrey, who kept the materials he received from the "Official Oscar Levant Fan Club." My sincerest thanks to Ned Comstock, University of Southern California archivist, for discovering this and many other Levant-related documents at USC.
5. The photo exists in the Levant Collection at USC, among a small number of photos taken on the program's set.
6. Document titled "NBC-TV PERSONALITY INFO," May 31, 1955. Hal Humphrey Collection.
7. Joan Shelley Rubin, *The Making of Middlebrow Culture* (Chapel Hill: University of North Carolina Press, 1992), 322.
8. A series of RKO film shorts was also produced of *Information, Please!*
9. "General Electric Guest House," *Variety*, July 4, 1951.
10. According to the sometimes reliable Internet Movie Database, Levant appeared on the show just one week in July 1951. http://imdb.com/title/tt0043203/epcast. (Accessed September 27, 2010).
11. Kashner and Schoenberger suggest Levant's devotion to Gershwin sidetracked his own career.

12. Originally aired January 28, 1956, KNXT.
13. Cecil Smith, "TV Scene," *Los Angeles Times*, March 6, 1958.
14. Fortunately, although no one saw fit to preserve Oscar's program itself, the local TV critics did follow it closely, and one can find out a lot about the content of the program, as well as Oscar's behavior, by reading the columns by Cecil Smith (*Los Angeles Times*) and Hal Humphrey (*Los Angeles Mirror-News*). Additionally, a transcript of another complete episode featuring James Mason (air date March 28, 1959) exists in the Levant Collection as well.
15. A thirty minute excerpt of an episode from just a few days earlier shows the piano playing and the pacing were standard. The studio audience, sitting very close to the stage, is visible. Hedda Hopper sits in it before coming on with Oscar. June does a commercial for Philco, who became a sponsor just the previous week (UCLA Film and Television Archive).
16. A couple of weeks after the Astaire episode, and after appearing on *The Eddie Fisher Show*, Levant participated in a local telethon raising funds for mental health education and treatment. Though Cecil Smith reported that Oscar got into a conflict with the fire department, which wouldn't let him smoke, there is unfortunately no footage or further description of what must have been a very interesting case of sick TV. (*Los Angeles Times*, May 25, 1958 and May 27, 1958.)
17. *Los Angeles Times*, June 26, 1958.
18. *Variety*, July 9, 1958.
19. Oscar Levant, "Noble, Vindictive Man!" *Los Angeles Mirror News*, August 6, 1958: 4.
20. Coincidentally, I found the street address for Oscar's house scrawled across a random notepad paper in the Ernie Kovacs collection, suggesting this other early TV eccentric made an attempt to visit Oscar.
21. *Los Angeles Times*, July 5, 1961.
22. *Variety*, September 15, 1965.
23. Ben Hecht, "Hooray for the Bad Taste Kid," *Esquire*, December 1958: 88–94.
24. *TV Guide*, July 5, 1958.
25. As evidence, note how the actual confession of his neuroses, which was so important on the network stage, comes in last with local fans.
26. *Los Angeles Mirror-News*, July 15, 1958.
27. *Variety*, June 15, 1960.
28. "Pitfalls of Commercial Techniques," *Television Magazine*, November 1953: 35–36.
29. Susan Murray, *Hitch Your Antenna to the Stars: Early Television and Broadcast Stardom* (New York: Routledge, 2005), 122.
30. *Los Angeles Mirror-News*, January 8, 1959.
31. *Los Angeles Times*, June 11, 1958.
32. *Los Angeles Times*, July 24, 1958.
33. Letter dated September 1, 1959 from "Official Oscar Levant Fan Club." Hal Humphrey Collection.
34. *Variety*, May 21, 1958.

Index

30 Rock, 150
9/11, 150

A
A&E Biography, 128
ABC, 33, 89, 111, 112, 114, 139
Adams, Don 28
Addams, Charles, 134
Adorno, Theodor 11, 12
advertising: criticisms of, 21, 23; and gender, 18, 59, 92; industry strategies, 86, 87, 120, 123; parody of, 47, 52–55, 75, 98, 100; in *Playboy*, 81; relationship to TV industry, 4, 7, 79, 111
Afghanistan, 150
albums: comedy, 5, 19, 26–27, 30–34, 88, 146; music, 11, 79, 83, 86, 88
Allen, Steve, 13, 24, 26, 84–85, 89, 114, 117, 126–128, 130
An American in Paris, 41, 131
Anderson, Christopher, 62, 112, 146
antitelevision, 128, 140–141
Army-McCarthy hearings, 60, 65, 147. *See also* McCarthyism
articulation, 18–19, 29, 49, 67, 73, 82, 100
Astaire, Fred, 47, 75, 96, 135–139, 141, 143
atomic bomb, 13, 24. *See also* Cold War
Avery, Tex, 122

B
Bakhtin, Mikhail, 65–66
Ballyhoo, 53
Barrymore, Ethel, 132
Barthes, Roland, 12–13,

Beat writers and culture, 27, 35, 111, 139
Bell & Howell Close-Up, 33
Bennett, Tony, 109
Berle, Milton, 25, 110, 113, 139
Berman, Shelley, 1, 10; albums, 26; on television, 15, 40–44, 125–126; routines, 24, 28–33, 147
Bernbach, Bill, 121
Blair, Walter, 26
Book-of-the-Month Club, 83
Boone, Pat, 45–46, 75
Bourdieu, Pierre 80–81, 86–87, 90
Brando, Marlon 40, 47, 78
brows. *See* culture: high vs. low
Bruce, Lenny: on comedy, 26–29, 40; as consumer culture, 88; as sick comedian, 10, 24, 43–44, 94, 96, 125, 147; on television, 76, 84–85
Burton, Al, 128, 133, 148
Bush, George W., 150

C
CBS, 1, 9, 113–114, 117, 131, 141
Caesar, Sid, 28, 71, 110–111, 143
Cahn, Sammy, 133
Caldwell, John, 78
camp, 51, 68, 80, 95
Captain Video, 59
Carlin, George 47
carnivalesque, 65–66
Celebrity Game, The 139
Chappelle's Show, 6, 149
Charles, Ray, 76, 89
Chevrolet, 133
children's programming, 61–62, 113, 115
class, 18, 27, 38, 40, 43, 67, 82, 147
Clinton, Hillary, 6
Cobweb, The, 126–127, 132

164 Index

Colbert Report, The, 6, 149
Cold War, 10, 20–21, 43, 50
Cole, Nat King, 84–85
Comedy Central, 5
comics (print): controversy, 51–53, 56; and gender, 59–60, 92–94; parody, 10, 71; readers, 62
commercial culture: 72–75; comedy as, 3–4; criticism of, 47, 61–62, 142–143; parody of, 53–55, 98; television as, 64, 108, 120–121, 133–134, 146. *See also* advertising
communism, 20–21, 61. *See also* Cold War
conformity: as cliché, 46, 80–81; and masculinity, 85–86, 112; and parody, 57, 69–70; as social problem, 21–22, 37, 51, 56, 74
consumer culture, 32, 74, 77–78, 99, 124. *See also* consumption, commercial culture
Consumer Reports, 53
consumption: masculine practices of, 79–84, 88; as stage of communication, 5, 11, 87; visual or media, 47, 51, 87, 92. *See also* consumer culture
Continental, The, 56–59
Corey, Irwin "Professor," 43
counterculture, 27, 34, 46, 49, 70, 75, 82, 86–87, 97
cult film, 68
cultural capital, 11, 80, 83, 87–88, 90, 93–94
culture, high vs. low: boundary blurring, 67–71, 130–131, 134; as brow levels, 25, 27–28; and sophistication, 83–87; on television, 64, 122, 140–141, 145

D

Dadaists, 36
Daily Show with Jon Stewart, The, 6, 117, 148, 149
Davis, Sammy, Jr. 84, 139, 141, 142
daytime programming, 98, 104, 113–116, 122
De Certeau, Michel, 8, 72–73, 99
Dean, James, 40
DeVol, Frank, 133
dialogism, 11, 13, 65–66, 108
Diller, Phyllis, 76
Disney, Walt, 54, 62, 64, 89, 146–147

Disneyland, 62–64, 72, 146–147
distinction, 27–28, 80, 83, 141, 146
domestic space, 40, 59, 78–80, 83, 88, 92, 95, 126
Douglas, William O., 141
Dragnet, 48, 56, 71
dramas, 41, 64, 89–91, 125, 141, 150
drug use: Lenny Bruce; 26, Oscar Levant, 41, 125–128, 139; pharmaceuticals, 64, 131, 138; references to, 95, 48, 133
Duggan, Tom 134, 142

E

Eames, furniture, 81, 88
EC Comics, 52, 96. *See also* Gaines, William
Eddie Fisher Show, The, 144
Ehrenreich, Barbara, 81, 88
Eisenhower, Dwight, 34, 46, 76
Emmy awards, 6, 62, 89, 138
Esquire, 77, 87–88, 92, 140

F

The Fabulous Fifties, 1–9, 14
Facebook, 150
Fadiman, Clifton, 130
Family Guy, 149
fans and fan letters: Ernie Kovacs, 98–100, 117, 120–121; Oscar Levant, 14, 137, 140, 144; *MAD*, 54, 67, 69, 150; and poaching, 72; *Playboy*, 91
Father Knows Best, 51, 78
Federal Bureau of Investigation (FBI), 11, 45, 50–51, 65
Federal Communications Commission (FCC), 2
Feldstein, Al, 33, 54
Ferguson, Bruce, 108, 119
Fitzgerald, Ella, 76, 90
Flanagan, Al, 140
Flintstones, The, 89
Food and Drug Administration (FDA), 53
Ford, Tennessee Ernie, 144
Foucault, Michel, 36
FOX News, 150
Frank, Thomas, 86
Frankenheimer, John 89
Freud, Sigmund: theories about jokes, 38–39, 42; popularity of, 39, 44, 73
Freed, Arthur, 131
Friedan, Betty, 9, 18

G

Gabbard, Glen O. and Krin, 39
Gaines, William, 33, 52–53, 60, 97
Garland, Judy, 138
Garroway, Dave, 64, 75
gaze. See voyeurism
gender, 40, 58–59, 80, 87
General Electric, 1
General Electric Guest House, 131
GI Bill, 18, 82
Gillespie, Dizzy, 84, 86
Ginsberg, Allen, 35
Gleason, Jackie, 25, 28, 45, 55, 66
Gobel, George, 28, 110, 144
Gregory, Dick, 34, 147
Gould, Jack, 114
Graham, Billy, 135
Gershwin, George, 132, 144
Godfrey, Arthur, 143
gossip, 143

H

Hall, Stuart, 5
Hanna-Barbera Productions, 89
Harper's Magazine, 27, 67
Hecht, Ben, 140
Hefner, Hugh. See *Playboy*
Hidden Persuaders, The. See Packard, Vance
Hill, Hamlin, 26
Hi-Fi stereo, 4, 54, 70, 88, 92
hip, 37, 45, 49, 82, 84, 86–89, 139
Hoberman, J., 12–13, 106, 107
Hoffman, Abbie, 74
Hollywood Squares, 139
Home, 113
Honeymooners, The 89
Hoover, J. Edgar, 45, 49–51, 65, 73, 75, 150
Hopper, Hedda, 141
Horkheimer, Max , 11–12
House Un-American Activities Committee (HUAC), 51
Howdy Doody, 61–62
humor, sense of: postwar changes, 15, 18, 20, 33; weapon against Communism, 20–21, in psychological tests, 38–39
Humphrey, Hal, 139, 142–144
Huxley, Aldous, 141

I

identity formation: and gender, 11, 82, 86; and mental health, 36, 40–41; and parody, 18, 49–50, 70, 73, 97, 147–148. *See also* articulation
immediacy, 58, 123
Information, Please! 41, 128, 130–132, 134
improvisation, 1, 107, 111, 115, 142, 143. *See also* spontaneity
intellectuals, 7, 67, 91, 111, 131, 134, 144
Internet, 150
Iraq, 150
irony, 3–4, 12, 51–52, 72, 91, 95, 98–99, 107, 134, 145, 149
Isherwood, Christopher 138–139, 141, 143

J

Jack Paar Show, The. See Paar, Jack
Jaffe, Rona, 85
jazz, 11, 28, 79, 82, 84, 86, 88, 94
Jenkins, Henry, 72
Jewish identity, 25, 31
Joey Bishop Show, The, 13, 128, 132, 139
Johnson, Lyndon Baines, 74
juvenile delinquency, 37, 40, 51–52, 60, 68

K

Kamen, Milt, 84
Kashner, Sam, 128
KCOP, 133–134, 137, 140
Keats, John, 21
Kefauver, Estes, 33, 37, 51–52, 60
Kelly, Gene, 131–132
Kennedy, John F., 33–35, 46
Kerouac, Jack, 112
KHJ-TV, 129, 137–138
King of the Hill, 149
Kirby Stone Quartet, 84
KNXT, 133
Kovacs, Ernie, 7, 10, 12, 50, 66, 98–126, 147–151
Krassner, Paul, 47, 89
Kurtzman, Harvey, 11, 33, 53–54, 64, 67, 96–97, 107, 118

L

Leave it to Beaver, 51, 68
legitimate culture, 130, 145
Lehrer, Tom, 28
Letterman, David, 6, 117
Levant, Oscar, 13–14, 41–42, 44, 94, 125–145, 148–149, 151

Levant, June, 136–139, 144
Levittown, 18, 68
Lewis, Jerry, 24, 107, 122, 141
Life Magazine, 25, 27, 69, 94, 109
liveness, 3, 58, 93, 128, 142
local television, 13, 113, 133, 140–142, 144, 145
Los Angeles, 13, 83, 125–133, 135, 144–145
Los Angeles Mirror News, 138
Los Angeles Times, 134
LPs. See albums
Lynes, Russell 27–28, 67, 69, 83

M

MacDonald, Dwight, 7, 11, 13–14, 79
MAD Magazine, 6, 10–11, 23, 44, 45–75, 96, 100, 118, 125, 145, 147, 150–151
madness. See mental health
Mailer, Norman, 80–81, 87
Man in the Grey Flannel Suit, The. See Wilson, Sloan
Martin, Dean, 107, 122, 141
Marx, Groucho, 132, 139
masculinity, 59, 76–97, 148
mass culture, 7, 11, 36, 52, 79–82, 95, 131, 145, 148–149
Masscult, 7, 12–13, 130, 145, 148
McCarthyism, 24, 26, 33, 60. See also Army-McCarthy
Mead, Shepherd, 94–95
Meader, Vaughn, 34
Memoirs of an Amnesiac, 128, 139
mental health, 29–31, 35–37, 43; in popular culture 39–42, 43, 125, 132
method acting, 40–41, 93
MGM, 131
middlebrow, 7, 27–28, 64, 67–68, 82–83, 85, 130–131, 141
Minelli, Vincente, 127
modern art, 11, 79–80, 94
modernism, 12, 36, 107–108, 116, 122, 130
Moore, Garry, 40
Murray, Susan, 123, 143
Murrow, Edward R., 2–3, 60

N

narrowcasting, 13–14, 126, 137
Nash, Michael, 105
NBC, 2, 98, 111–114, 116, 130, 132

Neuman, Alfred E., 47, 54, 69, 75, 79, 100, 149. See also *MAD Magazine*
neuroses. See mental health
Newhart, Bob, 26, 33, 90–91, 147
Nichols, Mike and Elaine May, 1–4, 7, 9, 12, 14, 28, 88
Nightlife, 139
Nixon, Richard, 35, 37, 43, 125

O

Ophir, Shai K., 76
Organization Man, The. See Whyte, William
Oscar Levant Show, The. See Levant, Oscar

P

Paar, Jack, 13, 41–42, 126, 128, 132, 139
Packard, Vance, 21, 23
parenting, 30–32, 50, 73, 80
parody: as criticism of consumer culture, 4, 45; defined, 9; varieties in *MAD*, 48; as carnivalesque, 65–66; as sophisticated taste, 79, 145; in fan letter, 99; in industrial and popular television economies, 146; as satire, 145; politics of, 147
Perry Como Show, The, 109, 144
personality tests, 22–23, 37–39
Peter Gunn, 15, 41–42
Phil Silvers Show, The, 48
Philco, 13, 137, 142
pills. See drug use
Playboy Magazine, 11, 44, 67, 76–97, 125, 148
Playboy's Penthouse, 11, 76, 83–87, 90–91, 97, 148, 151
Playhouse 90, 64, 89, 141
PM Magazine, 53
poaching, textual, 72, 117. See also De Certeau, Michel
Polan, Dana, 108
Politically Incorrect with Bill Maher, 5
politics, 1–2, 6, 19, 60–61, 72, 84, 112, 120; relationship to comedy, 25, 48, 147
Pollock, Jackson, 94
popular music, 133. See also rock music, albums
Popular Science, 87

postmodernism, 73, 108, 121–122
presence, 3, 58, 128
Price, Roger, 50
production style or mode, 136
programming strategies, 25, 48, 66, 80, 110, 112–116, 122, 128, 130, 144
Pryor, Richard, 147
psychiatry. *See* mental health
psychology. *See* mental health
Putterman, Barry, 113–114

Q

quality television, 4, 14, 62, 64, 79, 81, 89–91, 131, 141, 143, 147
quiz shows: 26, 97, 113–114, 121, 128, 130–131; scandals, 1–4, 7, 9, 91

R

race, 18, 34, 40, 83, 86, 147
radio, 3, 7, 68, 74, 112–113, 123, 125, 128, 130–131, 142
Radway, Janice, 83
Reader's Digest, 19, 68–69
Realist, The, 47
Rebel without a Cause, 40
records. See albums
Red Skelton Show, The, 141–142
Riesman, David, 22
rock music, 46, 70, 79, 84–85
Rose, Margaret A., 9
Rosen, Robert, 105–108, 122
Ross, Andrew, 87
Rowan and Martin's Laugh-In, 5
Rubin, Jerry, 74–75
Rubin, Joan Shelley, 130–131

S

Sahl, Mort, 24, 28, 29, 31, 33, 34, 88, 125, 145
Sarah Silverman Program, The, 6, 149
satire: as distinguished from parody, 9–10, 72; assessing politics of, 147–148; carnivalesque, 65–66; in *MAD*, 51, 53, 65; in comics, 56; in middlebrow culture, 130; in *Playboy* 89, 94; in postnetwork era, 6, 148–151, postwar significance, 5–6, 24–25, 33–34
Saturday Night Live, 5, 6, 113, 117
Schoenberger, Nancy, 128
science fiction, 55–56
Sconce, Jeffrey, 58

SCTV, 5
Second City, 34
Seeger, Pete, 91
self-reflexivity, 107–108, 110, 116, 123
sex: changes ideas about, 5; inhibitions, 38; and comics code, 52; in magazines, 77, 88; in parody, 71, 92, 108; and *Playboy*, 78, 80, 85, 92; on television, 76
sexism, 40, 148. *See also* gender
sexuality, coded references to, 116
Shaw, George Bernard, 141
Sheen, Bishop Fulton J., 113
Shepherd, Jean, 74
sick comedy, 10, 15, 19, 20, 24, 27–30, 42, 46, 125, 147, 148
Silverstein, Shel, 95
Simpsons, The, 149
simultaneity, 3
situation comedy, 25, 51, 73, 100, 111, 114, 119, 128, 146, 149
Skelton, Red, 141–142
sketch comedy, 2, 5, 111, 149
Smith, Cecil, 134, 137, 143
Smothers Brothers, 5
Sontag, Susan, 95
Sopranos, The, 6
South Park, 5, 148, 149
Spigel, Lynn, 46, 87, 92
Spock, Benjamin, 31
sponsors, commercial: 135–137, 141, 142; use of comedy toward, 142
spontaneity, 13, 111–112, 116
stereo. See Hi-Fi
Stevenson, Adlai, 34
Stojowski, Sigismund, 130
subject positions, 49, 73, 79, 97, 121
Sullivan, Ed, 45
Surrealists, 36

T

talk shows, 28, 30, 32, 41, 71, 83, 86, 89, 113, 121, 125–128, 134–135, 140, 144
alternative forms of,
Taschlin, Frank, 107, 122
taste: boundaries between, 69, 71, 145–147, 149; changing notions in postwar era, 27; related to masculinity, 76–97; elite vs. sophisticated, 79. *See also* culture, high vs. low
tastelessness, 27, 85–86, 142

Television Magazine, 142
That Was the Week That Was, 5
Time Magazine, 27, 43, 85, 136, 143, 144
Today, 66, 113, 115
Tonight, 98, 110, 113, 114, 117, 126
Treyz, Oliver, 89
TV Guide, 62, 91–92, 129, 140
Twilight Zone, The, 15, 32, 41
Two and a Half Men, 150

U
underground humor, 27, 47

V
Van Doren, Charles, 2–3, 9
Variety, 85–86, 131, 137–139, 142
variety shows, 41, 71, 76, 80, 83, 85–87, 90, 111–114, 121, 128, 131
vaudevillle, 25, 90, 104–105, 109–110, 122
video art, 12, 104–109, 115, 119, 123–124
voyeurism, male gaze, 80–82, 88, 92–94, 97
vulgar modernism, 12, 107, 122

W
Weaver, Pat, 112, 113, 123
Welk, Lawrence, 110
Wertham, Frederic, 51–52, 56
westerns, 26, 48, 70, 97, 99–106, 111–112, 115–116, 119, 123
What's My Line?, 113, 128, 139
White Negro. See Mailer, Norman
Whyte, William, 9, 22, 80
Williams, Raymond, 3
Williams, Tennessee, 138
Wilson, Sloan, 23, 35
Winters, Jonathan, 24, 28, 89
Wood, Natalie, 133
Words About Music, 133–134

Y
Yippies, 74–75, 147